SHAMEFUL VICTORY

Shameful Victory

The Los Angeles Dodgers, the Red Scare, and the Hidden History of Chavez Ravine

John H. M. Laslett

The University of Arizona Press
Tucson

The University of Arizona Press
www.uapress.arizona.edu

Printed in the United States of America

ISBN-13: 978-0-8165-0086-4 (paper)

Cover designed by Carrie House, HOUSEdesign llc
Cover photos: (*top*) New Routes to and from Dodger Stadium. Herald-Examiner Collection/Los Angeles Public Library; (*bottom*) Eviction of Aurora Vargas from Arechiga family home on May 8, 1959. Courtesy of UCLA Special Collections.

Publication of this book is made possible in part by the proceeds of a permanent endowment created with the assistance of a Challenge Grant from the National Endowment for the Humanities, a federal agency.

Library of Congress Cataloging-in-Publication Data
Laslett, John H. M., author.
Shameful victory : the Los Angeles Dodgers, the Red Scare, and the hidden history of Chavez Ravine / John H. M. Laslett.
pages cm
Includes bibliographical references and index.
ISBN 978-0-8165-0086-4 (pbk. : alk. paper)
1. Chávez Ravine (Los Angeles, Calif.)—History—20th century. 2. Public housing—California—Los Angeles. 3. Los Angeles (Calif.)—Politics and government—20th century. 4. Hispanic American neighborhoods—California—Los Angeles—History—20th century. 5. Land use—California—Los Angeles—History—20th century. 6. Mexican Americans—California—Los Angeles—History—20th century. 7. Mexican Americans—California—Los Angeles—Social conditions. 8. Los Angeles (Calif.)—Race relations—History—20th century. 9. Dodger Stadium (Los Angeles, Calif.)—History—20th century. I. Title.
F869.L86C438 2015
979.4'94—dc23
2015003060

♾ This paper meets the requirements of ANSI/NISO Z39.48-1992 (Permanence of Paper).

For Lois,
wife and fellow historian,
with love and gratitude

Contents

Illustrations

Figures

Maps

Acknowledgments

I wrote this book for several reasons: my interest in California's ethnic and minority history, the fact that I once lived near Chavez Ravine, and because of the major influence that the barrio's destruction had in shaping the historical memory of L.A.'s Mexican American community.

I am grateful to the Chicano Studies Research Center at UCLA for permission to cite material from the Michelle Kholos Brooks Collection of Manazar Gamboa papers (Collection 88). I am also indebted to Chronicle Books for permission to quote from the text of Don Normark's *Chavez Ravine, 1949* (1999), which contains a superb collection of photographs he took of the barrio not long before it was demolished.

My thanks go also to Jan Breidenbach for her expert advice on the history of urban renewal in Los Angeles and to William David Estrada of the history staff at the Museum of Natural History for reading the entire manuscript. The text was also read by my UCLA colleague Juan Gomez-Quinones and by Ric Salinas of Culture Clash, who advised me about its contents. Steve Ross read several chapters of an earlier draft, and Denis Deriev and Jack Levine helped prepare the manuscript for publication. I am grateful, too, to Kristen Buckles, Amanda Krause, Abby Mogollon, and other staff members at the University of Arizona Press for their guidance and advice.

Finally, I owe a special debt of gratitude to the survivors, relatives, and friends of the former residents of Chavez Ravine I interviewed for the project. They include Alicia Brown, Virginia Pinedo-Bye, Linda Delmar, Luis Santillan, Carol Jacques, and Dixie Swift.

Any errors that remain in the text are my sole responsibility.

February 2015

John Laslett
UCLA

Figure 1. Chavez Ravine before the evictions. Courtesy *Los Angeles Times*.

Figure 2. Chavez Ravine after the evictions. Courtesy *Los Angeles Times*.

Prologue

Most baseball fans today think of Chavez Ravine, located in Elysian Park less than a mile from downtown L.A., as the home of the Los Angeles Dodgers. Few among them know that, for almost a hundred years before the Dodgers began playing baseball there in 1962, Chavez Ravine was home to one of the largest and most celebrated Mexican American barrios in the American Southwest. Some of the settlers who built their homes in the ravine's rolling hills and meadows had lived there since the time of the Mexican Revolution. Because of its beauty and rural isolation, they called it their "Shangri-La."

Still fewer of California's present-day residents will remember the scandal that arose in the early 1950s when the Los Angeles City Housing Authority (CHA) razed the barrio to the ground in return for a promise to replace the residents' lost homes with public housing. The promise of public housing was never kept, and the scandal that resulted left many former residents homeless and spread widespread anger and unease throughout East L.A.'s poor, Latino community.

* * *

Having sold their homes to the city in good faith, Chavez Ravine's residents protested loudly against the evictions that occurred when the CHA used its power of eminent domain to force them out. But because they were poor Mexican Americans with little or no political power, their complaints were disregarded and the scandal was swept under the rug. City authorities behaved even more questionably when, in 1958, they sold the land from Chavez Ravine to baseball mogul Walter O'Malley for a suspiciously small sum as part of a deal to bring his legendary Brooklyn Dodgers baseball team to L.A. In their rush to bring first-class baseball to Los Angeles for the first time, the needs of one of the city's largest and most distinctive Mexican American communities were brushed aside.

The outlines of this scandal have been known for years. But neither the history of the Chavez Ravine barrio, nor the story of the deal that brought the Dodgers baseball team out west in 1959—it began playing in Dodger Stadium in 1962—have ever been fully told. Nor have the long-term consequences of this major episode in Los Angeles history been properly understood. The details of how, and why, the 3,300 Mexican Americans were evicted from their homes in the early 1950s are shocking and still hold lessons for us today. Some of the settlers refused to move; others protested at city hall. But most of the householders were forced to sell their homes—often at below market prices—and move in with relatives or become renters in far-off parts of the city.

Resistance to the evictions was especially strong during the last phase of the struggle in May 1959, when the last holdouts were dragged from their homes by sheriffs' deputies and their houses were demolished in front of their eyes—an episode replayed that same day on the evening news. It was the public exposure of this heartless act, as much as anything else, that imprinted the scandal on the public mind.

The mass evictions and the shady deal reached later to build Dodger Stadium on land formerly belonging to Chavez Ravine's homeowners raise many questions. Why did the Los Angeles City Council, having promised to build public housing for the evictees in June 1951, suddenly change its mind and refuse to build it six months later? Did L.A.'s city officials knowingly cheat the public by selling land to Walter O'Malley at a knockdown price? Was the contract they negotiated part of a secret conspiracy by a business elite willing to go to any lengths to bring Major League Baseball to Southern California for the first time in its history? What happened to the evicted tenants who lost their homes?

* * *

This book tries to answer these and many other questions. But it also places the Chavez Ravine affair in a broader social and historical context. It shows that the tragedy exerted a much greater influence on the history of urban renewal, and on the development of L.A.'s Mexican American community, than has hitherto been supposed. Exploring the early years of Chavez Ravine sheds fresh light on how minority ghettos come into being, how they grow, and how they come to terms with the demands of the majority in a white, Anglo-American city. The destruction of the barrio also

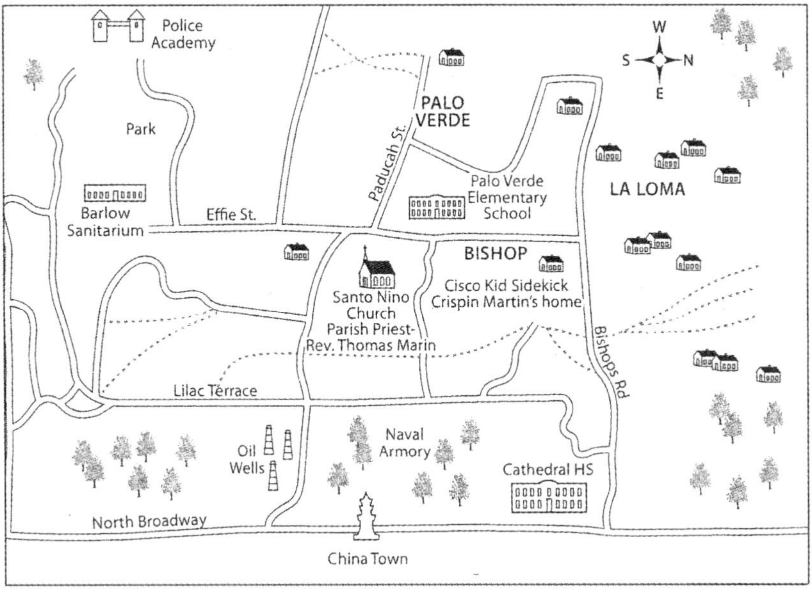

Map 1. Simplified map of Chavez Ravine's Mexican barrio

left behind a major cultural legacy in terms of poetry, drama, and the arts that has never been described before and still exerts an influence today.

Tracing Latino reaction to the mass evictions offers an inside look at the rise of Chicano political protest and how it influenced the growth of the Mexican American civil rights movement. The evictions took place at the height of the post–World War II Red Scare, prompting bitter political arguments in the Los Angeles City Council about minority rights, "creeping socialism," and the legacy of the 1930s New Deal. The 1953 election campaign, which put conservative mayor Norris Poulson into office, marked the end of the city's postwar liberal consensus. The election was largely fought over issues of slum clearance, minority evictions, public housing, and the neocorporate vision of Los Angeles' future that Poulson upheld. With Mayor Poulson's victory, L.A. politics swung markedly to the right—where they remained until the election of African American mayor Tom Bradley in 1973.

In addition, the destruction of the Chavez Ravine barrio raised public awareness about the history of spatial dislocation among L.A.'s minority populations, about the top-down character of L.A.'s urban renewal policies, and about redesigning post–World War II Los Angeles in the interests of its business elite. After the Watts uprising of 1965, renewed popular anger against the bulldozing philosophy of the L.A. Housing Authority led to a major revision in the redevelopment policies pursued by the housing authorities both in Los Angeles and elsewhere.

* * *

All of this, and much more, is discussed in the chapters that follow. No more than a routine episode in the business of the L.A. Housing Authority, the Chavez Ravine affair became a tragedy for the families who were evicted, many of whose lives were permanently disrupted. Could that tragedy have been avoided? Sadly, probably not.

This book tells the full story of the Chavez Ravine barrio, including its destruction and the consequences of that destruction for those who lost their homes, for the first time. The story is told through the opinions of L.A.'s politicians, baseball mogul Walter O'Malley, the Housing Authority, and—above all—the eyes of the residents of Chavez Ravine themselves. The answers Seattle photographer Don Normark received when he questioned the residents in 1999 about life in their Shangri-La offer glimpses into a close-knit, communal way of life different from the isolated, suburban existence most of L.A.'s white residents appeared to crave at that time. Normark's interviews took place many years after the L.A. Housing Authority condemned the Chavez Ravine barrio as a slum and forced its inhabitants to leave. Nevertheless, they provide an authentic taste of what life in the community was like.

Several of the answers to questions posed below are taken from the work of Manazar Gamboa, a brilliant but little-known poet, former prison inmate, and educator who grew up in Chavez Ravine and whose work is cited here for the first time. Gamboa's poems and short stories captured the essence of life in the ravine more successfully than those of any other writer. Several events from his life figure prominently in the narrative that follows.[1]

What Were Your Houses Like?

"My universe consisted of my father's garden; the four houses he built; fig, loquat, and apricot trees; eight parallel clotheslines; a pyramid-shaped brick incinerator, a garage, and a brick driveway.

"Because our house was built on a slope, its front was very high. Thirteen steps led up to a small porch and the front door. If you walked inside you'd be in the *sala* with its clothes closet, a high chest of drawers, and table—none of which matched. All the furniture had been handed down to us or bought used. On the walls were old family photographs and calendars with colorful pictures depicting la Virgen de Guadalupe and Jesucristo. To the left behind the sala was a tiny bedroom.

"Directly in front was the kitchen, which included the dinner table, stove, icebox, radio, dishes, and cupboard. The dinner table, a gift from one of my mother's employers, stood out from the rest of the furniture with its deep, dark wood—which was due partly to its natural hue and partly to countless elbows, arms, and hands rubbing over its surface. To the left of the kitchen was my parents' bedroom with hardly enough space to hold a double bed, a closet, and knickknack table. To the right was a low side porch. . . . Goats, rabbits, and chickens, in large numbers, ran around as if they owned the place. Often they could be seen wandering loose among the rocks and weeds of the high ground.

"Many of them, however, doubled as pets; even those that would eventually wind up being cooked and served with *frijoles, arroz y tortillas*, and sometimes with *nopales*; those lusty desert cacti that grew in generous clumps everywhere but never more than five feet. As for the barrio I grew up in, my street, Bishops Road, belonged to Palo Verde, but emotionally and geographically the two barrios were distant from each other. Ironically, the *gente* from my street had closer ties in both respects with the *plebe* from the other Chavez Ravine barrio, La Loma" (see map 1).

What Did You Learn in School?

"In Palo Verde there was Palo Verde Street School, the grammar school that I went to, which was located on a long stretch of flat land over the hill from Bishops Road. Another elementary school in that barrio was Paducah Street School. Some kids from our barrio attended this school, but kids from other barrios were bussed into it as well. Paducah Street School did not have a regular curriculum; its educational focus was centered on shops, gardening, and art. It was derogatorily called the 'dumb' school.

"When I went to school, I had to learn English. We didn't speak English at home; everybody was Mexican. We went barefoot to kindergarten, and all we did was paint and play games. They were trying to teach us the ABCs and the numbers, and I couldn't understand the teacher. But in the first grade I started right away. By the second grade I was already bilingual, reading and writing. And the teachers, Miss Wiggins, Miss Tucker, and Miss Lummis, none of them spoke Spanish. My parents were proud. They were trying to learn English from us. I taught my mom and dad to speak English. They could defend themselves after they learned."

Did You Go to Church?

"There were two churches in Palo Verde. One was Santo Nino Catholic Church, where Padre Tomas raged and stormed at the worshipers during evening rosaries and morning masses. Santo Nino took up a large lot on the corner of Paducah and Effie Streets. There was a Protestant church there, too, popularly known as La Iglesia Aleluya. I don't know what it was about because I never entered it. My friend Motie and his family were members of its congregation, but he never spoke of what occurred within its walls.

"Everybody tried to outdo each other with their altars. At every house that had an altar, we would stop and pray. We prayed and walked for about two and a half hours. You would pray and kneel. A good fifteen altars in the neighborhood. They put out whatever saint they wanted, mostly the Virgen de Guadalupe."

"That's not snow, those are eggshells. It's not winter, it's Easter, and someone just broke a *cascarone* over his head. You'd smile too. In the weeks before Easter, eggs are opened carefully by breaking a small hole in one end. The empty shells are dried, filled with confetti, and sealed with colored paper. On Easter morning loved ones are surprised when these bright egg cascarones burst over their heads."

Did You Ever Go Downtown?

"Sure. The old streetcars were fun to ride. One Red Car went to Canoga Park. Another Red Car went all the way down to San Dimas, Arcadia, Monrovia, and Azusa and another one to Long Beach and to Santa Monica. The number 5W Yellow Cars went to Eagle Rock. The main car went to Lincoln Park. The V Car went to Spring and Sunset. Fare was seven cents. The Red Cars were a dime. Sometimes we'd ride to the end of the line and stay in our seats and ride back. They wouldn't charge you if you didn't get off the car. They went down the aisle, bang, bang, bang, flipping the seats so they faced the other way. The conductor would get off and pull the cable down and wrap it up and then transfer his coin box to the front end. It was a lot of fun. I went on the streetcars to school."

Would You Call Yourselves Poor?

"People struggled to make ends meet. When women bought flour for tortillas they'd buy hundred-pound sacks because it was cheaper. One brand was El Faro, 'The Lighthouse,' another was La Pina. La Pina had a real nice pineapple in the background. These ladies made panties for their daughters out of the sacks. It was a joke among us kids. When girls got on the swings we used to watch and sing out, 'Hey, there's El Faro of the year. You can see the flour sack panties.' 'Hey, La Pina *en el aire*!' and all the guys used to run up and look. So, El Faro *o* La Pina *en el aire*, we'd hang out to peek, up in the air."

"Our parents showed us how to cook to make tortillas and tamales. Especially tortillas. Every day. We came home from school and my mother had a big pot of masa to make tortillas. My brothers would come home from work and go for tortillas with butter. They would eat and we would hit them. 'Don't touch them.' My father had to eat right away after work, and everything had to be set on the table—the chili, the beans, the rice, the meat, and the tortillas."

"Mother made our clothes. She'd cut out a skirt, cut a sleeve, just measuring with her fingers. She measured with her fingers how long the blouse was going to be. She sewed real pretty too. I learned a lot from her. I worked in the cafeteria at Palo Verde School. My sister used to bake the best lemon meringue pies because she learned from the cook at school. I danced at the Ballet Folklorico at Solano School with Mary Hilda Navarez and Julia and Margaret Navez. Their mother taught Mexican folk dances. My mother couldn't afford one of those dresses, but we'd borrow one."

What Happened When You Got Sick?

"Many families relied on the *curanderas*. One took care of my brother one time. He got real sick and my mother went to get her, and she said, 'Get him up.' So they got me out of bed. She spread a lot of newspapers on top of the bedsprings and then put the mattress back and put me back on there. She got a clear glass, filled it with water, and put an egg in the water (I was watching everything), and then she put the glass on the floor under the bed. She put candles on each post of the bed (I was craning my neck). She had plants and she waved them in front of me and then put the plants under the bed. In the morning she came back, got the glass from under

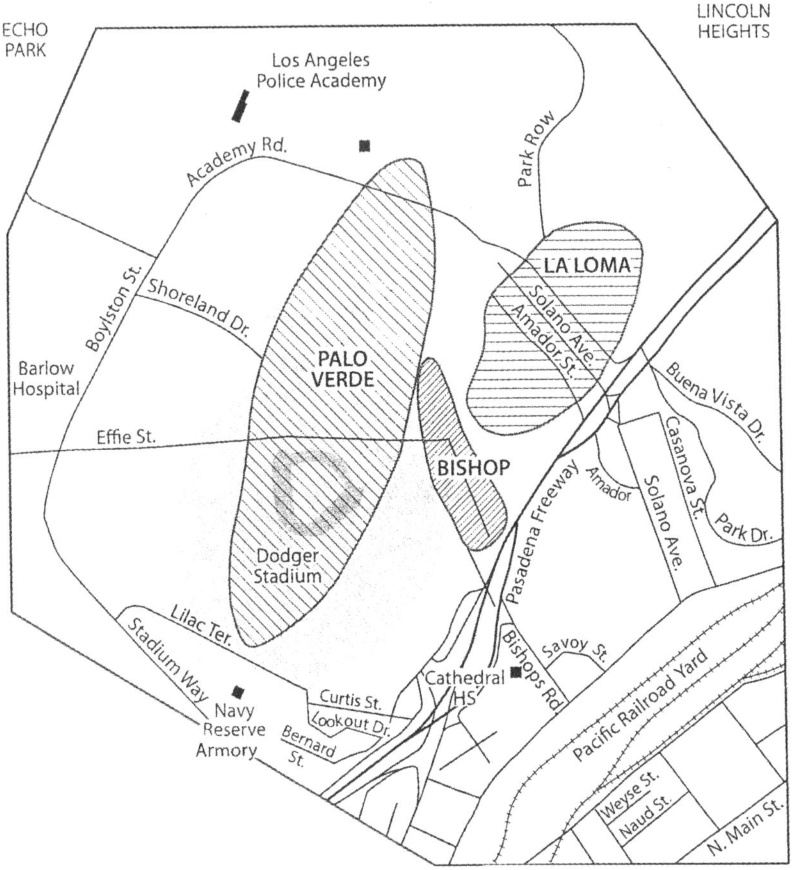

Map 2. Aerial survey of Chavez Ravine, with Bishop, La Loma, and Palo Verde delineated

the bed, took the egg out. She held it up and said that the egg had pulled the sickness out of my body. I felt better."

How Did Everybody Get Along?

"We guys from Palo Verde and the guys from La Loma used to bullshit a lot when we seen each other. We would greet each other and talk at parties, but that was about it. They had what they called federation dances at the Bishop playground or sometimes at the Solano School. We would go in there and mess around and drink beer and blow weed or whatever and dance. A lot of girls from other neighborhoods came, and that was how we communicated with each other. We seen each other at dances or meet down the street. We bullshit and so on, but that was as far as it went. I never did hang out with the Loma guys much.

I don't remember any gang fights around here. Never? Well sure, we had misunderstandings, like between Loma, Palo Verde, Bishop. But there never was any "We'll meet you guys over there" or anybody shooting. It was a time when I dressed like a zoot-suiter, but I was never in a gang fight. Neighborhoods like Alpine and Macy, where they were rivals, *they'd* fight it out, but I never seen it. Or Loma and Clover, they were always at it, but I never seen them in a gang fight. I was never involved, so I can't say anything. . . . But viva La Bishop. That was my neighborhood."

PART I

Building a Unique Barrio

CHAPTER ONE

Mexicans on the Hilltop

Gaining a Foothold, 1830–1929

"The majority of the people I photographed were born in the ravine. Most of their parents were from Mexico. Some had fled the Mexican Revolution; others were simply looking for a better life."

—DON NORMARK

"It was so beautiful up there, with the animals, the fresh wind from the ocean every afternoon, and the flowers and the trees. We thought we were in paradise. We called it Shangri-La."

—HELEN VASQUEZ

Early Arrivals

One day late in 1910 a battered truck with Mexican license plates drove down North Broadway toward the center of Los Angeles. Seated in the cab were two men who had driven the truck all the way up from Chihuahua, in northern Mexico. Crammed in the back of the truck with the family possessions were their wives and children. These were not the first immigrants to arrive in Chavez Ravine. Several hundred others had built houses there in earlier years. But the Antonio and Gomez families were among the first who settled there in order to escape the turmoil of the pre–World War I Mexican Revolution.

Crossing the Los Angeles River, the truck turned right up Bishops Road for several hundred yards before coming to a halt in front of the steep hills of Chavez Ravine, a remote, rural area about a mile northeast of downtown Los Angeles. Located in Elysian Park, Chavez Ravine was surrounded by city streets on three sides and by the Los Angeles River on the fourth. Stiff from their long drive, the Gomez and Antonio families got out of their truck, stretched their legs, and joined other newcomers milling about in a grassy area that had been marked off into housing sites. The ground was strewn with furniture, boxes, and other personal possessions.

"Buenos dias, bienvenidos; mi nombre es Jorge Rosas," said a stranger. "We have the lot next to yours."[1]

Joel and Reluccia Gomez unloaded their possessions onto the plot of land assigned to them. Later designated 1760 Bishops Road, the house they built would remain their family home for more than forty years, until it was torn down by the Housing Authority of the City of Los Angeles (HACLA) in 1951. Along with the other new arrivals, the two families set to work to help build each other's houses. Mutual help of this kind had long been customary among Mexican village families struggling to build their first home.[2]

Who were Joel and Reluccia Gomez? Why did they settle in Chavez Ravine rather than in L.A.'s original Plaza area or in one of the many established urban barrios that had sprung up on both sides of the Los Angeles River? Joel Gomez, who remained a laborer for most of his life, was born in 1886 in the Apache highlands of la Sierra Madre Occidentale. He met and married Reluccia in 1909 while working as a janitor at her Catholic school in Clifton, Arizona. The young couple moved north the following year and eventually sired eleven children. Their youngest son, who took the name Manazar Gamboa when he became a writer, was born in Chavez Ravine in 1934.[3]

Chavez Ravine was difficult to get to, and most of its land was undeveloped. Through the 1930s and 1940s the scattered settlement, which consisted of three subbarrios named Bishop, Alta Loma, and Palo Verde, lacked paved roads, street lights, or a proper sewage system, still less any decent shops or places of entertainment. Also, it was a long walk down to North Broadway and the major shops on Figueroa and other downtown streets. Boyle Heights, for example, on the other side of the Los Angeles River, seemed a far more appealing destination. It possessed dance halls, a wide variety of stores, a street life, and a mixed Mexican and Jewish population.[4] Did it not offer more opportunities for employment, advancement, and enjoyment than the three remote, primitive-looking villages on the top of the hill?

Why Did They Call It Shangri-La?

The answer to the previous question is undoubtedly yes. But there were many reasons why the inhabitants of Chavez Ravine came to cherish their community and why they became so indignant when the City of Los Angeles forced them to leave it in the 1950s. For one thing, land there was

Figure 3. Women climbing hill to Chavez Ravine from downtown. Courtesy *Los Angeles Times*.

much cheaper than it was in Boyle Heights or Belvedere. If newcomers lacked the money for a down payment on a regular house, which many of them did, they could build their own homes in Chavez Ravine room by room, in a manner more suited to their limited resources.

A second reason for preferring Chavez Ravine, paradoxically, was its isolation. The remoteness of the ravine from governmental authority enabled members of the community to practice traditional forms of Mexican village culture without running up against the disapproval of white bureaucrats or the LAPD. For example, there were several *curanderas* (native healers) of Indian descent among the early settlers. For years they were able to deliver babies and practice their ancient arts with little fear of complaints from doctors in the local hospitals.[5]

A third reason for the ravine's appeal was its rural atmosphere and natural beauty. Each of its three subbarrios was nestled in a separate canyon surrounded by meadows, clumps of trees, flowering bushes, and—in the early years, at least—ample land for planting orchards, grazing animals, and growing vegetables. Carol Jacques describes the view from her parents' house as a girl in the 1940s: "From the top of the hill I lived on, we could look down past the trees and see the police academy. Our neighborhood was a wonderful world of color. Yellow and orange canaries in our house; turquoise and green parrots in our neighbors' houses. Bougainvilleas flowering everywhere. Flower gardens in front of almost everyone's home."[6]

Carol Jacques's grandfather, Lorenzo Ayala, migrated to Los Angeles from Puruandiro, Michoacán, in 1907. He began his new life in Southern California by picking up new arrivals from the Southern Pacific train station with a horse and buggy and transporting them to the original Mexican settlement area around Olvera Street. By 1909 Lorenzo had saved up enough money to send for his wife, Arcadia, and their children. A little later he bought two lots in Palo Verde—one to build his family home on and the other for growing corn and raising chickens, pigs, and goats. Obeying his mother's wishes, Carol's uncle Thomas (then nine years old) carried the family's metate, an old-fashioned stone device for grinding corn, all the way from Mexico. In a city where manufactured tortillas were readily available, it turned out to be unnecessary. But because it had once been essential to her family's way of life, Carol Jacques regarded her metate as "a symbol of life."[7] It now adorns the mantle in her Mount Washington home.

Besides being beautiful, the pastoral setting of the ravines and hilltops, with their acres of cultivable land, was of great practical value to poor, rural migrants who came from the peasant communities of northern Mexico. It enabled them to supplement their meager cash wages by raising goats, chickens, pigs, and even some cattle, without (as they thought) contravening the city's sanitation and zoning regulations. During the Great Depression of the 1930s these additional sources of meat, along with fruit, vegetables, and eggs from their orchards and backyards, saved many a poor family in Chavez Ravine from begging on the streets or becoming dependent on New Deal welfare agencies.[8]

In addition, the unfenced surroundings of the ravine were a wonderful playground for children. They could run free, climb trees, and pursue all manner of childhood adventures in relative safety without encountering traffic or coming up against the LAPD. Several old-timers recalled the fun they had as kids in the teens and twenties when, during hot summer days, they flew kites and scrambled down the hill to swim, build dams, and play in the Los Angeles River.[9] There were more modern pleasures, too. Sally Munoz remembered fondly how, every Friday and Saturday night in Alta Loma, local youths attached a stolen jukebox to the overhead electric wires. "Kids would come from all over. We had the best jukebox in the world, and everybody'd be dancing up there under the only streetlight we had. We had a real good time. We had happiness."[10]

These pickup dances in the dirt roads of the barrio lacked the sophistication and excitement of a night out at L.A.'s big downtown music halls and jazz clubs. But when they could afford it, youths from Chavez Ravine on weekends eagerly attended concerts by Lionel "Chico" Sesma, Paul Lopez, Don Tosti, and other up-and-coming Latino artists at Betty's Bar in Boyle Heights and at Club La Bamba on Olvera Street. Or they took their girls dancing at the Avedon Ballroom near Our Lady of Lourdes Catholic Church in East L.A., where the Armenta Brothers and Sal Chico played a mixture of swing, rhythm and blues, and boleros for both cholos and straight kids. Playing in a Mexican band, or—for the very few—getting a record label of one's own, was one of the few avenues of upward mobility for these working-class youths. Going to hear jazz greats like Dizzy Gillespie and Buddy Collette on Central Avenue also helped break down racial barriers.[11]

The isolation of Chavez Ravine from the rest of L.A. was only relative. Besides jobs and weekly shopping trips to stores on North Broadway and the downtown central market, young men from the ravine established sports teams to play against other Mexican clubs in the city and went out in the evenings to play their guitars in nightclubs or visit the movies downtown, in Echo Park, Lincoln Heights, Chinatown, and elsewhere. Housewives shopped frequently at the Mercado Plaza at the corner of North Main and Republic Streets, which featured a soda fountain as well as a meat market and a wide variety of Mexican goods. On weekends, ravine families might catch one of the Red Cars and venture as far away as the beach in Santa Monica. To the disapproval of their parents, youths with cars (although few had them in the early days) cruised the downtown streets to pick up girls, visit bars, and hold parties in secret hiding places back in the hills.[12]

Nevertheless, the relative isolation of Chavez Ravine did have its downside. As seen in the experience of Reluccia Gomez, who had eleven children, of whom only five survived, in the early days the birthrate in Chavez Ravine was extremely high. With no trained doctors readily available, babies were frequently delivered by a midwife. Unfortunately, the result, again evident in Reluccia Gomez's case, was a high rate of infant mortality. In 1929 the infant mortality rate for L.A.'s Mexicans in general was 104.4 per 1,000 live births, compared to only 39.6 per 1,000 births among the white population. In Chavez Ravine the infant death rate was even higher.[13] Poor diet and lack of medical care were also responsible for a relatively high incidence of tuberculosis and other diseases of poverty.

Evidence of the impact of tuberculosis on the community can be seen in a moving story Manazar Gamboa later wrote about the death of his eighteen-year-old sister Lina, which happened when he was five:

> I ran into the kitchen, everything and everyone was silent. The curtains were drawn; the room was dark. It smelled of medicine and the sweet, pungent odor of burning wax. On top of the bureau, two candles were burning before a large picture of La Virgen de Guadalupe. From a large, wooden crucifix hanging high on the wall, Christ tilted His head and looked down.
>
> My mother was sitting stiffly on a chair beside the old sofa. Her high cheekbones were damp; the beads of a limp rosary intertwined between her fingers. Lina was stretched out on the sofa. A gray blanket covered her frail body up to the neck. She lay on her side, facing the room. Her eyes were closed.
>
> "*Ven, Manuel.*" My mother held her arms out to me, but I couldn't move. My mother pulled me into her arms. "Manuel," she spoke softly. "Lina has gone to heaven. God wanted her to be with him—just like he wanted my other six children."
>
> "What do I care about God!" I screamed. "What about me!?"[14]

Despite the obstacles created by emergencies like this, the steep hillsides of Chavez Ravine helped to protect its residents from nativist whites and other outsiders who despised the immigrants' poverty and made fun of their "quaint" way of life. Carol Jacques remembered how she was sneered at by white passersby on her daily walk with her *tia* (aunt) along Sunset Boulevard to the St. Francis of Assisi Catholic school in Silverlake. One white girl, whose house they passed on Lilac Terrace, would "yell racist names at me, like 'squaw' or 'greaser.'" When Carol and her mother got on the bus, white women would move to different seats uttering words like "dirty Mexican." Carol also had to endure racist remarks on the way back home. But, she added, "I always felt safe when I was back in Chavez Ravine."[15]

Early History of the Ravine

Who were the predecessors of the Gomez family and the other early residents of the area? And why was this remote series of gullies and hills, high above the rapidly growing city of Los Angeles, called Chavez Ravine?

Elysian Park was established as a city park in 1886, and it immediately began to develop some of the facilities that can still be found there today. But despite its lack of paved roads, piped water, or electricity, Chavez Ravine (formerly called Sulphur Ravine) contained a smattering of settlers, small farmers, and those looking for a cheap place to build their homes as far back as the 1840s.[16]

Julian Chavez, a settler from New Mexico after whom the area was named, began purchasing land "for agricultural purposes" in the late 1830s.[17] The city census of 1836 listed him as a twenty-seven-year-old laborer. In the next city census, however, Chavez was described as a prosperous and influential citizen. During the Mexican-American War of 1846 to 1848, he was made *juez de aguas*, judge of the waters. This was an important job in a city where the river regularly flooded and there were few other sources of irrigation.

During the smallpox epidemics that broke out in 1850 and 1880, Chavez Ravine was used as the L.A. County "pest farm" to care for the Mexicans and Chinese who suffered from the scourge, and in 1854 the Hebrew Benevolent Society Burial Ground was deeded some land on the south side of the main canyon.[18] Both of these developments suggest that in its early days the ravine was seen by L.A.'s tiny group of middle-class whites as a remote and inhospitable area to which undesirable immigrants and nonsalubrious activities could conveniently be assigned.

Whatever his loyalties during the Mexican-American War, landowner Julian Chavez developed a successful political career after it was over. In 1852 he was elected as one of the first members of the Los Angeles County Board of Supervisors. In 1870 and 1871 he served as councilman in the city's first ward, serving alongside such influential pioneers of modern Los Angeles as Henry Dockweiler and Prudent Beaudry. Julian Chavez died in 1879 at the age of seventy, with most of his large land holdings in Chavez Ravine still intact. After his death his heirs sold off most of it into small holdings and residential lots.[19]

Not long after the establishment of Elysian Park, when numerous palm trees and other vegetation were being added, the local press began commenting on how beautiful not just the park was but also the undeveloped areas of the ravine itself. In 1902 Alfredo Solano's son-in-law, Dr. Walter Jarvis Barlow, found the "ideal location" for his tuberculosis sanatorium on Chavez Ravine Road at the southern edge of the park. The site was described as "untouched meadow land set amidst rolling hills, and even better, next to the city-owned Elysian Park, a protective barrier that seemed to insure against future encroachment by any future development."[20]

Chavez Ravine and the Mexican Revolution of 1910 to 1920

It was not until the Mexican Revolution broke out in 1910 that significant numbers of Mexican immigrants began settling in Chavez Ravine itself. They were not the only ones to end up there. In the 1920s, when progressive reformer Christine Sterling began her campaign to "restore" Olvera Street, several hundred Italian and Mexican families from Sonoratown, who had lost their homes to urban renewal, also moved there.[21] During the preceding decade, however, migrants fleeing from the chaos created by the downfall of the dictator Porfirio Diaz dominated the flow.

Before the revolution, it was customary for the father or the eldest son, as the most capable breadwinner in an immigrant family, to start the process of roundabout migration that ended up—often some time later—with an entire family of Mexican immigrants settling in Los Angeles. In most instances the women and children would be sent for later. Joel Gomez, Manazar Gamboa's father, followed this pattern. Having worked for a few months in silver mines on both sides of the Mexican border in 1909, he returned home to Chihuahua. A few months later he ventured north again, crossing the border at Juarez–El Paso, and traveled northwest by train along the recently completed Santa Fe Railroad to Los Angeles. After staying there for several months, he went back to fetch the rest of his family.[22]

During the Mexican Revolution itself, however, when large areas of the country were threatened by warring factions and the loss of land, entire families from Sonora, Chihuahua, and other states in northern Mexico began moving directly to L.A. in order to escape food shortages and the threat of social breakdown. In one extraordinary incident Carol Jacques recalled how the ranchero (landowner) for whom her grandfather worked came across her grandmother and their young children in an open field. One of the children, Carol's aunt Agapita, appeared to be starving from malnutrition. As an act of kindness, he cut open the stomach of one of his cows and placed the child in its belly, where she was able to absorb enough nutrients to accompany her mother and brother on the journey north.[23]

It was no coincidence, either, that the Gomez family entered the United States through the Juarez–El Paso crossing point. Records show that close to 60 percent of all Mexican immigrants who settled in Los Angeles in the early years of the twentieth century crossed the border there. This was partly because several major railroads from southern Mexico

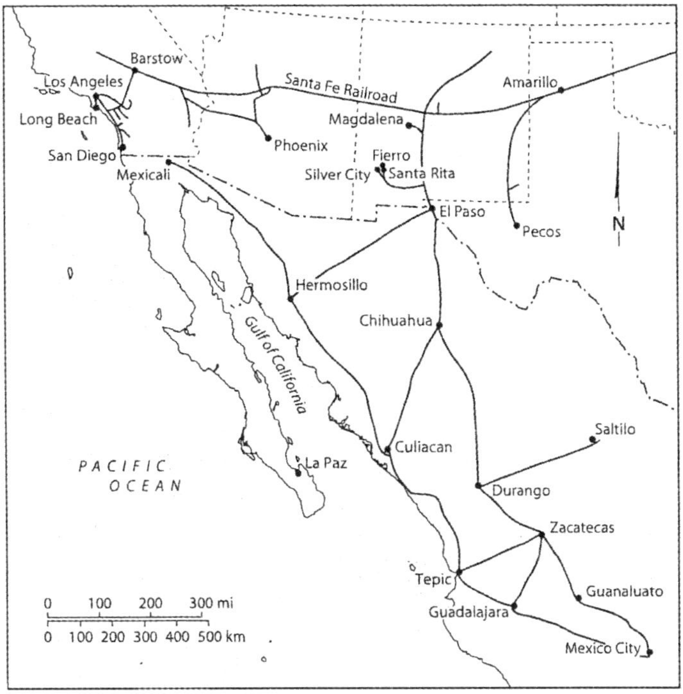

Map 3. Railroads connecting Mexico with Los Angeles, 1910

converged in El Paso. In addition, El Paso possessed a number of factories and railroad shops where migrants could earn additional money before completing their journey to L.A. Some migrants stayed there long enough to learn new skills, learn a little English, and familiarize themselves with the American way of life.[24]

The Juarez–El Paso international border in Texas, where large numbers of refugees destined for Los Angeles crossed over into the United States, was also a center of revolutionary activity. Juarez, on the Mexican side, became one of the main suppliers of arms and ammunition to rebels fighting to overthrow the Diaz regime. In 1906 Enrique and Flores Magon, leaders of the anarcho-syndicalist Partido Liberal Mexicano (PLM)—which later established its headquarters in L.A.—planned an uprising against Diaz in Juarez, only to be betrayed by informants.[25]

Despite this, few of the emigrants traveling through northern Mexico who ended up in Chavez Ravine appear to have had any direct involvement with the 1910 revolution. This was probably because they were attempting to escape from the violence and social chaos that accompanied the revolution, instead of getting caught up in it. As Manazar Gamboa puts it in his epic poem "Memories Around a Deserted Barrio," his father ran away from the Sierra Madre Occidental in 1897, "with the fangs of hunger gnawing at his stomach."[26] Deliberately avoiding Juarez, he made his way directly to Los Angeles.

Nevertheless, a few Chavez Ravine residents did recall incidents from the conflict. In 1949 Rudy Flores, of Palo Verde, told Don Normark that his father had been present when Pancho Villa and his forces marched into his home village in the state of Durango. Villa hated the Catholic Church because of its support for the Diaz regime. Hostility toward the repressive policies of the Church was standard practice among Mexican revolutionaries, as it had been among secular radicals ever since the time of the French Revolution. Pancho Villa ordered his soldiers to destroy the plaster statues of saints in the village church. He then spoke to the landless Indians in the area and urged them to join his cause. "Follow me," Pancho Villa told the Indians. "We have to get rid of all of them landlords."[27]

In the pre–World War I period, curious residents from Chavez Ravine who ventured downtown on a Sunday afternoon attended some of the political rallies held in the Plaza. They heard soapbox orators protesting the arrest and trial of the Magon brothers in the L.A. courts, "free speech" advocates defending the syndicalist doctrines of the Industrial Workers of the World (IWW), and socialist and left-wing trade unionists (some of them from nearby Italian Hall) arguing in favor of social and economic justice.[28]

Years later Carol Jacques told me that her grandfather, Lorenzo Ayala, was a Magonista—a member of the Mexican Land and Liberty movement—who acquired his political opinions by reading *Regeneracion*, the political paper of the Partido Liberal Mexicano. Another of her relatives, Magdaleno Contreras, became a Communist. His son was nicknamed Kropo, short for the Russian anarchist leader Peter Kropotkin. In the 1920s and 1930s quite a few former anarchists and other radicals from the Mexican revolutionary movement joined the Southern California branches of the American Communist Party. Most of them kept their heads down, however, because of the danger of being red-baited.[29]

In 1916 the Magon brothers, who were tried several times for seditious activities in Los Angeles, established a small, radical commune in Echo Park, about a mile west of Chavez Ravine. But they were never able to disentangle themselves from the arm of the law. Enrique Magon was sent back to Mexico, and Ricardo Magon died in a U.S. prison in Fort Leavenworth, Kansas, in 1923.[30]

Religious and Educational Practices in Chavez Ravine

During the 1920s the number of immigrants who crossed the border from Mexico into the United States increased, owing partly to ongoing violence in Mexico and partly to the dramatic growth of the City of Los Angeles and the jobs it provided. L.A.'s population rose from 250,000 in 1914 to more than 2 million in 1930.[31] Another factor was the passage of legislation by Congress in 1924 that reduced European immigration to a trickle, thereby redoubling the demand for cheap Mexican labor in the American Southwest. It was also during this period that the population of Chavez Ravine expanded most rapidly. It rose from about 1,200 in 1918 to more than 2,000 by 1930.[32] What social and economic developments influenced the community as it continued to grow?

Let us look first at religion. Although the barrio's residents were open to a wide range of secular influences, the Catholic faith played an important role in their lives, just as it did among European immigrant communities in cities in the East like Chicago and Cleveland who sought spiritual reinforcement by building their own churches in a new and uncertain world. Because of the relative isolation of Chavez Ravine, its first-generation residents appeared to be more traditional in practicing their faith than Mexican immigrants were in more cosmopolitan, urbanized barrios such as Belvedere and Boyle Heights.

The social activities of the Catholic Church played an especially important role in the lives of the women in the community. For young girls, their first communion was an event of great importance. One young woman remembered how proud she was when her aunt was made a member of the Altar Society of L.A. Iglesia de Santo Nino de Atoche. "These ladies would make clothes for the statues of the saints and decorate the altar with beautiful flowers from their gardens. At Christmas time, the altar was filled with huge, bright red chrysanthemums. Great big bouquets of white lilies adorned the altar on Easter mornings. . . . I loved it."[33] Carol Jacques also enjoyed the ceremonies at Santo Nino Church on Effie Street when she was a little girl. She especially remembered how colorful the church ceremonies were in Palo Verde compared to the more sober services held in the Church of Saint Francis in Silverlake, where she attended elementary school.[34]

Father Tomas Matin, the Austrian-born priest who conducted services at El Santo Nino Church, was a respected local figure. During his long career he presided over innumerable church fiestas, baptisms, weddings, and Saints Days, which were often held outdoors and accompanied by processions and communal meals prepared by the local women. In bad times Father Tomas dispensed coupons to poor children who attended mass regularly. The coupons were then exchanged for clothes or toys that had been donated to the church by charitable organizations. Occasionally, Father Matin also provided shelter for illegal Mexican immigrants who hid in his church. The Los Angeles Archdiocese reproved him for this.[35]

For children, attending mass in one of the ravine's two small churches was not always as dull as it might seem. Several former residents remembered Saturday afternoons in the church hall when they watched rented comedies like *Rin Tin Tin*, *Laurel and Hardy*, and westerns featuring Tom Mix, Roy Rogers, or Hoot Gibson. Many barrio children drifted away from the faith when they grew up or were absorbed into the secular, urban culture of downtown L.A. Others deliberately repudiated Catholicism in favor of some other belief system. But even the agnostics among them remembered with affection the fiestas and public church ceremonies they spent with their families in El Santo Nino Church.[36]

Educational issues in Chavez Ravine were more complicated. The barrio had two elementary schools, one in Palo Verde and the other on Paducah Street. The latter only offered very basic instruction, and it gained a reputation for admitting those children who spoke no English. Other educational organizations such as the Woodcraft Rangers (similar to the Boy Scouts) also established branches in the ravine. After graduating from elementary school the children went by bus or Red Car to Central Junior High on North Grand Street or to Nightingale Junior High School. In the early days, almost none of them went on to college. According to one estimate, even this low assessment of scholastic achievement in the ravine was overoptimistic. In 1945 some of the kids were still failing to complete elementary school. Among the better-performing children, the average period of schooling was from four to five years.[37]

Around the time of the First World War, Los Angeles became a fashionable center for religious revivals—a place where evangelical ministers and high-minded progressives sought to socialize recent immigrants into Anglo-American norms of behavior, which they believed to be necessary for individual prosperity and spiritual salvation. In 1915 the California state legislature passed the Home Teacher Act, which mandated special teachers to visit homes and teach the basic principles of sanitation, domestic economy, and the duties of American citizenship. "Sanitary, hygienic, and dietetic measures are not easily learned by the Mexican," wrote one reformer, betraying the condescending attitude toward Latinos that characterized much of L.A.'s white population.[38]

Although disrespectful of Latino culture, the Home Teacher Act at least purported to have the best interests of Mexican American schoolchildren at heart. But the overall attitude of the Los Angeles School Board and its employees toward Latino students was deeply racist. White school superintendents felt no shame about verbalizing contempt for their Mexican American charges. Minority children had "lower moral standards" than white children. They were "lazy, have no ambition, and won't take advantage of opportunities offered them."[39] Although L.A.'s schools were not officially segregated, officials took advantage of the city's "whites only" residential covenants to place thousands of them into special "Mexican schools" that emphasized vocational education at the expense of academic instruction. This was just as true of the schools in and around Chavez Ravine as it was of the other schools in East L.A.[40]

Because of their relative isolation, Chavez Ravine's elementary schools experienced even higher rates of absenteeism than most regular city schools. Playing hooky in the nearby woods and hills was a constant temptation. So, too, was slipping out of school early to help mother at home or, for boys, taking part in pickup games or tinkering with one of the innumerable broken-down cars that lay in the ravine's vacant lots and alleyways.

For most barrio students, however, the main stumbling block to any kind of social advancement was learning—or not learning—the English language. Spanish was spoken almost universally in the home and at church, but it was supposed to be taboo at school, where in the early days all the teachers were white and rarely spoke Spanish. Some of the ravine's early settlers were illiterate even in their own language, so learning English, which was essential if one was to climb out of the barrio, was far more of a problem then than it is now. In fact, learning to read and write English well, which seemed unnecessary in the monolingual, daily life of the barrio, became a critical dividing line between those who learned to flourish in the Anglo world and those who did not.

For some pioneer families in Chavez Ravine, maintaining the dominance of Spanish was also a source of cultural pride. Among adolescents, it could even become a means of resisting adult control. One day in 1939, for example, when five-year-old Manazar Gamboa began speaking English at home, his mother snapped, "Don't come to me with your English! Speak *our* Spanish."[41] This incident evidently encouraged Manazar to resist learning English at Nightingale Junior High School. Many years later,

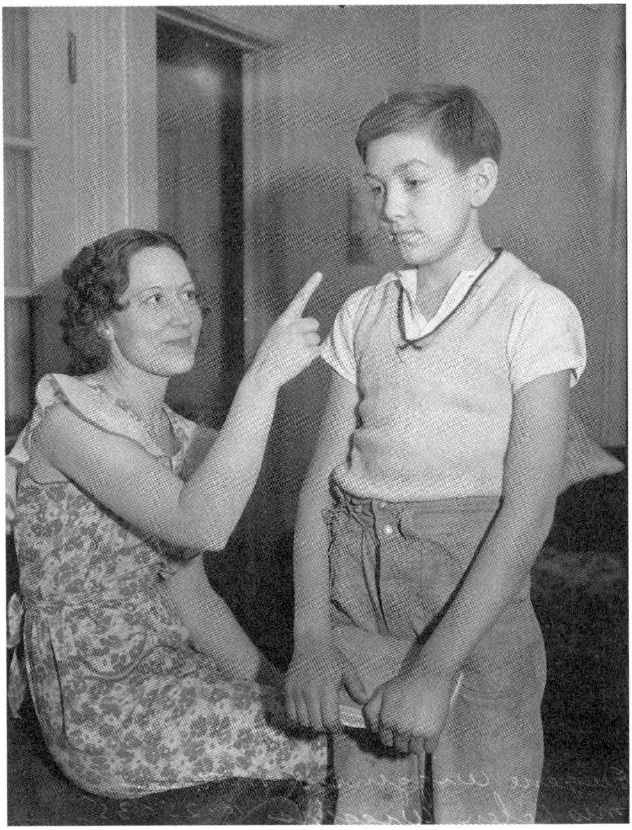

Figure 4. Miss Wiggins reprimanding a boy at Palo Verde School. Courtesy *Los Angeles Times*.

in an interview, he said that his rebellion over the language issue also influenced his subsequent descent into criminal behavior. "My rebellion was so complete that I didn't really speak English until I was eighteen. That was also when I was first sent to prison for armed robbery."[42]

Getting a Job

How typical of Chavez Ravine's adolescents Manazar Gamboa's youthful rebellion over learning English was is unclear. But in addition to white stereotypes about the "laziness" or "stupidity" of Mexican workers, the language issue was one of the main barriers they encountered in their efforts to secure decent jobs. Anecdotal evidence suggests that a few adult males from the ravine acquired skilled positions in the nearby Southern Pacific Railroad yards or as printers, restaurant owners, and garage mechanics. But for the most part they worked for low wages as laborers digging ditches, restaurant employees washing dishes, or unskilled workers toiling at poorly paid service jobs in bakeries, slaughterhouses, and packing plants. Willie Segura remembered that his father managed to keep the same job as a skilled molder in a downtown iron foundry for almost forty years. His dad was lucky, he said, "because in those days they didn't hire no Mexicans at all."[43]

One industry that did employ significant numbers of Mexican men was brick making, owing to Chavez Ravine's large clay deposits. At a time when Los Angeles was expanding rapidly and bricks were still used for home construction, the brick and tile making industry employed more than forty thousand male laborers throughout the city. This had been an important occupation for Mexican Americans ever since the original "Zanja Madre" (Mother Ditch) municipal water supply had been laid down in the early nineteenth century. Except for the skilled tile makers, the wages of these brick makers averaged no more than twenty cents an hour. Many brick makers came from the Mexican state of Jalisco. One writer states that "Simons brick workers and their families epitomized the working poor, Mexican poor of industrial Los Angeles."[44]

At least three brickyards existed in Chavez Ravine. Joel Gomez, Manazar Gamboa's father, worked for several years in one of them. Machines did some of the work, such as digging clay from the nearby clay pits. But stacking the heavy clay bricks into the giant kilns and then, after they had cooled, throwing them down from the kiln roof to catchers loading the bricks into trucks twenty feet below was an arduous and dangerous task carried out exclusively by hand. A bad catch could break a nose or jaw or do even more serious damage.[45]

We can catch a glimpse of the debilitating nature of work in a brickyard in the following exchange between Joel Gomez and his son that occurred when they passed by the La Ladrillera brickworks one day, on their way to downtown Los Angeles:

> "Oh, look, there's La Ladrillera brick works, where I worked," said my Dad. "I hated that brickyard! It was dirty. Red dust got into our lungs. The weight of the bricks bent our backs. New bricks scraped our hands until they were raw. And the bosses yelled at us like we were animals. By the end of the day I hated everyone," Dad said, "especially the bosses!" "I

seen the workers going home," Meno [Manazar] replied. "They looked like broken dolls."[46]

In comparison to working in a brickyard, laying track for Henry E. Huntington's Pacific Electric Railway (nicknamed Red Cars) was a coveted occupation. At least forty men from Chavez Ravine worked as railroad tracklayers in the 1920s and 1930s. Sometimes they were away from home for weeks at a time. They were housed in labor camps, which the P. E. Company built as temporary shelters as Huntington extended his suburban Red Car system all across the Los Angeles Basin. Elsewhere in Southern California, Mexicans who worked for the Southern Pacific Railroad earned an average of $1.25 per day, while Greeks earned $1.60 and Japanese laborers $1.45 for the same work. These wage differentials provided further evidence of a nativist bias against "lazy" and "unreliable" Mexican "greasers," which lasted among some employers until World War II and beyond. But in downtown Los Angeles, where the Pacific Electric Co. had to compete with the Southern Pacific and the Santa Fe Railroad companies for labor, Huntington paid his workers $1.85 per day, no matter their ethnicity.[47]

It was relatively rare for the women of Chavez Ravine to work outside the home in the early days. Some of the wives and daughters earned extra money by carrying out traditional female tasks at home, such as taking in laundry or sewing garments for white middle-class housewives. But Louis Ruiz remembered his mother leaving home every morning to work for regular wages as a seamstress in the garment district at 7th Street and San Pedro—an occupation that became increasingly common among the next generation of Mexican girls. A few men from the ravine also worked in the upholstery lofts (making cushions and other items) in L.A.'s booming furniture shops downtown. As for Louis Ruiz's father, he worked as a laborer and mechanic for the Los Angeles Red Cars.[48]

It may be that Chavez Ravine's peculiar geographical position distorted the employment patterns of its male population. But their jobs were unlikely to have differed very much from those of Mexican men in the city as a whole. According to the 1930 census, 31.1 percent of L.A.'s Mexican men were employed in manufacturing (the majority of these were laborers: only 13.2 percent were in the skilled trades); 18 percent were full-time farm workers; 16.8 percent of the men were engaged in transportation (mostly as tracklayers or railroad laborers); and 5.4 percent were engaged in the retail trades, usually as Mexican store owners or as behind-the-counter servers. Only 2.6 percent of Mexican men and women held

Figure 5. Mexican tracklayers working on the Red Car lines. Courtesy Huntington Library, San Marino, California.

professional or clerical jobs. Some of the small number of men listed as professionals were musicians who performed in nightclubs or for street entertainment.[49]

The one occupation in which entire families from Chavez Ravine—men, women, and children—could participate was earning extra cash by harvesting crops during the summer in the fields and ranches that stretched north, south, and east beyond the Los Angeles Basin. Seasonal harvesting has, of course, remained a full-time job for large numbers of Mexican laborers in Los Angeles County until today. Many of the ravine's families looked forward to their yearly summer expedition because it enabled them to renew old friendships among the growing stream of seasonal laborers who came north from Mexico to work during the harvest season or with those who remained in the United States year-round but moved from one state to another picking and planting different crops.[50]

As soon as school let out in June or July, dozens of ravine families began planning for the annual "trip to the crops." It was acceptable for women and girls to join in and earn extra money because they remained in the company of their husbands or parents. The families loaded up their old trucks and cars and drove north up Route 5 to harvest nuts, vegetables, and fruit or down south to the Imperial Valley to pick melons. They often

Figure 6. Mexican families harvesting walnuts in summer. Courtesy *Los Angeles Times*.

formed a caravan of cars along the highway, in case someone needed help with a flat or a breakdown. Once they got to their destination, the harvesters would camp together in tents or in the rudimentary shelters provided by the ranch owners or growers. The kids, especially, loved these expeditions and thought of them as vacations. "My dad and mom raised seven of us," remembered Sally Munoz. "It was fun. They would take us up north to pick tomatoes, grapes, and walnuts in Whittier. We were always late when school started, about a month and a half late. I could never catch up. It got to a point where I went to school just to be going, I guess. One of my brothers graduated. He was the only one of seven that did."[51]

These summer trips were not always joyful. Albert Elias recalled how, after his family returned in 1938 from a long trip picking plums, grapes, and tomatoes for a few cents a box, they had less money left over than they had when they left home. "Dad emptied all his pockets, all the money he had, and my mom took all the money out of her purse and put it there on the table. They had $7.50. From the whole summer. I think they had more when they left in June."[52]

Manazar Gamboa left a vivid memory of his first boyhood experience of summer harvesting. His memoir shows us how, in the overcrowded houses of Chavez Ravine with numerous boys and girls crammed into a tiny space—or in a summer tent, as in this example—sexual initiation sometimes occurred earlier than it did among middle-class whites. The following lines paraphrase parts of "Buttonwillow," one of Gamboa's best poems:

> My family is picking cotton. My mother drags a ten-foot canvas sack behind her—a white, giant worm glowing in the sun. She stoops over to drag it, her hands move rhythmically, picking soft, white, cotton balls from the low, claw-like plants. It is hot . . . hot . . . hot. . . .
>
> Slowly, my head goes down. I fall asleep on the peaceful, cotton-stuffed sack . . . to the rhythm of the picking, and the dragging, and the swaying, and the rays of the burning sun.
>
> At night, we sleep in the back of trucks, on the ground, or in a big, old tent that has my cousins, and two teenagers from other families I do not know. It is hot in the tent. . . . I can see Alcina's half naked body in the dark. She has jet black hair, pretty eyes, and a smooth, curving body. . . .
>
> "Meno, would you like to touch me?" she whispered. I was embarrassed—didn't know what she meant. I moved away a little. Alcina was quiet for a while. Then she slid closer to me, put out her hand, and touched me on my thing. She giggled. "Here, Meno, put it here," she whispered. I did. It felt warm and nice. It was the first time.[53]

Social Tensions and Relations with Police

In 1924 the training of LAPD officers began at the Los Angeles Police Revolver and Athletic Club in Elysian Park. Ironically, given the long-standing racist practices of the city's white police force toward Mexicans and other ethnic minorities, the police academy at first had quite good relations with the Chavez Ravine community. It ran a boy's club for the youths in the barrio and allowed the kids to swim in the pool next to its training facility.[54]

But as time passed, the LAPD grew harsher in its treatment of the residents of Chavez Ravine, especially its youth. Based on their experience in World War I, law enforcement authorities expected an increase in lawless behavior as World War II approached, and the number of juvenile arrests in East L.A. more than doubled from 1939 to 1945. To some extent, this increase resulted from the need to enforce wartime regulations, such as the nighttime curfew. It was also due to misleading daily reports about "zoot suit gangs" and "Pachuco gangsters."[55] But the newly repressive treatment also stemmed from public fear of Japanese air attacks, as well as from anxiety about a loosening of public morals that supposedly resulted from the huge influx of newcomers—including many single and married women—who came to L.A. in search of war jobs.[56]

It has since been established that these fears were exaggerated. But reports of increased LAPD vigilance, sometimes accompanied by indiscriminate violence, were quickly picked up by the inhabitants of Chavez Ravine. "I saw them [police] beat a Mexican kid from Palo Verde for no apparent reason," recalled Vince Delgado of Alta Loma in January 1940. "He was handcuffed in a SWAT car and led away. They caught him (running, hands cuffed behind him!) and beat the heck out of him. Kicked him, hit him with the sticks."[57]

The growing harshness of the police response can also be explained by the increasing presence of neighborhood gangs, even though they were less brutal and violent during the 1930s and 1940s than they subsequently became. "They had gangs," stated Vince Delgado. But he was reluctant to admit that they posed a serious problem in Chavez Ravine. "They never really bothered anybody," he added, disingenuously. "The guys used to drink or smoke pot. I never saw them with needles or anything like that. I never saw them with guns."[58] Despite this disclaimer, anxiety about gang behavior was expressed by first-generation Mexican American mothers whose children were born in Chavez Ravine and who were unable to control with the same degree of authority they had been able to exert in Mexico's more traditional society.

Evidence in support of this concern is provided by the unruly behavior of an increasing number of Chavez Ravine youths, angry at their lowly status, who were willing to risk jail by breaking the rules. Among them were Manazar Gamboa and his childhood friend Frankie. Even before they were ten, both of these boys began taking drugs and indulged in a series of youthful pranks like stealing rabbits and exploding live bullets picked up from the police academy's firing range. At first, these pranks appeared fairly harmless. But within a few months they had deteriorated into serious crime.

Serious trouble started when Manazar and Frankie began imitating the behavior of a group of older boys, some of whom were unquestionably gang members, who developed the habit of walking down into Chinatown and North Broadway at night to steal automobiles. The youngsters learned how to hot-wire cars, drive them around town for a time, and then take

Figure 7. A young ravine resident fixing his car. Courtesy *Los Angeles Times*.

them back up into Chavez Ravine. They would strip the vehicles of their saleable accessories, such as hubcaps and tires, and then abandon them or hide them in the brush.[59]

It was no coincidence that Manazar and Frankie chose car stealing as their way to get ahead in the world. In the 1930s and 1940s the desire to own, or at least get a hold of, a car was just as much of an obsession among young Mexican American men in the ravine as it was among young white males in the L.A. suburbs. Those who could afford it customized their vehicles by adding original upholstery and double rearview mirrors from Tijuana, as well as acrylic enamel or lacquer paint jobs. In Boyle Heights, the owners of corner service stations and auto repair shops would lend their facilities to ambitious young men, encouraging them to turn out "custom jobs."[60]

Manazar Gamboa and Frankie were too young to go this far. But in 1948, when Manazar was fourteen, a joyride he and Frankie took in a stolen car had disastrous, long-term consequences. High on beer, they drove a late-model Chevy at high speed along the Avenue of the Palms up through Elysian Park, where they were caught by police:

> "Open the hood!" The cops found the hot wire, cuffed us, then
> Took us down to Georgia Street jail, near Venice and Pico
> "Name?" "Meno Gomez." "Age?" "Fourteen." "Address?"
> "1760 Bishops Road." "Well, this doesn't just mean Juvenile Hall,
> you Goddam punks. It's gonna mean a hell of a lot more!"[61]

The sequel to this incident shows how brutal the LAPD could be, even when it was dealing with young boys. Manazar and Frankie were booked at the Georgia Street jail and led down to the cells:

> The hall was in semi-darkness. The silhouettes of several boys leaned against the cubicle doors. "Who are you?" several silhouettes called out to the newcomers. "Hold it down, assholes," said the guard, striking one boy in the face with his nightstick. "Fuck you, bull!" said the other boys, surging angrily into the light. Straightaway whistles blew, nightsticks flew, and several more boys fell to the floor! They were beaten for ten minutes or more. The other silhouettes quickly disappeared.
>
> The jailor kicked Frankie in the balls and shoved him, gasping, into cell number 2. CLANG! Then he pushed me into cell number 4, knocking me to the ground and laughing as he did so. CLANG! It was the first of many times I was to hear steel against steel, depriving me of my freedom and future![62]

Modernization and Social Change

The pleasure that families from Chavez Ravine took in harvesting fruit and cotton by hand on their summer trips—a task seen by many whites as demeaning and old-fashioned—did not mean they wanted to remain stuck in the same preindustrial habits they had earlier followed in Mexico. To the contrary, their main purpose in coming north to Los Angeles was to get away from the semifeudal way of life that had restricted their lives south of the border and to embrace the new opportunities available in a modern American city such as Los Angeles.

When they first arrived most of the settlers' wives made all (or most) of their own clothes and those of their children by hand. In the remoter Mexican villages, few stores sold ready-made garments. But these women quickly realized that it was quicker and cheaper to buy mass-produced blouses, skirts, and pants from the garment district in downtown L.A. than it was to make them themselves. Several hundred young Chicana women and girls from Chavez Ravine ended up working there.[63]

It was the same with kitchen utensils, newspapers, radios, iceboxes, and store-bought food. On Saints Days or other special occasions, traditional foods continued to be prepared and presented in the time-honored manner. But on most weekdays, ravine families now ate mass-produced items sold by local Mexican-run stores that prepared the items to fit immigrant tastes. On weekends, even newcomers to Chavez Ravine eagerly adjusted their habits to take in American-style movies, boxing matches, horse races, and other modern entertainments.[64]

Despite the poverty and lack of education of most residents, a few of them also experienced upward social mobility, even in the first generation. For example, Carol Jacques's aunt Juanita became a school teacher. After beginning his career as a baker's assistant, her uncle Pete graduated from USC with a degree in pharmacology and bought a pharmacy on 6th Street in downtown L.A. Carol's mother worked in a cosmetics factory on Vermont Avenue in Hollywood, while her uncle Sisto bought a gardening business.[65]

In the 1920s and subsequent years, other developments that occurred in the area around Chavez Ravine showed further modernizing tendencies at work. To the north beyond Riverside Drive, expensive, middle-class homes—complete with two-door garages—were built in the terraces that led down to the Los Angeles River. Several silent movies were made in Elysian Park, which enabled some of the ravine's residents to secure temporary jobs as extras or laborers building the sets.[66]

These modernizing tendencies did not mean that second-generation immigrants in Chavez Ravine abandoned all of their Mexican traditions. Most of the barrio's young people still spoke Spanish at home and attended the Mexican Catholic church. Not all of them became U.S. citizens. What these modernizing tendencies did mean, however, was that the new generation underwent a complex process of acculturation in which they adopted those aspects of the American way of life that were either useful or necessary to their progress in U.S. society, while at the same time retaining the elements of Mexican culture they still valued. Unlike their children, few first-generation inhabitants of the ravine became full-fledged American citizens in the Anglo-American sense of the word, despite efforts of the post–World War I "Americanizers" to "cleanse" them of their Mexican heritage. Instead, in their own time and in their own way, they evolved a unique set of behavioral characteristics that today we would label "Mexican American."[67]

In 1928 an anonymous Mexican American writer for *La Opinion*, L.A.'s leading Spanish-language newspaper, wrote a series of articles that provided a more detailed description of the geography and way of life of the three subbarrios that made up the Chavez Ravine community. His descriptions show us how far that way of life had changed since the latter part of the nineteenth century and how far it had not.

First, and nearest to downtown, was the smallest subbarrio, Bishop, which in its early years contained about one hundred families but by now had expanded up the hill to the point where Bishops Road met Pine Street and crossed Effie. Its *gente*, or better-off elements, built their houses higher up on the slopes of Bishops Canyon. Behind Bishops Canyon stood the second, larger barrio of Alta Loma. In 1920 a post office and a shop that carried American foods as well as flour, tortillas, and beans had been added to serve the people there. To the west lay the third, even larger, barrio of Palo Verde. The most telling sign of modernization was the fact that scattered among the houses and shacks all across the ravine one could now see automobiles in various states of repair.[68]

The writer in *La Opinion* also made some shrewd observations about community relations. They are especially noteworthy in light of the fact that, because of the ravine's isolation, welfare agents and city bureaucrats were unable to exert the same degree of social control there that they did in other parts of Los Angeles.

> In the barrio, "vatos" and "jainas" (boys and girls) start playing together when they are toddlers. They form neighborhood groups by the age of nine. Throughout puberty they play organized games and go through their early troubles together. Kids and adults alike hang out on their front porches and talk, laugh, tell stories, initiate romances, socialize. By their early teens the "vatos" and "jainas" have formed strong bonds. And from these strong bonds comes the formation of their own law. And their law is real! It may have flaws, but in most cases it is more respected than the law of the state, because, unlike the law of the state, the law of the barrio is made by its own "gente."[69]

Historically, some degree of cultural separation has always existed between the U.S.-born generation of Mexican Americans and the immigrant generation of recent arrivals from Mexico. As we have already seen, some of the latter group continued for a time to earn their living as peripatetic workers, employed by Southern California ranchers, railroad companies, and mine operators who operated in the borderlands between Los Angeles and the Mexican border, before they settled permanently in Los Angeles. These generational differences quite often provoked disagreements between the two groups over issues ranging from religious observance to courtship and gender roles and from childrearing practices to questions of national identity. By 1928, *La Opinion* observed, these differences between the American-born and immigrant generations had become more marked. "These [young] leaders, also, are real. They do not buy their positions by spending money on political campaigns as do government bureaucrats. They grow into leaders by showing strict adherence to their barrio's law. In the case of Chavez Ravine, the law of the minor does not always jive with the law of the adult. And because each group was determined to back up its particular beliefs, a division took place between the traditional generation, those born in Mexico, and the new generation, those born in the U.S."[70]

The only sensibilities that clearly transcended this generational divide (and not always then) were loyalty to family, neighborhood gangs, and to the barrio community as a whole—especially when it was threatened from the outside, as the Chavez Ravine community was in the 1950s in the struggle over evictions and the loss of homes.

Conclusion

Such was life in Chavez Ravine in its heyday between World War I and the Great Depression. Its people were poor, its children frequently wore ragged clothes and went to school without shoes, and the barrio still lacked most elements of modern urban infrastructure. But the intimacy of its neighborhood life and the uniqueness of its geography created an organic, self-made community with a strong sense of place and of pride in its own identity and traditions. Unlike L.A.'s other downtown barrios, which often included Jews, Asians, and African Americans mixed in with the Mexican population, the loyalty of its residents was largely undiluted by the presence of other ethnic groups. The privacy made possible by the ravine's rolling hills and canyons clearly contributed to the strong sense of community loyalty that was such a marked feature of the inhabitants.

The loyalty of the ravine's residents to their barrio was cemented in other ways, too. According to the population census, a majority of the houses in the ravine were first occupied in the years from 1910 to 1930 by families with many children. This suggests the presence of multigenerational families who built up the community in its early years and passed their cultural traditions down from one generation to the next. Memories of caring grandparents loomed large in the reminiscences of many of the residents. To be sure, by the 1920s, when they learned English and the secular ways of the big city, some of these children rebelled against both their parents and the threat posed by the dominance of orthodox Anglo-American culture by dressing differently, dancing the jitterbug, learning swing music from African American and Jewish musicians, or by leaving the community altogether.

But the persistence with which third- or even fourth-generation descendants from Chavez Ravine returned to Elysian Park year after year in the 1970s and 1980s to picnic and share their memories of the time before "the great eviction" suggests a community pride that remained strong long after Bishop, Alta Loma, and Palo Verde had been razed. In July 1988 Natalie Ramirez was still sufficiently incensed by the evictions of the 1950s that she wrote the following in a letter to a member of the Dodger baseball club administration who had spoken slightingly about the ravine in its pre-Dodger days. "How dare any of you call Chavez Ravine a wasteland or a slum?" she wrote. "Maybe it wasn't Beverly Hills, but it was home to a lot of people, my family included. Doesn't anyone want to recognize us because we are Mexicans?"[71]

This gibe, delivered after two generations of change in which the lives of most of L.A.'s Mexicans had significantly improved, not only shows how much the scars left by the evictions of the 1950s still hurt. It also touches on the question that probably rankled most of all—the extent of Anglo-American racial prejudice and condescension. This was an issue that, during the years of the Great Depression and World War II, would affect the residents of Chavez Ravine even more directly than it had before.

CHAPTER TWO

Prelude to a Crisis

Race, Patriotism, and Public Housing in Depression and War, 1929–1949

"Mexicans received the lowest welfare benefits on a scale that gave whites the highest, with Blacks in between. Welfare officials also tried to force people off the rolls and into the agricultural fields in order to break strikes."

—DOUGLAS MONROY

"When the [Zoot Suit] rioting finally stopped, the Eagle Rock Advertiser *mournfully editorialized: 'It's too bad the servicemen were called off before they were able to finish the job. . . . Most of the citizens of the city have been delighted with what has been going on."*

—CAREY MCWILLIAMS

Chavez Ravine and the 1930s Depression

Many people believed at the time that the Great Depression that followed the stock market crash of 1929 was less severe in Los Angeles than it was in the nation's other big cities. It is true that the good weather and agricultural surpluses produced in L.A. County made the crisis somewhat easier to deal with than it was elsewhere. But in terms of unemployment, families on welfare, and other indexes of loss, the Depression was just as serious in Southern California as it was in other parts of the country. Indeed, for Mexican Americans on public relief it may have been even tougher, since the City of Los Angeles was more reluctant to spend public money on the unemployed than most other big cities in the United States were.[1]

Catholic Charities, which was administered by the Los Angeles Archdiocese, was the main source of private relief for Mexican families, including those in Chavez Ravine. But its resources were limited, and as the number of unemployed grew, families in the ravine found themselves relying more and more on what they could produce from their own backyards and from their harvesting trips into the hinterland. Labor groups protested that Mexican immigrants were taking jobs away from native-born whites, and ravine residents who worked downtown found themselves being replaced by white employees, who pressed the City of Los Angeles to hire only U.S. "citizens."[2] In August 1931, the state legislature in Sacramento passed the Alien Labor Act, which made it illegal for any business doing business with the state to employ "aliens" on public works.[3]

No official statistics exist regarding the extent of unemployment in Chavez Ravine during the Great Depression, but it probably differed little from the 15 percent to 20 percent that prevailed in the rest of East L.A. In March 1934, a reporter for the *Echo Park Advertiser* met up with a group of eight women in Alta Loma and asked them how many of their husbands were out of work. Two said their husbands earned a few dollars a week delivering goods or cleaning railroad cars, while three others reported that their husbands "stayed home and did nothing."[4] Thirty-eight-year-old Mary Elucia, who had four young children, reported that her husband had been laid off by the Pacific Electric Company in 1932, had been out of work ever since, and had spent his few remaining dollars on drink. "If it wasn't for the [Catholic] charity," she added, "I would have nothing." Her family ate "the chickens, rabbits and squirrels Joseph catches, and some roots and apples we have in the yard. We've had no milk or cornmeal for months, and the baby has gotten sick."[5]

Another woman told the *Echo Park Advertiser* that her husband had gone back to Mexico eight months ago to try to sell his father's vacant house in Durango, and she had not heard from him since. Still another woman, who had been evicted for failing to pay her rent, reported that she had moved with her three children into her daughter's house. The two combined families between them had one son and an elderly man working—the latter, whose pay had fallen to six dollars a week, for an ice delivery company. Until the previous fall her son had worked three days a week digging flood control ditches for the City of L.A. But he had been told he would soon be replaced by "someone else—probably a white man."[6]

The county and state relief system that emerged to aid the unemployed was also discriminatory. The number of welfare cases in Los Angeles County more than doubled from 1929 to 1931. But only U.S. citizens were eligible to apply for assistance, and when Mexicans were questioned about their status the percentage of them on relief fell dramatically, from 21.5 percent in 1929 to 12.5 percent in 1931.[7] After the federal relief programs started by President Roosevelt in 1933 came on line, the system became somewhat more equitable, a development that was remembered by some of the families in Chavez Ravine with gratitude. "I used to go with my Dad down to *la comisaria* [federal relief office] to get a gunny sack . . . to Echo Park," recalled Tony Montez. "He'd go in line [and] get packages of beans, navy beans, garabanzos, stuff like that. Everything was so scarce. But it made a difference."[8]

Albert Elias on the other hand, who grew up in Palo Verde, remembered how hard it was to get either adequate relief payments or enough work to keep the wolf from the door. "[In] one week he could be a gardener, a cement finisher, construction, roofer, you name it," his son stated. "They used to work until the job was done and then they used to lay him off. He never had a steady job until 1938 or 1939, when the United States knew they were going to war."[9]

Perhaps the most moving account of the impact of the Great Depression on the residents of Chavez Ravine came in a memoir, written years later by Manazar Gamboa (called Meno in this story) about the occasion in 1938 when he and his father walked three miles from their home on Bishops Road to the Grand Central Market in downtown L.A. in search of food. The fact that they left home at 5:00 in the morning to prevent their neighbors from witnessing their departure suggests that they did not want to reveal how badly off they were. (Notice also, in the following passage, that Joel Gomez refers to the white American tourists who frequented Olvera Street as "the real wetbacks." This tells us something about how Mexican Americans resented being stigmatized by the use of the term.)

> "That little shrimp house is too expensive for us," Papa said as they traversed Chinatown, pulling their wooden wagon behind them. "Everything in Chinatown is. We'll eat in the market."
>
> "Olvera Street is empty," said Papa after they had gone a little further. "It's too early for the turistas, Meno. Do you know that most of the people who come here are turistas? They are descendants of those wetbacks who came here from Europe." "I didn't know they called them wetbacks," said Meno. "Well, if you think about it, they're the real wetbacks, not us," Papa added. "After all, they crossed the Atlantic."[10]

Papa and Meno walked on in silence until they reached the Grand Central Market on Alameda and Seventh. The clatter of hundreds of trucks being unloaded, the hubbub of voices, and the whistles and roars of the trains that brought many of the provisions to market made them pause and hold their ears for a moment, before beginning to shop.

"That's too expensive for us, Juan," Papa says to a man who wants them to buy fresh fruit. Papa waits until the market man has gone, then walks surreptitiously over to a pile of discarded fruit lying on the ground and quickly loads up the wagon.

Another man sees Papa. "Hello, Alfredo, how did you do?" "Not bad, but everything is so expensive!" Alfredo pulls a bottle of tequila out of his jacket, and Papa takes a healthy drink. Good byes all round. . . . Papa and Meno feel apprehensive as they get nearer to home, and their neighbors are able to see they only brought back discarded fruit.

Roco's mother is hanging out clothes on the line two doors down from their house. She looks up as Papa and Meno pass by, glances at the wagon, and shakes her head disapprovingly.

"Everyone can see we're bringing home rotten fruit," says Meno, in dismay.

"Half rotten," retorts Papa. "Don't worry, we'll cut the bad parts out."[11]

Nativism and the Deportation Scare

Aside from poverty and unemployment, the most damaging experience for L.A.'s Mexican community in the Depression years, including those in Chavez Ravine, was the wave of nativist sentiment that swept over much of L.A.'s white community during the course of the decade. Its main manifestation was a federally sponsored program of forced "repatriation to Mexico," which was carried out from 1931 to 1935. The main purpose of the repatriation program was to get Mexican immigrants off the relief rolls and to rid L.A. of immigrant workers who were said to deprive native-born whites of their jobs. But racial scapegoating was clearly involved. As Manazar Gamboa later put it in one of his essays:

> White Americans blamed unemployment on Mexicans;
> those very same people whom they had imported
> to do their dirty work, and they took harsh
> measures to eliminate "the problem."[12]

In January 1931 Charles P. Visel, head of the Los Angeles Committee to Coordinate Unemployment Relief, announced an LAPD sweep of the Plaza area, the first of several designed to frighten immigrants into leaving the city voluntarily. Many immigrants without citizenship papers took the hint and went back across the border without being forced to do so. In February police chief Steckel alarmed the Mexican community even more when he claimed that it was responsible for "most of our crime problems." He said that henceforth, when his officers arrested a suspected illegal immigrant, "attention will be paid not only to the person under arrest, but to all members of the family."[13]

The most alarming experience, however, befell those who were rounded up and put on trains to take them back across the border. In the frenzied roundups that preceded the deportations, Mexican residents of L.A. who already had their citizenship papers were sometimes put on trains as well. The first of these trainloads left Los Angeles on March 23, 1931, and was followed by several others in subsequent months. By 1934, almost a third of L.A.'s Mexican population of about one hundred thousand had been sent back across the border.[14]

How many Chavez Ravine residents there were among the deportees is unclear. Anecdotal sources record only one, but there were probably others. Isabella Fierro Rodriguez recalled that her father "in 1932 took off voluntarily to Mexico, to Chihuahua because of the depression." He did so, she said, before "they"—the deportation authorities—"could catch him."[15] Rodriguez took his four-year-old daughter Isabella along with him, as well as the clothing and furniture he had bought in Los Angeles, to give to family members back in Chihuahua. Isabella was raised in Mexico for the next ten years. But her father brought her back to L.A. in 1943 when wartime jobs became easier to get.[16] Many Mexican deportees later returned to the city for the same reason.

This was not the only deportation incident to affect the residents of Chavez Ravine. One day in September 1932, an LAPD patrol car drove up Bishops Road behind a group of young Mexicans walking home after a trip downtown. Getting out of the car, the police told the young men to report to the downtown deportation office the next day. But when the officers started to write down their names, the young men ran off up the hill and hid in some bushes. The patrol car, lights flashing, searched for them for about half an hour before giving up the chase. It was rare for the LAPD to carry out searches of this kind in the ravine. They usually left policing up to the staff and trainees at the police academy, which was located nearby in Elysian Park. At a community meeting held in Bishop a few days later, several older residents urged the young men of the barrio to stay indoors at night until the scare blew over.[17]

The effect of this deportation campaign on the Mexican community was traumatic. It divided families, threatened barrio communities, caused dissension in Latino civic organizations, and—by reducing the overall size

Figure 8. Mexicans awaiting deportation at Union Station. Courtesy *Los Angeles Times*.

of the Latino population—undermined numerous family-owned businesses. According to one historian, those who returned to Mexico sometimes felt like strangers in their native land, while those who remained in L.A. became more suspicious of the Anglo community and hunkered down in places like Chavez Ravine and the urban barrios on the east side of the Los Angeles River.[18]

The racial scapegoating that accompanied the deportation campaign also increased the sense of uncertainty among Mexican Americans about their identity and made the recent immigrants among them more pessimistic about their future in the United States. At the same time, the draining off of large numbers of single men and youths who were sent back across the border accelerated the rise to prominence of the second Latino generation.[19]

Patriotism, Prejudice, and Latinos in the Military

Despite Chavez Ravine's relative isolation, its residents shared the same feelings of excitement, loyalty, and fear of Japanese invasion that America's entry into World War II raised throughout the rest of Southern California. Included in one of Manazar Gamboa's short stories is an imaginary conversation between two women from the ravine who travel through downtown on a Red Car. It captures the heightened tensions the women feel as they pass by the crowded bars, the sidewalks filled with GIs with girls on their arms and the new mixture of people on the city streets.

One of the women calls out the names of the movie houses and gambling joints that youths from the ravine were accustomed to visit at night in the downtown area—the Million Dollar, the Kozy, and the Central on Third Street and the Roxy, the Arcade, and the Cameo on Fifth. Then she catches sight of St. Peter's Dance Hall and exclaims, "I'll never know why the church rents its hall to irresponsible people. Lots of kids who go there are Pachucos." She adds disapprovingly, "It's supposed to be for dancing, but they drink, get into serious fights, and who knows what goes on behind the building." Her companion also grows agitated as she points out La Copa de Oro, famous for being a rough bar: "A man was killed there the other night."[20]

Although the impact of the war was not as extensive in Chavez Ravine as it was, say, in Long Beach, where overcrowding led to a temporary breakdown in municipal services, in one respect preparations for war were just as striking there as they were in other parts of the city. In 1940 the city bought land on the ravine's southern edge in order to build the million dollar Naval Reserve Armory. The white middle-class officers who staffed the armory, with their starched uniforms and military bearing, came from a different world from the scruffy, working-class Mexicans who lived in the ravine farther up the hill.

Built out of California granite, in a Mediterranean style that contained hints of colonial Spain, the armory looked, in the words of one observer, "every bit the frontier outpost standing watch over the surrounding enclaves of the local population."[21] It symbolized the growing power of the modern state, with which the Mexican community had already clashed painfully in the forced repatriation scheme of the mid-1930s. Most of the residents of Chavez Ravine looked on the Naval Reserve Armory with distaste.

Distaste for the presence of the Naval Armory, however, did not prevent Mexican Americans from being any less patriotic than other citizens of

Los Angeles, despite doubts about their loyalty held by the white majority. They collected newspapers, increased their cultivation of produce, and purchased Liberty Bonds with just as much fervor as the rest of the city's population. "Most of us were more than glad to . . . serve in the war," noted one study of the Mexicans' role. "We felt that this was an opportunity to show the rest of the nation that we too were also ready, willing, and able to fight for our nation. It did not matter whether we were looked upon as Mexican, Mexican Americans, or belonging to a minority group; the war soon made us all genuine Americans . . . available immediately to fight and defend our country."[22]

A similar willingness to enlist in the military was evident in Chavez Ravine itself. Manazar Gamboa, who was six years old in December 1941, remembered how quickly attitudes toward Japan changed after the attack on Pearl Harbor. "Even the comic books were different," he recalled. "The Japanese were depicted as monkey-types with buck teeth. Germans were [a] bulldog-growling sort called Krauts or Jerries."[23]

It is impossible to know just how many volunteers (or conscripts) from the ravine entered the U.S. military during World War II. But Gamboa remembered with pride the day on which several volunteers from his Bishop subbarrio, who had recently joined the famous 82nd Airborne Division, were blessed by Father Tomas in Santo Nino Church. He also observed what he saw as a significant rise in macho behavior after war had been declared. "The instinct to fight and risk physical danger was accelerated among our young men," he wrote. "Movies, speeches, newspapers, newsreels, etc., all gave out a very clear and strong message: it's all right to kill your enemy."[24]

Along with the city's white population, the residents of Chavez Ravine expressed few qualms about the internment of L.A.'s more than one hundred thousand Japanese American citizens in the spring of 1942, even though this act was not without negative consequences for the Latino community. With the departure of the "wicked Japanese," L.A.'s newspapers turned their attention, even more fully than they had done before, to the supposedly widespread criminal behavior of L.A.'s Mexican population. Relatively minor crimes, such as the snatching of a woman's purse, were blown out of proportion. At the end of 1942, in response to a request from a U.S. government fearful of undermining wartime unity, the Los Angeles press cut back on this sensationalist coverage. But it started up again the following spring and reached a climax at the time of the 1943 Zoot Suit Riots.[25]

Figure 9. Youths from Chavez Ravine served proudly in World War II. Courtesy *Los Angeles Times*.

Despite more military decorations given to Mexican American soldiers in World War II than to any other minority group, the contribution young Latinos—including those from Chavez Ravine—made to the U.S. war effort was never given the same acclaim that the record of white soldiers received. In this respect, the role of Mexicans in the military fell into the same category as that of similarly disappointed African Americans.[26] Another source of increased racial tension was the Bracero Program of 1942, which brought a significant number of new Mexican laborers into the city to make up for the loss of white workers who had joined the military. Although their contribution was sorely needed, the uncouth manners of the new workers from Mexico who replaced the white workers led to numerous disparaging remarks, and the number of racial incidents increased.[27]

By 1942 more than 250,000 new workers seeking war jobs had moved to Southern California from all over the country. They included African Americans from the Deep South (some of whom moved into the houses vacated by the Japanese in Little Tokyo, which was now called Bronzeville) and more than 125,000 white, and some black, women who became "Rosie the Riveters" in shipbuilding and aircraft factories in Long Beach, El Segundo, and elsewhere. It was the housing shortage caused by this sudden influx that prompted L.A. city authorities to develop their interest in the need for public housing.[28]

Few of these World War II newcomers impinged directly on the lives of the inhabitants of Chavez Ravine. Most of the wartime factories were too far away from the barrio for its residents to get jobs in them, even if they had possessed the skills to do so. After union leader A. Philip Randolph's threatened March on Washington protesting racial discrimination in wartime hiring, President Roosevelt issued his famous Executive Order 8802 of June 1941, which supposedly opened up jobs in the defense plants to everyone without regard to color, creed, or national origin. As a result, sixteen-year-old Isabella Fierro from Alta Loma found a job at an aircraft factory on Alameda Avenue making seats and doors for fighter planes, where she was "treated very nicely," despite the fact that her uncle felt that she was too young to work outside the home. Her friend Alice Martinez, who lived nearby, got a job in the same plant.[29]

But few other residents from the ravine were fortunate enough to join them. This was partly because most of L.A.'s major defense plants were located many miles away from the East L.A. area. But it was mainly because most employers took it for granted that Mexican workers lacked the skill to work in the defense plants and were only capable of taking unskilled, poorly paid jobs.[30] Although they did not say it openly, many—if not most—defense contractors also refused to employ Mexicans on racial grounds.

In addition, when the Fair Employment Practices Commission held hearings in Los Angeles at the end of 1941 it paid less attention to discrimination against Mexican workers than it did to discrimination against African Americans. Thus Palo Verde's Albino Real, who got a job as a blacksmith's helper in a foundry producing weapons parts, died of smoke inhalation without an inquiry into his death being held.[31] Some Chavez Ravine residents were taken on to fill in for whites who joined the armed forces but nearly always in heavy, laboring jobs or in unskilled positions in the food preparation, garment, or retail trades. Two middle-aged Mexicans from the ravine, Bernardo Ruiz and Luis Castello, were among the very few Mexicans lucky enough to be hired as replacements for absent white trolley conductors on the Pacific Electric's Red Car system.[32]

Anecdotal evidence about the lack of technical skills among Chavez Ravine's residents was confirmed by the statistical data provided by the 1940 population census. Only 12 percent of those employed in the ravine were reported to be skilled artisans or craftsman. The bulk of its male labor force continued to be described as operatives, service workers, or laborers.

In fact, the only significant difference between the 1930 and the 1940 censuses, as far as the ravine's population was concerned, was the fact that in 1940 a higher proportion of its residents were American-born, compared to ten years previously. Among its foreign-born residents, 918 (61 percent) came from Mexico, while the rest were divided between Italians, Germans, and a scattering of East Europeans. With almost four children per family, 31 percent of the ravine's population was under fourteen years of age—a much higher proportion of minors than was present among white, middle-class families on the city's West Side.[33]

Pachucos and the Zoot Suit Riots of 1943

Let us go back to what the two women from Chavez Ravine who traveled through downtown on a Red Car said about the young people who called themselves Pachucos and Pachucas. Who were they, and what impact did they have on the residents of Chavez Ravine? A few people saw them simply as a cadre of young adults who wanted to draw attention to themselves by parading down the streets in a new style of dress.

It is true that the clothes and hairstyles of the Pachucos and Pachucas departed markedly from the fashions worn by civilians at a time of wartime austerity. The Pachucos wore slicked, long black hair, ending in ducktails; their shirts were cleaned and pressed; their flared-out pants were pegged tightly at the ankles; and they wore double-soled cordovan shoes. "Wearing the zoot" meant something slightly different for the young women who called themselves Pachucas. They favored pompadour hairstyles and wore thin blouses, midthigh skirts, and sandals strapped over the calf in ancient Greek style. At a time when gender roles were in flux, the Pachucas' clothes may have derived some of their legitimacy from press photos of Rosie the Riveter and other female war workers who wore pants, overalls, and jumpsuits—a new fashion in wartime L.A.[34]

But the significance of the Pachucos went well beyond their manner of dress. Much of L.A.'s white public, and also the older generation of Mexican Americans in Chavez Ravine, saw their Bohemian life-style and provocative street habits as a source of serious concern. To the LAPD and most white educators, the Pachucos' swaggering style, offbeat music, and aggressive manners confirmed what they had always believed about Mexicans: that they were an inherently violent, uncivilized race who needed strong discipline to keep them under control. If anyone doubted this, the police argued, they had only to read about the "gang related" death in 1942 of

Figure 10. Pachuco dressed in typical clothes. Courtesy *Los Angeles Times.*

Sleepy Lagoon trial victim Jose Diaz, which the press distorted out of all recognition in its desire to make the racial stereotype stick.[35]

In reality, at a time when World War II was bringing about major changes in American social behavior, the Pachucos represented the avant-garde of a new generation of underprivileged Mexican Americans seeking an alternative cultural identity. They wanted to explore new forms of expression and to distance themselves both from the traditional mores of their Mexican American parents and from America's white, middle-class culture. They did so by embracing the new world of Latino jazz, flamboyant dancing, and sexual freedom; by developing a new street language, which they called Calo; and by asserting control over their own territorial space. In neighborhoods around Chavez Ravine such as Echo Park, Lincoln Heights, and Silverlake, this meant "claiming ownership rights" over specific streets, bars, dance halls, and movie houses and resisting any attempt by rival groups, the LAPD, or other community residents to reassert public control over them.[36]

As the racial temperature heated up following the internment of L.A.'s Japanese Americans in 1942 and the arrival in Los Angeles of large numbers of African American, Okie, and Arkie job seekers from the South, it was the territorial aspect of this new public assertiveness that held the greatest potential for neighborhood conflict. And it was the Pachucos' conspicuous clothing that made them into obvious targets during the Zoot Suit Riots. Even before the riots began in June 1943, military records showed that Pachucos were harassing soldiers on leave.

But it was when large numbers of white sailors, both those on leave from their ships and naval personnel who worked at the Naval Armory, took to the streets in the first week of June that serious violence began. This time the confrontation was much more serious. Fighting broke out when the sailors tried to pick up Chicano girls and when—in ignorance of neighborhood social boundaries—they entered the local bars, cafeterias, and movie houses the Pachucos considered part of their territory.[37]

That same evening a further group of about fifty sailors, followed by others in taxis and cars, left the armory with clubs, dumbbells, and other weapons concealed in their uniforms. Some of them invaded the Carmen Theater on Alpine Street (just south of the ravine) and beat up the dozen or so zoot-suiters who were watching the show. Shouting "Why aren't you in uniform?" the sailors stripped off the zoot-suiters' clothes, put them in a pile, and set them on fire. In retaliation, four boys in zoot suits cornered Seaman Second Class Gene Crosland as he was returning to the armory and terrorized him by brandishing their switchblades in front of his face.[38]

Pachucos and the Residents of Chavez Ravine

How did the residents of Chavez Ravine react to the Zoot Suit Riots and to the rise of the Pachuco phenomenon? Despite the reference earlier to a visit being paid to the ravine by military personnel, there is no evidence that the Pachucos caused a major disturbance there. But that does not mean that some, at least, of the ravine's residents did not react strongly to what was going on in the streets below. In a play he wrote many years later, Manazar Gamboa inserted several lines of dialogue between ravine residents who exchanged views about the riots and the Pachucos.

Although fictional, these exchanges probably reflected the views of Chavez Ravine's residents fairly accurately. In the first exchange, Jando, a soldier on leave from his unit in the 82nd Airborne Division, complains bitterly about the double standard that enabled the U.S. military to enlist young Mexican men into the army, while at the same time allowing agents of that same military to beat up on Mexican American civilians simply because they wore different clothes:

> DON MIGUEL—reading from a newspaper: "A whole caravan of taxi drivers gave the navy men free rides and they launched a reprisal attack on the Chicanos in East Los Angeles. They tore up everything, beat up the kids, the girls, whoever was there. Then, when the 'vatos' [Mexican guys] came, the sailors took off."
> COOKIE: "They call them the Zoot Suit Riots? They should call them the Gringo Riots!"
> JANDO: "They think 'muy chingones!' just cause they got the 'jura' [law] backing them up. Yeah! They didn't 'twist' the sailors. They threw the 'vatos' and their carnelas [girlfriends] into jail! Is this why I joined the Airborne?!"[39]

In the second exchange, ravine residents try to explain the new sense of identity the Pachucos were striving for by contrasting their views with what they assumed L.A.'s young, white radicals believed in. The future Chicano movement, explains Don Miguel, would not espouse "your typical revolution." Instead of adopting the social agenda of mainstream white radicals, Pachucos were searching for "a new way of being themselves." In this exchange Gamboa again appears in the guise of the six-year-old Meno:

> MENO: "What do you mean by that, Don Miguel?"
> DON MIGUEL: "Sometimes a people has to rebel so it won't be a carbon copy of another."
> JANDO: "That's right, we don't want to be like the gringos, but we don't want to be like 'old Mexico' either."
> TIN: "So what do we really want?"
> DON MIGUEL: "To be what we want to be, not what somebody else wants us to be. A good example is the new language you pachucos have invented. You call it 'Calo,' right?"
> COOKIE: "You like that, Don Miguel?"

DON MIGUEL: "Yes, of course, especially the humor. To be able to switch from English to Spanish, and then to Calo within the same sentence, gives Chicanos a way of expressing their real thoughts better than anything else."[40]

When World War II came to an end, many Mexican American veterans, like many African Americans who also served in the armed forces, entertained hopes for a better future. Having fought for the values of democracy against a racist Nazi regime in Germany, they were no longer willing to wait indefinitely for the full privileges of U.S. citizenship. In practice, however, although some Mexican Americans from Chavez Ravine were able to take advantage of the GI Bill to improve their education, few of them experienced any immediate improvement in their job prospects, any more than black veterans did.[41] The anger many ravine residents later expressed at being evicted from their homes may also have been exacerbated by the dashed expectations they entertained in the immediate postwar years.

Two Competing Views of L.A.'s Postwar Future

The complex mixture of hope, anger, and disappointment that affected the residents of Chavez Ravine as World War II came to an end provides a compelling backdrop to the housing shortage—amounting to a crisis—that resulted from the massive influx of war workers and their families who came to Los Angeles during the course of the conflict and after.[42]

Before we examine the response of city authorities to the postwar housing crisis and to the role public housing played in their efforts to find a solution, we need to understand the mind-set of the politicians planning L.A.'s future. Since the turn of the century Southern California's white, Protestant elite had been trying—with considerable success—to transform the city from a small, dusty cattle town into the commercial capital of the American Southwest. The explosion of population and industry that accompanied World War II encouraged the city's leaders to raise their sights still further. They now wanted to transform L.A. from a commercial center into a modern, industrial metropolis capable of taking its place alongside New York and Chicago as one of America's foremost cities.[43]

It was in this context that the conflict between the so-called community modernist and corporate modernist vision—a concept introduced by urban sociologist Don Parson—came into the open. The idea of corporate modernism, which triumphed in L.A. when Mayor Norris Poulson was elected in 1953, can be defined as inner-city development for commercial purposes on a monumental scale. In 1946 Albert C. Martin, head of one of the city's oldest architectural firms, called it "the devotion of the urban core to large banking interests . . . [and] large government centers, with all of their support buildings."[44] New residential housing was to be confined largely to the suburbs, with private builders attracting lower-class home buyers to the outskirts by reducing the per-unit cost of house building through standardized production techniques.

The departure of middle-class whites to the suburbs exposed a growing number of blighted downtown areas such as New Chinatown, Bunker Hill, and the Plaza area inhabited by a mixture of poor whites and minority groups, many of whom lived in substandard housing. Poor neighborhoods generated far less tax income than the properties of affluent whites did, giving urban reformers an incentive to tear them down. According to a survey conducted by the Works Progress Administration in 1939, more than 10 percent of the city's housing stock was "substandard," lacking bathtubs and inside toilets and in various stages of disrepair. Some homes were considered unfit for human habitation.[45]

In the eyes of the corporate modernizers, all such areas of substandard housing, which included the barrio in Chavez Ravine, needed to be removed if their development plans were to succeed. In a 1943 article in *Architectural Forum*, a city planner sympathetic to this approach used the language of tooth decay to describe how to deal with L.A.'s slum areas. "How can we fix decay?" the planner asked. "The way a dentist does—by cleaning out the infected area and guarding it against further trouble."[46] In other words, by removing all the dilapidated and substandard housing and rebuilding the slum areas altogether.

The community modernist school of thought agreed about the need for slum clearance. But its attitude toward how this should be done, as well as toward other aspects of urban redevelopment, was significantly different. In 1946 liberal urban planner Mel Scott saw redevelopment as offering the city an opportunity to reconstruct its blighted areas as balanced residential neighborhoods that would cater to citizens from a wide range of social classes.

The reforming mayor of Los Angeles, Fletcher Bowron, put it this way in a radio broadcast he made to the city in 1951: "Community redevelopment will make new sections [of the city] out of old, put attractive buildings in place of eyesores for *all of our citizens*" (my italics).[47] Liberally inclined community modernists also saw public housing as one of the key tools to facilitate this process. Corporate modernists, on the other hand, believed that the new housing required as a result of the postwar shortage should be built exclusively by the private construction industry.[48]

The idea of building publicly owned housing to replace substandard dwellings dates from the efforts of progressive reformers such as Jacob Riis, who condemned the slums of New York in the years before the First World War. The public housing movement was boosted by the passage of the federal Housing Act in 1937 as part of President Roosevelt's New Deal. During World War II ten public housing projects were constructed in Los Angeles to accommodate the influx of war workers, including Ramona Garden and Aliso Village. The latter project, on First Street and Mission Road, was the nearest to Chavez Ravine. These projects were built with the support of liberal mayor Bowron, the L.A. branches of the National Negro Congress, and El Congreso del Pueblo de Habla Espanol. Ramon Welch, general secretary of El Congreso, urged the L.A. City Council to pursue federal funding for a more extensive public housing program.[49]

During and after World War II the debate over public housing was exacerbated by the question of race. Initially, accommodations in federally funded housing projects were allotted according to L.A.'s existing patterns of housing segregation. As the influx of war workers grew larger, however, some newcomers demanded that this policy be abandoned in favor of a "first come, first served" approach, a policy that would have given African Americans an advantage. This proposal was strongly opposed by Arkies and Okies and other white defense workers who came from the South. The situation was further complicated by liberal demands that all of L.A.'s public housing facilities be integrated, no matter the racial composition of the neighborhood. The race issue was never satisfactorily resolved, and it caused a great deal of bitterness.[50]

The Housing Shortage and the 1949 Housing Act

By far the strongest reason for increasing the number of public housing projects in Los Angeles was the housing shortage, which by the end of World War II had reached crisis proportions. The shortage was exacerbated by the return of thousands of GIs from the European and Pacific theaters, the release of Japanese Americans from detention camps, and the fact that many of the war workers who had come to L.A. during the course of the conflict decided to stay in the area. By August 1945 as many as 162,000 families were living in tents, garages, trailers, and firetrap hotels all over the city. In 1946 the California Reconstruction Commission estimated that as many as 280,000 additional housing units would be needed to end the shortage.[51]

While the housing shortage was serious for everyone, it was particularly severe for minority families and employees. Despite federal regulations prohibiting discrimination in Federal Housing Administration and Veterans Administration loan guarantees, racially restrictive covenants continued to be used in L.A. to prevent the sale or renting of private homes to blacks, Mexicans, Asians, and Jews. Even the celebrated Supreme Court antidiscrimination decision in *Shelley v. Kraemer* of 1948 did not make privately negotiated racial covenants illegal. It only made them unenforceable in court. *La Opinion* published numerous articles on the housing shortage, noting that even successful Mexican businessmen, college graduates, and decorated veterans were refused the right to buy a home in white neighborhoods.[52]

The problem was made even worse by the resumption of L.A.'s freeway construction program, which had been put on hold during the war. In October 1945 five hundred families from the northern part of Bunker Hill, many of them Filipinos and Mexicans, were issued eviction notices to make way for the construction of the Hollywood and Santa Ana freeways. The neighborhood Freeway Anti-Eviction Committee, which foreshadowed the protest committees later established to oppose the demolition of Chavez Ravine, led a march on city hall, only to be told that it was too late to reroute the roadways.[53]

In March 1945 Mayor Fletcher Bowron sent the following telegram to President Roosevelt: "I appeal to you for help in connection with a critical shortage of housing in Los Angeles."[54] His plea fell on deaf ears. FDR was too ill (he died the following month) and too preoccupied with bringing the war to a successful conclusion to deal with the housing situation. Soon after he took office President Truman established the Veterans' Emergency Housing Program and appointed Wilson W. Wyatt as a national "housing expediter" to take charge of it. But for a variety of reasons, including the shortage of building materials and the opposition of Republicans in Congress, the program was ineffective. In June 1947 the *California Eagle*, the city's premier black newspaper, complained that only 35,000 new housing units had been constructed throughout the entire country during the preceding year. "That's just 965,000 units short of the goal of one million units a year set by Wilson Wyatt," the paper noted wryly.[55]

The thousands of veterans who returned to Los Angeles from the Pacific theater, including Mexican American veterans from Chavez Ravine, were particularly upset. They were greeted as heroes at the dockside in

Long Beach by their families and city officials, only to find either that there was no low-cost housing available or that they could not afford those homes that were for sale. A number of stopgap measures were hastily enacted to help them. The L.A. City Council decreed that the Quonset huts and other temporary housing put up during the war would not be torn down but made available to veterans. The L.A. Housing Authority was also authorized to build 1,500 so-called Basilone Homes in the San Fernando Valley to relieve the pressure. Most of the financing and materials for this project were provided by the state and federal governments, using methods similar to those used in public housing.[56]

These stopgap measures proved inadequate. On January 10, 1947, two thousand supporters of the L.A. Committee for Veterans Housing, which included several volunteers from Chavez Ravine, camped out overnight in Westlake Park to dramatize their displeasure. In a speech at the campsite, veterans' leader Norris Helford demanded to know "why our country had no trouble furnishing us with guns and ammunition but now offers us only excuses instead of homes?"[57] Several campers displayed posters demanding increased federally sponsored public housing.

Protests like this, along with the slow pace of private construction, disconcerted the leaders of the private construction industry. They were particularly worried by the support gained by housing reformers for Proposition 14 in November 1948, which proposed an additional 100,000 rental housing units to be built by local housing authorities and funded by the state. Save for the role allotted to private construction companies, this scheme advocated public housing in all but name.[58] In Los Angeles the leader of the No campaign was Fritz B. Burns, an influential property developer who made millions erecting suburban housing tracts all over Southern California. Burns argued that the private housing industry was perfectly capable of ending the housing shortage but had been prevented from doing so by government bureaucracy. In the November 1948 election, Proposition 14 was defeated by a two-to-one majority, demonstrating the political power of the private construction industry and the reluctance of the Los Angeles public to spend public money on "socialist" projects.[59]

But for once in L.A.'s history the champions of private enterprise did not have it all their way. Dismayed by the defeat of Proposition 14, minority and left-liberal groups rallied their forces and continued to exploit rising public anger over the housing shortage. The community solidarity stimulated by wartime practices such as shared housekeeping practices, communal living, and the construction of child care centers for "Rosie the Riveters" also gave credence to the public housing campaign. In 1947, for example, an article in *Harper's Bazaar* suggested that the emancipated women of postwar California did not wish to return to the isolation of privately built homes, which had made them into "mere servants for their husbands and children."[60]

What finally put supporters of public housing in Los Angeles in a position of power—even if only temporarily—was the passage of the new Federal Housing Act in 1949. Previous postwar efforts to pass a new housing bill had been stymied by the Republican majority in Congress. But President Truman's unexpected reelection in 1948 injected new life into the measure. Forced to act by a large number of powerful pressure groups (including the NAACP, both the AFL and the CIO, the National Conference of Mayors, and various veterans' and women's organizations), Congress finally adopted a housing reform bill in July 1949.[61]

The 1949 Housing Act was not a complete victory for public housing advocates. Title 1, which provided loan guarantees and capital grants for slum clearance and urban redevelopment, provided plenty of scope for the private construction industry. Title 2, however, gave the reformers the opening they had been waiting for. It sanctioned "federal contributions and loans to local housing authorities for the construction of 810,000 units of public housing over the next six years."[62] Not all of Mayor Bowron's supporters espoused these provisions in the 1949 act out of principle. Rather, the city administration and the CHA embraced the public housing provisions of the legislation because of the desperate shortage of housing in Los Angeles and the need to embrace any and all means to alleviate it.[63]

It is important to acknowledge these limits to the success of the public housing movement in Los Angeles in order to understand the fragile and temporary nature of the political victory it won. Nevertheless, minority residents, slum dwellers, veterans' organizations, and Angelenos without homes were overjoyed when, on August 8, 1949, the City Council unanimously directed the CHA to contract with the federal government to build 10,000 new units of public housing in Southern California.[64]

During this long debate about the need for new housing, the residents of Chavez Ravine did little more than watch and wait. But they pricked up their ears when rumors circulated that the ravine had been chosen as the site for the first new public housing project. Many of the ravine's residents at first thought that the new project would be built on vacant land and that the barrio itself would remain intact.[65] But, with the newspapers full of articles about slum clearance, astute leaders in the barrio quickly grasped the reality: their cherished Shangri-La was threatened with demolition and might soon disappear.

PART II

Public Housing, Evictions, and the Impact of the Red Scare

CHAPTER THREE

"Struggling to Keep Our Homes"

The Evictions Crisis, 1950–1952

"This letter is to inform you that a public housing development will be built on this location for families of low income. . . . The house you are living in will be included. . . . You will be visited by a representative of the Housing Authority who will inspect your house in order to estimate its value. . . . Later you will have the first chance to move back into the new Elysian Park Heights development."

—CITY HOUSING AUTHORITY, JULY 24, 1950

"It's absolutely the tragedy of my life. I was responsible for uprooting hundreds of people from their own little valley and having the whole thing destroyed."

—FRANK WILKINSON

Why Was Chavez Ravine Chosen for Demolition?

In July 1950, nine months after Los Angeles signed its contract with the federal government to build 10,000 new units of public housing in Southern California, the CHA made it official—the new public housing project would not be built on vacant land.[1] Instead, all three subbarrios in Chavez Ravine would be demolished, and their residents would be rehoused in a single large public housing project to be named Elysian Park Heights.[2]

The choice of Chavez Ravine was confirmed by a Department of Health report, which condemned the Chavez Ravine barrio as "the worst slum in the city."[3] Was this sweeping conclusion justified? Not altogether. The quality of houses in the ravine varied considerably, depending on their age and the resources of the families who owned them. About a quarter of the homes were well-built structures constructed out of standard building materials. A third were in poor condition, while the worst dwellings were ramshackle structures put together with old packing cases, pieces of lumber, and trailers without wheels. Unfortunately for the residents, it was these dilapidated structures that caught the public eye. According to a survey taken in 1949, a third of the houses had no toilets, 377 of them lacked bathing facilities, and 174 were without running water. But these totals were no worse than the proportion of homes lacking these same facilities in places such as Belvedere, Watts, or Sonoratown.[4]

Despite these housing deficiencies, most residents of Chavez Ravine resented the fact that their neighborhood was labeled "substandard." Many of them had built their houses with their own hands and improved them little by little over the years. "How dare they call it a slum!" one homeowner declared. "My family has been here for thirty years, and I would choose nothing else."[5] The ravine's defenders also pointed out that most of its housing stock had been built in the 1920s, before L.A.'s building codes had been brought up to date. If the barrio was in poor condition, the fault lay partly with the city itself, which for years had refused requests from the residents to grade its dirt roads and put in proper drainage and street lights.[6] Resident anger at the condescending language used to describe their cherished neighborhood revealed the racial biases that were built into the controversy and became a prime factor in uniting the community against the CHA's plans to tear it down.

On paper, the plan handed down to justify the demolition of Chavez Ravine seemed quite reasonable. It acknowledged the strong community spirit in the barrio, commended the fact that the level of juvenile delinquency was lower there than it was in L.A.'s other downtown barrios, and recognized the need to keep the existing community together, as far as possible, by building the new public housing complex in the same area that the barrio now inhabited. The plan also took note of the different income levels of the tenants in the different subbarrios and recommended that Elysian Park Heights contain a range of new rental properties that would accommodate these different income levels. "Everything possible must be done" the document added, "to gain the widespread approval of the redevelopment program both by [the] site occupants and by the general public."[7]

Doubts About the Demolition Plan

The redevelopment plan was drawn up by Drayton Bryant, Reginald Johnson, and other city planners who were sensitive to the residents' needs.

When they set about implementing the plan, however, the slum clearance agents—who came from a different part of the CHA's office—behaved ruthlessly. They made little or no attempt to prepare Chavez Ravine's residents for what was coming or to explain to them why such extensive destruction was necessary. They focused almost exclusively on the demolition aspects of the blueprint and carried them out in a rigid and autocratic fashion.[8]

It was not just the residents of the ravine who questioned the wisdom of the City Housing Authority's demolition plans. When Howard L. Holtzendorff, director of the CHA, chose architect Robert Alexander to draw up a plan for Elysian Park Heights, he at first refused to do so because he questioned the wisdom of razing the three existing subbarrios and moving the residents into a quite different environment. But Holtzendorff insisted, urging him to recruit an established partner to help him design the project. Alexander managed to secure the cooperation of the distinguished Austrian émigré architect Richard Neutra, who had a practice in nearby Silverlake.[9]

Alexander and Neutra were pleased with their lucrative contract but taken aback to find that the CHA wanted to accommodate as many as 17,000 residents on the new Elysian Park Heights site. These additions meant adding more than 10,000 new tenants from Bunker Hill and other slum areas to the 3,764 residents who currently lived in Chavez Ravine. Such a high density forced the two men to include thirteen high-rise towers in their design—a feature they both considered inappropriate. Had these thirteen high-rises been built, they would have transformed Elysian Park Heights into a giant public housing complex like those in New York and Chicago, which turned into havens of drug dealing, petty crime, and social degeneration.[10]

The discomfort of the two architects increased still further when they visited Chavez Ravine itself and saw that its houses were nearly all one-story, single-family homes with yards, vegetable gardens, and orchards spread out across a wide area. Contrary to what they had been told, the visitors also found the ravine's residents to be "well-adjusted" and many of their houses capable of repair. Robert Alexander even went so far as to call the final plan for Elysian Park Heights "a complete disaster."[11] Friend and fellow architect Clarence Stein agreed with him. Stein even asked the project's site planner, Simon Eisner, how he could justify destroying all of Chavez Ravine's existing homes and gardens and moving its semirural residents into new and alien surroundings. "When I learned of the 13-story buildings," Stein added, "I became an opponent of public housing."[12]

These doubts reflected the views of an emerging school of city planners who rejected demolition as the best method of dealing with urban slums. This school was led by Jane Jacobs, author of *The Death and Life of Great American Cities*, which would be published in 1961. Jacobs recognized the demoralizing effect of uprooting people and forcing them to move into totally different environments. By destroying old neighborhoods, city planners risked undermining the vitality and cohesion of the very areas they were attempting to improve. However, the ideas of this alternative school of urban planners, which we shall examine at greater length in a subsequent chapter, were unacceptable to the Los Angeles city planners of the 1950s. They were convinced of the superiority of their bulldozing techniques.[13]

Some left-wing critics of the CHA's slum clearance policies even accused it of deliberately exaggerating the number of substandard buildings in Chavez Ravine to strengthen its case for demolishing them. In an early 1950s court case, a real estate company with property interests in the ravine argued that many of the condemned houses there could have been made to conform to the Los Angeles building code simply by requiring landlords "to enforce the [city's] building and health ordinances."[14] The prosecuting attorney in the case also deplored the idea of forcing residents who were already homeowners into selling their houses and becoming renters dependent on the public purse.[15]

Behind these arguments lay the still more difficult question of the proper definition of a slum. The L.A. Department of Health, like most city health departments in the United States at this time, defined slums exclusively in terms of sanitation, living space, and the propensity of overcrowded buildings to disseminate disease, crime, and "immoral behavior"—the latter a tendentious phrase sometimes used as cover for racial prejudice.[16] These criteria were, of course, important. But this definition neglected the beneficial effects of Chavez Ravine's wide-open spaces, its cultivated backyards, and its high level of community morale. These benefits were difficult to quantify. But the inhabitants of the ravine and their white allies regarded them as crucial to the residents' well-being.

None of these considerations, however, carried weight with the CHA's planning staff. The final design for Elysian Park Heights, shown in figure 11, included three churches, three schools, a 1,500 person auditorium, and a shopping center. But it also contained the aforesaid thirteen high-rise apartment towers, four of which are shown here. On a positive note, the project's planners said that Elysian Park Heights "should contain groups of varying religious, language, and ethnic backgrounds."[17] The

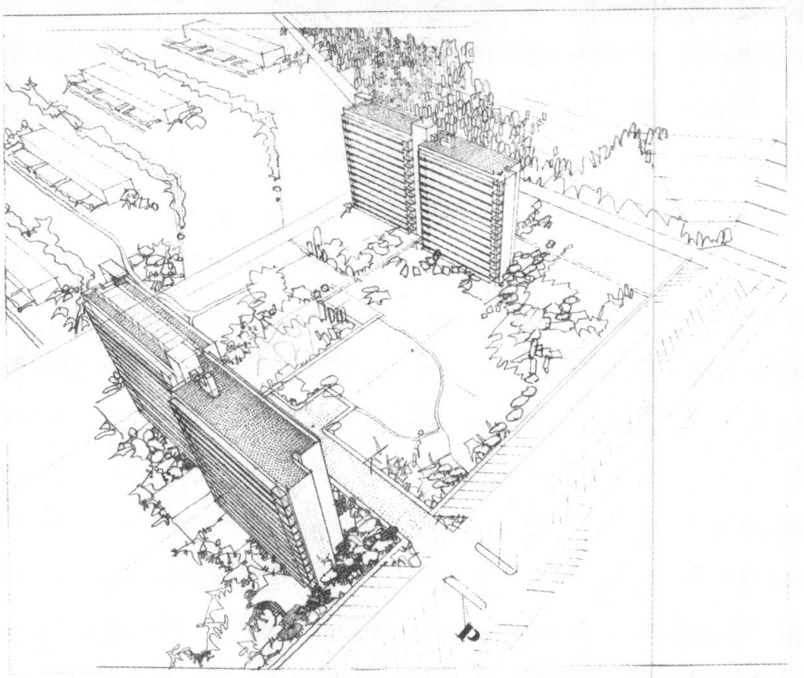

Figure 11. Proposed high-rise towers in Elysian Park Heights. Courtesy Dion Neutra, architect, and Richard and Dion Neutra Papers, Department of Special Collections, Charles E. Young Research Library, UCLA.

existing tenants were told that, in exchange for selling their current houses to the city, they would be permitted to return to the new public housing project after it was finished and given first choice among the proposed new houses and apartments.[18]

In reality, however, these promises were misleading. For one thing, they took no account of the fact that Chavez Ravine residents who already owned their own homes—a group that included almost half of its existing population—were not eligible for public housing. Families in which the main wage earner was a non–U.S. citizen were disqualified, too. They would have to take the money they received from the forced sale of their houses and find accommodations elsewhere.

The officials of the City Housing Authority also neglected to tell the residents that the Elysian Park Heights complex would take more than two years to build. Fears were expressed that when the ravine's residents moved out, even if only temporarily, they would be unable to afford the rents in the private housing market and would run afoul of the racial covenants that limited the areas where Mexicans could live. In several cases, these fears turned out to be justified.[19]

For the time being, however, these reservations were set aside. In the summer of 1950 Frank Wilkinson, the CHA's enthusiastic young public relations officer, distributed notices of the impending demolition plan to all the ravine's residents. He urged them to sell their houses to the Housing Authority, in return for the promise of new accommodations in Elysian Park Heights. If they did not sell their houses voluntarily to the CHA, they would be forced to do so under the city's power of eminent domain.[20]

Early Signs of Community Protest

As he tramped back and forth across the dusty hills of La Loma, Bishop, and Palo Verde, Frank Wilkinson was surprised to find, in the first sign of the furor shortly to erupt, that he was greeted with skepticism by many residents and with outright hostility by others. Carol Jacques remembered the consternation that Wilkinson's visit to her house created: "One of the worst days of my childhood was when THE MAN came to our house. . . . He spoke to the family: nothing could be done; the city was exercising its power of eminent domain; we were being evicted. It was a really bad day because Aunt Gap couldn't stop crying. She called a family meeting. All the family members came to our house. I didn't know what was going on. I know now that the papers [we were served] were the beginning of the eviction process and the beginning of the end of my idyllic little world."[21]

For an activist who later became known as a champion of the downtrodden, Frank Wilkinson's surprise at the opposition he encountered as he toured Chavez Ravine may seem rather strange. It can be explained, at least in part, by his youthfulness and social background. Born in 1914 as the son of a wealthy medical doctor in Pasadena, Frank was a Hoover Republican during his youth. He witnessed extensive poverty and social injustice when he traveled throughout Europe in the 1930s during the Great Depression.[22] According to his own account, however, when he first began working for the CHA he was an "extremely naïve" supporter of the pre-1914 progressive school of urban reformers. The leaders of this movement believed that, as experts in city planning, they knew what was best for working-class families better than the families did themselves. When he started working for the CHA, Wilkinson assumed that the "slum dwellers" of Chavez Ravine would automatically prefer public housing to their current accommodations.[23]

But when he actually met some of the residents (as opposed to contemplating the CHA's public housing plans in a bureaucratic blueprint), Wilkinson was startled to encounter a number of politically astute homeowners who had already participated in previous protest movements against the destructive impact the city's postwar freeway building program had had on the Mexican barrio communities of East L.A. They had no wish to give up their houses, still less sell them to a group of unknown white bureaucrats simply on the strength of a written notice offering them accommodations in a public housing project that had yet to be built.[24]

Despite these early signs of opposition, the CHA began buying up homes in Chavez Ravine in December 1950. Some of the more gullible residents were so excited by the immediate offer of cash that they sold their houses straightaway. In some cases this strategy paid off, but in others it did not. Take the case of Beto Elias, who lived in La Loma. To his son's irritation, Beto accepted the CHA's offer of $9,600 for his house straightaway, even though he later realized it was worth a lot more than that. "How come you didn't talk to me before you sold?" his son asked when he came home from work. "Now we have to move whether we want to or not."[25]

Beto Elias looked for a new house outside Chavez Ravine that was large enough to accommodate all eight members of his family and eventually found one in Lincoln Heights. Having lived for years in the ravine, however, he was unfamiliar with prices in L.A.'s racially restricted housing market. At $15,000, his new house cost far more than his old one in the ravine. The additional loan he was forced to take out plunged his family permanently into debt. Other residents who sold their houses too hastily made similar mistakes.[26]

Most of Chavez Ravine's residents, however, especially those who spoke little English and knew nothing about the L.A. housing market, were suspicious of the CHA's intentions. Having lived through—and perhaps experienced—police violence, the Zoot Suit Riots, and other forms of racial discrimination during World War II, they had good reason to be cautious. Some of them may already have been displaced from their homes once before as a result of the demolition of part of old Sonoratown—the Plaza area where the earliest, pre–Civil War settlers had stayed. They preferred to sit tight rather than sell their homes, especially when they had no concrete evidence of what they were exchanging them for. As one observer put it, "Not only were their dwellings better than no homes at all, they were really *home* to these people. . . . So they were frightened by the thought that they would be torn down."[27]

According to his memoirs, when faced with these difficulties Frank Wilkinson (who was now a secret member of the Communist Party) tried to get help from the scattering of Mexican-born Communists who lived in Chavez Ravine. This was a risky thing to do when the Cold War was at its height, especially when the leaders of the ravine's protest movement, after it began in earnest a few weeks later, made it clear they wanted nothing to do with the Communists. Nevertheless, as cosupporters of public housing, Wilkinson hoped his fellow Communists would be able to persuade a larger number of residents to sell their homes.[28]

Just who Wilkinson's "fellow Communists" in Chavez Ravine were is unclear. An influential party branch, or "cell," certainly existed in the Echo Park/Silverlake area during the 1940s. But there is no direct evidence that Communists—or, more particularly, Mexican American Communists—were present in the ravine itself.[29] Wilkinson may have been referring to the role Alice McGrath and her husband Tom McGrath, who moved to Echo Park in 1940, played in establishing the Sleepy Lagoon Defense Committee, which had raised money to defend the twenty-six young Mexicans wrongly accused of murder in the notorious Sleepy Lagoon trial a few years earlier.[30]

But whatever help Wilkinson was able to drum up from his radical friends, it did very little to persuade residents in the ravine to sell their homes and leave the neighborhood. Impatient with the slow pace of house sales, CHA agents stepped up the pressure on the homeowners by engaging in high-pressure tactics. They offered to raise their cash payments for the houses, then threatened that if the owners refused to sell, any subsequent cash offers would be lower. Some CHA officials went even further. Esther Rodarte, a middle-aged woman who owned a small grocery store on Paducah Street, remembered how CHA agents visited her home late one night and threatened to condemn her property (meaning the city could tear it down straightaway) if she did not accept their terms. She called this "terror tactics designed to get rid of the residents in short order."[31] Late in 1950 the *Daily News* ran a series of scare articles, allegedly at the CHA's suggestion, describing the ravine's housing as a "crime-ridden health trap" that deserved to be torn down immediately.[32]

Some of Chavez Ravine's residents were also panicked into selling by rumors, which the CHA did nothing to allay, that if they did not sell quickly the fire department would set fire to their homes or the LAPD

Figure 12. Bulldozed home in Alta Loma, circa 1951. Courtesy *Los Angeles Times*.

would be sent in to arrest all those who refused to leave. Still other residents sold their houses because they did not want to be the only holdouts left on their street. "Once a few started selling," Rudy Flores recalled, "it breaks the chain." All the CHA really wanted, he added, "was the land; . . . Maybe they wanted the bricks, the windows, the doors. You [the resident] took what you wanted and left the rest. . . . A lot of people were still living there. They didn't want to leave."[33]

Those residents who decided to stay put sometimes quarreled with one another as to how best to proceed. They became angry with their neighbors who sold their houses and left without putting up a fight. Geneva Williams, who decided to leave early in the eviction process, remembered an Italian neighbor who was one of the holdouts. "She was almost crazy, she was so angry about losing her home. When I drove by, she would lean on her four-foot chainlink fence and spit at me. She absolutely hated me because I had decided to sell my home."[34] Still others became upset when they saw that after one or two homeowners on a street decided to sell their houses to the city, the rest followed suit in a hurry, out of fear that they would be left as the only people remaining on their block and would get nothing for their homes.

But as the number of departing residents increased, those who decided to stay and fight city hall realized that the time had come to make a stand. If they did not, it might be too late. Outside the ravine, opinion on the issue also became more heated. Those in favor of public housing as a replacement for slum buildings included the liberals who supported Mayor Bowron, the Citizens Housing Council, numerous church bodies, Mexican American civic leaders such as Councilman Edward Roybal, the NAACP, and—for the time being at least—a majority of the twelve members of the City Council. The opposition was led by the *Los Angeles Times*, suburban Republicans, the downtown business elite, and the city's powerful real estate lobby.[35]

Not all liberal groups who supported public housing did so for the same reasons. Mayor Bowron was a progressive Republican who, when first elected mayor of Los Angeles in 1938, had embraced most of President Roosevelt's New Deal. After World War II, however, he moved somewhat to the right and maintained his support for public housing largely as a response to the city's chronic housing shortage, rather than as a matter of principle.[36] Unionized workers also displayed a variety of attitudes. Socially conscious trade unions like the International Ladies' Garment Workers' Union (ILGWU) upheld public housing as a matter of social justice, whereas more conservative unions such as those in the building trades did so because of the new construction jobs it would generate.[37] Church opinion was similarly divided. Cardinal Francis McIntyre and other conservative priests at the top of L.A.'s Catholic hierarchy disapproved of the "socialist" character of public housing. But Monsignor Thomas O'Dwyer, head of the Citizens Housing Council and a friend of Frank Wilkinson, was a fervent supporter.[38]

Nevertheless, most white liberals agreed that razing slums and replacing them with low-cost public housing open to all races would improve living standards, reduce poverty and crime, and pose a welcome challenge to the racially restrictive housing covenants that prevailed in the city's private housing market. Even before the post–World War II Red Scare heated up, many of their opponents, especially the Small Property Owners Association (SPOA), rejected public housing as a form of "creeping socialism" that threatened the private enterprise system. Some enlightened businessmen also favored slum clearance and urban redevelopment. But they argued that L.A.'s need for more housing was being adequately met by private developers such as Fritz Burns, who was increasingly recognized as the leader of the anti–public housing lobby.[39]

Chavez Ravine Residents Take on City Hall

Such was the alignment of interests when, on April 26, 1951, opponents of the city's plans for demolishing Chavez Ravine attended the hearings of the City Planning Commission. A large crowd of supporters stood outside waving signs reading "MacArthur Was Kicked Out—Are We Next?" "Don't Believe Them [the CHA]—They're Trying to Take Your Land!" and "Priests Should Stick to Religion—and Not Meddle in Politics." (The reference to General Douglas MacArthur was to his dismissal by President Truman during the Korean War; the priest reference concerned the pro–public housing activities of Monsignor Thomas O'Dwyer.)[40]

Howard Holtzendorff spoke first on behalf of the City Housing Authority. Chavez Ravine, he said, was the "keystone to the entire future of replanning downtown Los Angeles." Calling it a "large, partially vacant area blighted by substandard housing," he praised the proposed Elysian Park Heights public housing project as the best solution to the problem of slum clearance.[41] G. G. Bauman, the lawyer who represented much of the ravine community, disagreed. Rejecting the idea that the area was blighted, he reiterated the residents' view that if city authorities would enforce the building and sanitation codes properly, most of the housing in the area could be brought up to standard. There was still time to do this, he argued, if only the CHA would support the idea. "We could keep the property in [private owners'] hands . . . and keep it on the tax roll without building high cost public housing for low rent."[42]

To the dismay of Howard Holtzendorff, Frank Wilkinson, and other leaders of the CHA, virtually all the ravine's residents at the hearing lined up behind Bauman in rejecting public housing as a solution for Chavez Ravine's problems. In doing this they also went against the advice of most civic leaders in the Los Angeles Mexican community, many of whom had endorsed public housing in their social programs. By rejecting public housing the ravine's residents were, in effect, breaking ranks with El Congreso and other Mexican organizations that favored public housing and lining themselves up on the side of the conservative supporters of the privately run real estate industry.[43]

Why did the ravine's residents deliberately reject the views of their middle-class allies on the question of public housing, especially when on other issues they opposed the conservative policies of L.A.'s business elite? Their decision reflected the complexity of Mexican American civic life in the post–World War II era. Virtually all the inhabitants of Chavez Ravine were working class, many of them semiliterate. Many of their families had earlier lived in rented cottages owned by the landlords who ran the haciendas (large-scale ranches) in rural Mexico by whom they were employed. Hence their strong desire to own homes of their own, no matter how primitive. If they could buy or build a house of their own, they were no longer dependent on the largesse of the frequently autocratic landowners.

In addition, unlike the relatively small group of middle-class Mexican Americans who inhabited Los Angeles in the World War II period, very few of Chavez Ravine's working-class residents were conversant with the underpinnings of the state-oriented welfare philosophy of the New Deal. Indeed those residents who had earlier sympathized with the anarchist outlook of the Partido Liberal Mexicano (PLM), and who remembered the oppressive Porfirio Diaz regime in prerevolutionary Mexico, were likely to have been suspicious of state power, whether it was exercised by agencies of the left or the right.[44]

Thus the residents' reluctance to sell their homes was based partly on the pride in ownership they had developed about their homes, many of which they had built with their own hands, and partly on their unwillingness to break cherished community bonds. But it was also based on their belief that owning a private home, instead of being dependent on an unsympathetic landlord, was one of the hallmarks of the American dream. Like African American veterans returning from World War II, the Mexican American residents of Chavez Ravine wanted to end their public perception as outsiders. They wanted to be accepted as first-class citizens entitled to all the rights and privileges that went along with it. Throughout U.S. history one of the key indicators of personal success among immigrant groups has always been—as it is still is, to some extent, today—the ability to purchase a private home.[45]

Asserting Their Rights as American Citizens

Agnes Cerda, secretary of the Chavez Ravine Community Association, expressed this point of view better than any other residents who addressed the Planning Commission. Speaking as a "taxpayer and American citizen," she likened the Mexican American homeowners of the ravine to the

European immigrants who had come to the United States in search of liberty and had become integrated into American life by buying or building their own homes. "Take away our homes," she said, "and you are taking away our incentive to be good, American citizens." Mrs. Cerda had a son who would shortly leave to fight in the Korean War. "Is he going to fight over there," she asked the members of the commission indignantly, "and [then] have to come back and have to fight . . . here for a home he hasn't got? Would you put your mother out of your home to give it to the Housing Authority? You would not!"[46]

Frank Sanchez, who owned several properties in La Loma, also stressed the role home ownership played in developing a sense of patriotic loyalty to the United States and how that loyalty could be compromised if the homes were taken away. "If this plan goes through," he said—meaning the plan to evict the residents from their homes and place them in Elysian Park Heights—"I assure you there will be 1,100 families that will not be as American, with attitudes they should not possess. I am sure if you label us as 'Reds' from now on it will be the fault of the Housing Authority group which has no right to push people around, as they have been pushing 1,100 families in Chavez Ravine."[47]

Although they were unaware of it, by expressing themselves this way the ravine's residents were employing language very similar to the rhetoric used by white migrants from the Midwest who had moved to Southern California in the 1920s and 1930s and settled in the new, industrial suburbs of South Central L.A. They, too, saw home ownership as their ticket to acceptance and economic security. One resident of South Gate, looking back on that era, told an interviewer, "When you're raising five kids and you want security you pretty much think you need to own a place. . . . If you couldn't buy a house you were at the bottom, floundering around, trying to survive. Home ownership meant nobody could evict you."[48] Chavez Ravine's residents had also come to believe that no one could evict them from their privately owned homes. This was why they became so frightened and angry when they found that the CHA could use the power of eminent domain to do so.

It should be remembered, too, that in the 1920s many of the homes constructed by white settlers in L.A.'s industrial suburbs were self-built, just like many of the homes in Chavez Ravine.[49] The difference, in the eyes of the CHA, was that whereas white settlers from Iowa and Indiana who built their own homes were seen as sturdy pioneers following a time-honored American tradition, Mexicans who did the same thing were often seen as breeders of slums.

Despite the thoughtful arguments ravine residents used to challenge the Elysian Park Heights project, the City Planning Commission approved it by a large majority. But the matter did not rest there. Along with threatened homeowners from two other public housing projects, the residents of Chavez Ravine were given permission to appeal the Planning Commission's decision to a special session of the City Council scheduled for June 21, 1951. Those hearings were even more raucous than those at the Planning Commission. Hundreds of people packed the City Council chambers, chanting demonstrators marched up and down outside, and some of the speakers were booed.[50]

Speaking in favor of public housing were representatives of twenty-six civic organizations, including veterans, minority, religious, and labor groups. Most of them repeated the same arguments they had used earlier, adding that private developers had failed to produce enough new housing, that human rights should prevail over property rights, and that the benefits of public housing to the community outweighed the damage it did to the interests of a few individuals. In a rare endorsement of the CHA's public housing plan by a Chavez Ravine resident, Trinidad Rodriguez of the United Railroad Workers of America stated that the Elysian Park project would be particularly helpful to ravine workers like him who worked in the nearby Southern Pacific railroad yards.[51]

The anti–public housing representatives also made many of the same points they had made in the previous hearing but this time in more vociferous language. Bertha Winters declared that L.A.'s public housing scheme was "the biggest invitation to political graft that ever disgraced this community."[52] And Manuel Cerda echoed the arguments of the conservative champions of private enterprise when he stated, "The people of my district don't want to be renters. They want to be honest taxpayers. We don't want anybody else to pay our taxes." Finally, he said, "We don't want to be socialized."[53]

Despite these objections, on June 26, 1951, the Los Angeles City Council voted to deny the appeal of the anti–public housing lobby. It granted the CHA permission to proceed with the demolition of the barrio in Chavez Ravine and build Elysian Park Heights in its place.[54] Little did any of those present realize that, only six months later, the City Council would reverse its decision. On December 26, 1951, the Los Angeles City Council would declare—this time amid a welter of Cold War rhetoric—that its $110,000 contract with the federal government for public housing was null and void. The reasons for this sudden about-face are addressed in the next chapter.

Expressions of Anger and Loss

Once the formal purchase and demolition of the houses in Chavez Ravine began in earnest, the number of residents remaining there rapidly declined. By December 1952 more than two-thirds of the homeowners, believing further resistance to be futile, had packed up their belongings, sold their houses to the City Housing Authority, and left. Fewer than two hundred holdouts still remained.[55]

The desire of the holdouts to stay was reinforced by the negative experiences of those who left, only to suffer discrimination and hostility in their new neighborhoods. As Mrs. de Leon of Bishop put it, "There are families that have moved into the city and . . . have come back to us and have tears in their eyes. They say that they are not accepted outside."[56] Others found it difficult not only to come to terms with the loss of their old homes but also with the loss of the traditional way of life that went along with it. Alfred Zepeda spoke of how his father saw the evictions as a chance to move to a better area of town but of how his eighty-one-year-old mother was unable to adjust to her new Anglo-American neighborhood. "All her life, she spoke Spanish; she had neighbors she could communicate with just by watering her flowers, talking across the fence. All of a sudden she had no one, and she died the next year. That was the worst part of the whole thing."[57]

Some of those forced to sell became so angry at what had happened to them and their families that they were radicalized by the experience. Prominent among this group was Carol Jacques: "I was really angry. I had lost my home, I had lost everything that I knew, everything I'd been so happy with, and then I lost my brother [who died at age nine]. I believe that anger turned me toward political action, starting with the Chicano movement. . . . That probably would not have happened had I not felt so uprooted and at such a loss when we were moved out of Chavez Ravine."[58]

Several of those who left also described the fears and anxieties that caused them to move. Anita Cano, who was eight years old when her family left the ravine, remembered how "rumblings [rumors] began that if you didn't move they were going to bulldoze you in the night while you [were] asleep. I was old enough to understand about bulldozers, and the adults were terrified. . . . One of my uncles, Ramon Contreras, said, 'I'm not moving, they'll have to drag me out by the feet dead.' He had a rifle and was going to make a last stand. It was kind of a tense situation, but finally they were able to talk him out [of it] with an offer of money."[59]

By the end of 1952 the once cheerful, bustling neighborhoods and cultivated gardens of La Loma, Bishop, and Palo Verde were largely silent and deserted. Few barefoot children played hopscotch in the alleys anymore, and not many rusting old jalopies kicked up the dust as they clambered painfully up and down the dirt roads. "Weeds were growing," remembered Zeke Contreras, who lived at the top of Bishops Road. "Everything was left neglected, deserted, and abandoned. . . . They were wrecking some houses below, but a lot of the houses were still in place. By then we had most of Chavez Ravine to ourselves. But it was kinda lonely. Us and the coyotes."[60]

A special sense of indignation was registered by the Catholic parishioners of La Loma, many of them women, who mourned the demolition of the Iglesia del Santo Nino. Only a few months before it had been the main focus of their community life. Several articles about the church appeared in the *Torch Reporter*, a newsletter published by former residents. "The destruction of this beautiful church was nothing less than 'a sacrifice to Satan,'" wrote one angry parishioner. Another woman remembered sadly how its decorations had been "bulldozed like garbage" and wondered what had happened to the church's bell, its silver candles, and other relics. If they were sold for cash by the head of the diocese, Cardinal Francis McIntyre, she reasoned, the bulk of the money should be spent to reimburse needy, evicted parishioners who had "toiled and sweated to build [up] our house of worship."[61] Any remaining cash should be used to buy gas for other poor residents so that they could attend mass elsewhere.

Other former residents, surprised to find oil company employees digging under the land that had formerly belonged to them, protested angrily to the CHA about its failure to mention oil rights in its dealings with the evicted families. Few of the residents even knew that they possessed rights to the oil under their land until city authorities began leasing it out for exploration, by which time it was too late for most of them to do anything about it.[62]

One of the most poignant memoirs of the evictions came from an elderly widow named Alice Martin, who was one of the few remaining pioneers to have begun her life in Chavez Ravine before World War I. She and her husband had owned 1456 Davis Street in La Loma for more than thirty years. In the spring of 1951 Mrs. Martin was out of town when the CHA issued an order condemning her rental properties. She hired an attorney to contest the order, but instead of doing as she wished he pressured her (like other lawyers who tried to exploit ravine property owners) to sell her rental houses to the CHA for less than they were worth. When that tactic failed, the lawyer paid some local youths to roll boulders down on her tenants' homes, panicking several of them into leaving. As a result Mrs. Martin lost most of her rental income. Adding insult to injury, the attorney then forged her signature to a document authorizing the sale of her own house for less than she had specified. He also deducted more than $2,000 for his fee—all without her knowledge or consent.[63]

Mrs. Martin refused to back down. Returning to Los Angeles, she managed to have the sale declared illegal and recovered her property, staying in it until the last of the holdouts were evicted in May 1959. Despite her vindication, Mrs. Martin wrote an angry letter of complaint to the *Torch Reporter* attacking the hypocrisy of the CHA's initial circular letter of July 24, 1950, which had promised the residents that, after buying their houses for a fair market price, it would give them "every assistance in finding another home." In reality, Alice Martin commented bitterly, "another home" was "nothing more than the open street."[64]

Mrs. Martin's next-door neighbor also published a letter of sympathy on her behalf in the *Torch Reporter*. In it she explained that the confused behavior of some of the Spanish-speaking residents resulted from their failure to understand the law and the ins and outs of the Los Angeles housing market. But she also made it clear that the residents were led by a politically sophisticated group of Mexican Americans (especially women like herself) who were fully aware of their rights and determined to fight for them. "We Americans," she wrote angrily, "who pride ourselves on fair play, protecting the underdog, [and] preserving dignity and self-respect for the common man, [have been forced to] stand by and see a whole population defrauded of their heritage at the whim and pleasure of a few bigoted men." The CHA "told us that the house you live in and the ground it is situated upon is to be used for a Public Housing Project, then the whole project went up in smoke. So much for America's principles!"[65]

CHAPTER FOUR

Political Consequences

The Defeat of Public Housing and the Triumph of Corporate Modernism, 1950–1953

"The Housing Authority is a natural target for communist infiltration because the people who are forced to live in public housing units are more apt to be socially maladjusted."

—CALIFORNIA HUAC

"On May 26, 1953, with a record high voter turnout, Norris Poulson defeated [Mayor] Fletcher Bowron by a margin of around 35,000 votes. . . . The Red Scare in public housing was . . . the major issue that led to Poulson's victory."

—DON PARSON

Public Housing and the Los Angeles City Council

Why did the Elysian Heights public housing project go up in smoke? The short answer, of course, is that on December 26, 1951, the L.A. City Council voted to repudiate its earlier decision to authorize its construction. But the issue was more complicated than that. For one thing, the City Council lacked the authority to cancel the loan it had accepted from the federal government all by itself. During the early 1950s the City Housing Authority, Mayor Bowron, and the courts all insisted either that the public housing program be continued or that the loan from the Federal Housing Administration be repaid.[1]

The City Council had several reasons for changing its mind. Some of them reflected the Red Scare hysteria then sweeping the country; others were local in origin. Tiny by European standards, the Southern California branch of the American Communist Party (CP), with almost five thousand members, reached its peak membership from 1945 to 1947.

This was due partly to doubts among white liberals about the harshness of President Truman's Cold War policies and partly to the strong support the Communists gave to the struggle for civil rights in L.A.'s minority communities.[2]

Having underscored the Soviet threat that resulted from the Russian takeover of Eastern Europe, President Truman increased the fear of domestic disloyalty in 1947 when he mandated a loyalty oath for federal employees. In Southern California, anxieties about domestic treachery expanded still further when the House Un-American Affairs Committee conducted its dramatic hearings into Communist influence in the motion picture industry, which resulted in the blacklisting of the Hollywood Ten.[3] In the 1948 presidential election, which Truman unexpectedly won, the Democratic Party split between its regular members and supporters of Progressive Party candidate Henry Wallace, who angered many voters by accepting help from the Communist Party. The result of these political divisions was an overall weakening of support for Truman's Fair Deal reform programs and a growing disregard for the civil rights of radicals and dissenters on the part of anti-Communist liberals.[4]

In turn, these developments reawakened the long-standing tradition of red-baiting among Los Angeles' civic elite. That tradition went back at least to 1911, when the *Los Angeles Times* and the business community combined to defeat a moderate Socialist candidate for mayor by falsely claiming that he was a revolutionary.[5] In 1949 and 1950, a new generation of conservatives hailed the expulsion of Communist-influenced unions from the AFL and the CIO, both in Los Angeles and in numerous other cities.

Fears of domestic betrayal grew still greater when the Communist Party officially went underground, and they reached a new peak when the United States began to suffer military setbacks in the Korean War. These setbacks reinforced concerns about "the loss of China," strengthened the search for domestic scapegoats, and increased the political clout of the conservative military-industrial complex that was emerging in Orange County. The expense of the Korean War also resulted in cutbacks in domestic spending, including money for public housing.[6]

At the same time, the Los Angeles construction industry at last began producing enough privately financed homes to satisfy demand. In response to the emerging economic boom, real estate magnate Fritz Burns built multistory apartment complexes in North Hollywood, Westchester, and Pasadena and constructed shopping centers in various parts of the L.A. Basin. Together with his allies in the Home Builders Association, the

Small Property Owners League, and the Chamber of Commerce, Burns established the Committee Against Socialist Housing. He and his supporters also began making political donations to Edward Davenport and other members of the City Council to persuade them to withdraw their support for public housing. "While the socialist-minded do-gooders foist government-constructed housing upon the population," wrote one of Fritz Burns's allies in the *Valley Times* in May 1951, "the cost to the taxpayers for constructing such housing will be several times that of the same buildings built by private contractors on a competitive basis."[7]

Another reason why supporters of public housing lost their majority on the Los Angeles City Council was the fallout from the so-called Burke affair. In October 1946 it was discovered that Sidney Burke and his wife, who were known members of the Communist Party, were living in the wartime Rodger Young public housing project, even though Burke was not technically a veteran of the U.S. Armed Forces for which the project had been designed. The CHA evicted Burke and his wife and suggested they be offered a place in the Channel Heights housing project instead.

But that did not satisfy the City Council. On October 16, 1951, it voted 11–1 to ban the Burkes from any of L.A.'s public housing projects. Councilman Ed Davenport claimed that the Burke case "heightened the conviction of many citizens, whose money builds Federal Housing, that the projects are targets of Communist propaganda and fertile fields for cultivating the support of the subversive groups who would change the American way of life to that of the communism of Russia."[8]

From this point on, public housing became increasingly associated in the public mind with the Soviet menace and with Communist efforts to gain influence among L.A.'s workers, racial minorities, and Jewish community groups. The liberal insistence that the projects should remain integrated (a contentious point in World War II) also exacerbated the distaste with which most white, middle-class voters, and some second-generation Mexican Americans, now regarded the issue. In fact, not long after the Burke affair, the California Senate's Committee on Un-American Activities—the Tenney Committee—drew a specific link between communism, public housing, and race. It labeled the racial minorities who lived in public housing as "socially maladjusted . . . and therefore more susceptible to the blandishments of clever Communists than the average person."[9]

Another issue that, in conservative eyes, was used improperly by the left to enhance the power of the state (and therefore to increase support for public housing) was that of rent control. During World War II the federal government had imposed rent control throughout the United States as a way of keeping living costs down. After the war ended, the real estate industry lobbied to have rent control abolished. In February 1950, Burton E. Edwards of the Los Angeles Apartment Owners' Association made an impassioned speech decrying rent control as "un-American." In July the City Council adopted a resolution declaring that a housing shortage no longer existed in Los Angeles, while urging the federal government to allow rent decontrol to go forward. The issue became embroiled in the courts until it was finally resolved in favor of decontrol.[10]

Finally, in August 1951 a resolution was put before the City Council requiring all local Communists to register with the LAPD. During the chaotic debate that followed, L.A. Communist leader Dorothy Healey called Councilman Davenport a "two-bit Fuehrer," which caused an enormous row.[11] By this time public housing had become so tainted with the brush of socialism that most of the councilmen who had formerly constituted a majority in favor of it announced that they would no longer support it. The tipping point came on December 3 when Councilman Harold Harby changed his position. Harby was an oil executive who had worked at various times for Shell and Richfield Oil. In a speech he denounced public housing as "the creeping cancer of socialism [that] will bring us to statiesm [*sic*] . . . and social decay."[12] As a result of all this it came as no surprise when, on December 26, 1951, the City Council voted 8 to 7 to reverse its decision of six months earlier and declared the federal public housing contract to be null and void.

As already noted, however, this did not put an end to the matter. On January 3, 1952, Mayor Fletcher Bowron vetoed the council vote, declaring that the city had entered into a contract with the federal government that it could not abrogate unilaterally. In response the City Council—now at odds with the mayor—decided to put the matter to a referendum in the form of Proposition B, to be held on June 3, 1952. It took this decision despite the fact that, in the meantime, the California Supreme Court ruled that the city could not unilaterally cancel its federal contract, meaning that the referendum would have no legal standing.[13] The decision to hold the referendum provided the first evidence that the Los Angeles City Council was prepared to act with dubious legality with respect to the housing issue.

As the referendum campaign heated up, the housing issue became ever more deeply entangled with Cold War politics, personal antagonism, and accusations of disloyalty. At a May conference on the issue presided over by Mayor Bowron, more than fifty demonstrators marched around city hall declaring that "the mayor is a dictator" and that "all Commies, progressives, and socialists are for public housing."[14]

Figure 13. Los Angeles City Council arguing over public housing. Courtesy *Los Angeles Times.*

The Yes on Prop. B (pro public housing) campaign was coordinated by Citizens for Slum Clearance and supported by the same coalition of labor unions, religious leaders, and liberal Democrats that had backed public housing before. They argued that if the housing contract was canceled, $13 million would have to be repaid to the federal government and that the large sums due to be spent on servicing existing slum areas could be avoided if they were replaced by new public housing projects. Despite this, Proposition B lost, 379,050 votes to 258,777.[15]

Armed with this evidence of the electorate's desire to repudiate the scheme, on August 18, 1952, Mayor Fletcher Bowron, accompanied by CHA director Howard Holtzendorff, met with President Truman and leaders of the Federal Housing Administration in Washington, DC, in an effort to limit L.A.'s public housing program. The federal government was willing to make concessions. Two days later, they returned with a scaled-down version of the agreement that removed the thirteen high-rise buildings from the Elysian Park Heights project (a concession, perhaps, to architect Richard Neutra's doubts about its viability) and reduced the number of public housing units required in the Los Angeles contract from 10,000 to 7,000.[16]

Mayor Bowron, Howard Holtzendorff, and the other leaders of the CHA hoped that these changes would placate opponents of the public housing program and allow the rest of it to proceed. They were wrong. Encouraged by the rise to prominence of Senator Joseph McCarthy, and declining public interest in the social engineering programs of the New Deal, the real estate industry and its allies remained implacably opposed, pointing out that the compromise agreement the mayor had secured still required the city to spend $83,000 on new housing projects. "If the public housing program is wrong, as a majority of the citizens of Los Angeles and of the City Councilmen believe," asserted the *Los Angeles Times* on August 21, 1952, "then it is as wrong at 7,000 units as it was at 10,000."[17]

Figure 14. Anti–public housing demonstrators at City Hall. Courtesy *Los Angeles Times*.

The Downfall of Frank Wilkinson

The June 1952 defeat of Proposition B favoring public housing, and the growing preoccupation of the U.S. government with the Soviet threat, gave conservative critics of public housing in Los Angeles good reason to believe they had their liberal opponents on the run. Imagine their delight, therefore, when they managed to get their principal antagonist, CHA publicity director Frank Wilkinson, exposed as a Communist and dismissed from his job.

The reason for this was that, unknown to Wilkinson, Los Angeles Police chief Parker compiled a secret dossier concerning his party membership. Wilkinson's membership was exposed during the course of a routine court hearing in August 1952 on housing conditions in Chavez Ravine, when he was suddenly asked about his political beliefs. Felix McGinnis, attorney for the plaintiffs in the case, asked, "Mr. Wilkinson, what organizations, political or otherwise, have you belonged to since 1928?" Taken by surprise, Wilkinson described the political clubs he had belonged to as a student at UCLA, but when McGinnis pressed him further he paused, as if he smelled a rat. After hesitating a few moments he replied: "I do not feel that I want to answer this question, . . . If necessary, I would hold that to answer such a question might in some way incriminate me."[18]

The audience gasped. By this time Senator McCarthy's tactic of using witnesses' invocations of the Fifth Amendment as evidence of their guilt was well enough known that it was assumed by many audience members—correctly, as it turned out—that Wilkinson was a covert Communist. After a brief intermission the questioning was resumed, and Wilkinson again refused to answer. When the day's court session was over Director Howard Holtzendorff immediately suspended Wilkinson from his duties pending further inquiries, and the City Council demanded a full-blown investigation of the CHA by the California Un-American Activities Committee (not the House Un-American Affairs Committee, or HUAC) headed by Senator Jack Tenney. This was agreed to. The next morning, a one-inch headline appeared on the *LA Times*' front page: LID BLOWS OFF HOUSING: TOP AIDE SUSPENDED; RED INQUIRY DEMANDED BY CITY COUNCIL.[19]

State senator Jack Tenney was a somewhat eccentric public figure—he also wrote popular songs—and well known as a bitter foe of communism. His committee had a history of making wild and unsubstantiated allegations. In April 1945, for example, it blamed the Zoot Suit Riots on "communist-inspired racial agitation"—an assertion for which there was no evidence. When the committee first tried to question Wilkinson he was in the hospital undergoing knee surgery. In a sign of the committee's zeal, one of its agents tried to serve Frank with a subpoena while he was still in the operating room. Failing this, they pinned the subpoena on his hospital gown.[20] After Wilkinson had recovered, the hearings were resumed, and the committee deployed Senator McCarthy's well-known "guilt-by-association" technique by claiming that Wilkinson had attended meetings of "Communist front" organizations such as the Los Angeles Workers School and the National Negro Congress.[21] In the eyes of public opinion, these associations were enough to prove that the suspect was a member of the Communist Party. It was no credit to the committee's methods that in this case it happened to be right.

The Tenney Committee also ignored numerous letters testifying to Wilkinson's character and to the depth of his commitment to the Chavez Ravine slum clearance project. In his letter on Wilkinson's behalf, for example, attorney Stanley Moffatt linked the Tenney Committee's investigation to previous attacks by right-wing conservatives against the Los Angeles public housing program. "I hope you will continue to stand firm against the vicious, Fascist forces that are trying . . . to destroy Public Slum Clearance and Housing Projects which were fostered by the great Franklin Roosevelt."[22] When Wilkinson again refused to cooperate by asserting his Fifth Amendment rights, he was permanently fired from his position at the CHA. Four other staff members of the CHA suspected of Communist Party connections (Sidney Green, Adina Williamson, Fay Kovner, and H. L. Sunshine) were also fired.[23]

During these hearings it also became apparent that the Tenney Committee was eager to expose Communist influence among teachers and in the Southern California labor movement, especially in public employee unions such as the American Federation of State, County and Municipal Employees (AFSCME) and the Los Angeles Federation of Teachers. Fears that left-wing school teachers were indoctrinating U.S. school children with un-American ideas were widespread at the time. During the 1950s more than thirty thousand teachers throughout the country were fired after being interrogated by federal and state authorities. Jean Benson Wilkinson, Frank Wilkinson's college sweetheart and now his wife, was an activist in the Los Angeles Federation of Teachers Local 430.[24]

Immediately after her husband was dismissed, Jean Benson Wilkinson was called on to give evidence to the Tenney Committee about her political beliefs. She was defended by the same lawyer as her husband, and she also lost her job after pleading the Fifth Amendment. The questioning "had nothing to do with education," she later reported. "They were just out to get us."[25] Along with five other schoolteachers, Jean Benson Wilkinson was formally dismissed by the Los Angeles Board of Education.

These dismissals put the Wilkinson family into a difficult position. "In thirty minutes," Frank later wrote, "I went from being one of the more respected citizens in city government to being an outcast."[26] Like thousands of other blacklisted employees, they found it extremely difficult to get another job. Jean helped sustain the family by working intermittently in private schools, and Frank received financial help from his friend Monsignor O'Dwyer. After about eight months, he was hired as a night janitor by a sympathetic Quaker who owned a department store in Pasadena. Early the following year, Wilkinson met Eason Monroe, a blacklisted English professor from San Francisco State College who worked for the ACLU, and was given a job writing for *Open Forum* about witch-hunt victims who fought back against the Red Scare. Shortly after that he secured a regular job with the Citizens Committee to Preserve American Freedoms, a group of liberals trying to protect freedom of expression and other civil liberties from being undermined by supporters of the Red Scare.[27]

By this time anti-Communist hysteria was so pervasive throughout Southern California that it threatened the jobs and reputations of men and women in all walks of life—including even the city's top elected public official. As previously noted, Mayor Bowron was not ideologically committed to the public housing movement. His main concern was to overcome the city's housing shortage and ensure that Los Angeles upheld its financial obligations under its housing contract with the federal government. But this did not spare him from the wrath of Cold War zealots. On September 2, 1951, he was subpoenaed to appear at an eminent domain hearing on housing in Chavez Ravine.[28] Upon leaving the building, Bowron was accosted by John Hoyga from the Small Property Owners League, who was one of the city's most vociferous opponents of public housing. "Didn't I warn you about Wilkinson?" Hoyga asked Bowron. The mayor did not believe that he had. When Hoyga persisted with his questioning, Bowron became annoyed and asked him what organization he represented. "I don't represent Communists," Hoyga stated. "Do you represent Joe Stalin?" Bowron asked sarcastically. "No," replied Hoyga, "but you do."[29]

Bowron lost his temper and took a swing at Hoyga. An aide intervened to prevent the conflict from escalating any further. Although he was unhurt, Hoyga later cast aspersions on Bowron's masculinity by telling the press that "it was like a woman's blow—a powder puff punch."[30] The incident seemed trivial and was laughed off by most citizens. Nevertheless, it illustrated how tense the political climate was and how sensitive

EXTRA

7¢ THE MIRROR

FINAL N.Y. STOCKS

Vol. IV - No. 284 76 Pages FRIDAY, SEPTEMBER 5, 1952 145 S. Spring, Los Angeles 53

MAYOR SLUGS HOUSING FOE

THE WINNAH—BOWRON BY ONE PUNCH

Bowron Hits Landlord With Fist in Court Row

BY ART WHITE, Mirror Staff Writer

The war over public housing in Los Angeles broke out on an old front today as Councilman Ed Davenport broke up another session of the City Council and on a new front as Mayor Bowron and a property owner engaged in a fist fight.

Bowron and John Hoyga, [illegible], of [illegible] S. Lake St., staged a one-punch brawl on the steps of a Superior Court building, hizzoner landing the single punch and the landlord landing the last word.

"It was like a woman's punch," said Hoyga, member of a small property owners' organization who provoked Bowron's wrath by accusing him of "representing Joe Stalin" in the dispute over $110,000,000 worth of public housing.

Figure 15. Mayor Fletcher Bowron loses his temper. Courtesy *Los Angeles Times*.

the defenders of public housing were about accusations of being pro-Communist. The disparagement of Bowron's masculinity also hinted at widespread public fears of homosexuality—another favorite target of conservatives in the 1950s.[31]

Public Housing and the Question of Race

Shortly after Mayor Bowron's scuffle with Hoyga another outburst of violence threatened to break out that was not at all trivial. On September 5 Councilman Davenport, who was known to drink heavily, introduced a resolution into the City Council naming Mayor Bowron a "co-conspirator" (i.e., a secret plotter) with Frank Wilkinson because of his defense of public housing.[32] When Davenport was rebuked by the council president for his choice of words, the councilman, displaying the hysteria that later led to a fatal heart attack, leapt to his feet and delivered a lengthy harangue against Mayor Bowron and all so-called disloyal state bureaucrats. The Mexican American councilman from the Ninth District, Edward R. Roybal, got up and tried to restrain him, whereupon Davenport—invoking the common stereotype that Mexicans were inherently violent—accused Roybal of having earlier threatened him with a knife.[33]

This accusation transformed a minor display of bad temper into a racially charged political incident. Racism had long been a half-hidden presence in the housing debate. As previously noted, the Tenney Committee alleged that Communist influence was more likely to develop in public housing units than in private homes because of the "high incidence of socially maladjusted racial minority groups."[34] Councilman Roybal was a respected former medical professional who had raised the political profile of L.A.'s Mexican American community by winning a seat on the City Council in 1949. He was understandably offended by Davenport's accusation, especially since the two men had already clashed in debates over proposals for a city-wide Fair Employment Practices Commission and the need to defend minorities against police brutality.[35] The Mexican Chamber of Commerce sent a letter to the City Council protesting Davenport's "vile, false, and defamatory statement," and Mauricio Terrazas of the Asociacion Nacional Mexico-Americana (ANMA) issued a statement that "any councilman who conducts himself in such a manner has no business to represent the city."[36]

Davenport responded to these criticisms by alleging that the Mexican Chamber of Commerce was "a Communist-front organization." He also tried to conceal the evidence of his ethnic slur by claiming that he was just "fighting . . . [to save] the homes of Mexican Americans in Chavez Ravine."[37] But this clumsy maneuver failed to appease the liberals on the city council. The *Daily News* called his antics unbecoming for a city councilman and demanded his removal from office. The incident eventually blew over. But it was a measure of how badly the Red Scare had corrupted L.A. politics that the Hearst-owned *Herald-Express* took Davenport's accusations seriously. It charged that the criticism of his behavior was a "frame-up," engineered by a "stacked deck of leftists."[38]

This incident enhanced the reputation of Edward Roybal, who was the first Mexican American to be elected to the City Council in the twentieth century. Frank Wilkinson, too, managed to retrieve his fortunes when he leveraged his job with the Citizens Committee to Preserve American Freedoms into a lifelong career as a defender of civil liberties.[39]

Even so, the attitudes both Edward Roybal and Frank Wilkinson adopted toward the plight of the residents of Chavez Ravine during the evictions crisis left something to be desired. In 1959, Roybal would give helpful legal advice to the last holdouts there when they were threatened with eviction.[40] But he was noticeably silent about the injustices done to the ravine's residents in the early stages of the crisis. This may have been because he was preoccupied with other matters or, as councilman for the Ninth District (which did not include Chavez Ravine), he felt that he had no responsibility for its residents. Nevertheless, as the sole Mexican American on the City Council during these years, and a staunch liberal on many other issues, it is somewhat surprising not to find him speaking out on their behalf when they were faced with mass evictions in 1951–1952.

Similar questions arise about Frank Wilkinson's behavior during the first phase of the crisis. He was not, of course, responsible for the failed effort to build the Elysian Park Heights public housing project, and he later expressed regret at the role he had inadvertently played in the eviction of the residents, calling it "the tragedy of my life."[41] Looking back at the central role he played in the eviction process, however, one wonders whether he knew about the bullying tactics the CHA agents used to force the residents to sell their homes or about the illegal tactics of unscrupulous lawyers like the one who took advantage of Mrs. Martin. If he was aware of these abuses, he did very little or nothing to stop them.

Also disconcerting is the absence from Wilkinson's memoirs and speeches during this period of any signs of sympathy for the plight of the dozens of poor Mexican homeowners he encountered on his early inspection trips to Chavez Ravine.[42] Later in life, Wilkinson frequently expressed regret about the failure of the Elysian Park Heights project. For instance, in an article written for *Frontier* magazine in the aftermath of the 1965 Watts Rebellion, he stated: "Had our plans been allowed to bear fruit, tens of thousands of African American and Mexican American children would have been lifted out of the stifling pressures of the ghettoes, into the good air of integrated, beautifully designed, low rent communities."[43] But even here Wilkinson, assuming—wrongly—that the ravine's residents would prefer public housing to their current homes, betrayed a certain racial insensitivity. This was because, in public at least, he never expressed an interest in what changes in their accommodations—if any—the residents of the ravine *themselves* wanted, as opposed to what white city bureaucrats like himself thought was best for them.

How is this paradox to be resolved? The answer, as I have already intimated, lies in Frank Wilkinson's early life and upbringing. He grew up in a wealthy family in a segregated Pasadena suburb where he had little, if any, contact with people of color. To his parents' chagrin, he embraced radical politics after he toured Europe with a college friend in the late 1930s and witnessed the impact of the Great Depression on European workers. This experience was largely responsible for his becoming a Communist. But he never got to know any of these European workers personally. Hence when he first took up the cause of social reform, he based his approach on the nearest progressive equivalent to the politics of his own white, middle-class family.[44]

This was to adopt the condescending, top-down model of the Los Angeles progressive movement of the World War I era, most of whose leaders, like Dr. John Randolph Haynes, were environmental determinists. Although their intentions were different, these progressives shared the Communist belief that planning experts like themselves knew what was best for immigrant slum dwellers without consulting them. Only later in life did Wilkinson learn to view the lives of minority families from the point of view of their own culture and interests. Frank's early naïveté on this matter was satirized in the 2003 play *Chavez Ravine*, where he is portrayed by the Culture Clash authors of the play as a well-intentioned but hopelessly ethnocentric do-gooder (see chapter 8 in this volume). In one scene based on his own career in the CHA, an ebullient Wilkinson leads architect Richard Neutra up into the hills above downtown, then turns to him and asks, in a mocking, sarcastic voice, "Aren't these rolling hills of Chavez Ravine a perfect site for . . . your modular, low-slung, abstractly asymmetrical buildings!"[45] Neutra's character in the play was far more skeptical than Wilkinson about the suitability of his public housing architectural designs, as he was in real life.

By the end of 1952, with Mayor Bowron on the defensive, Frank Wilkinson fired, and Edward R. Roybal preoccupied with other matters, any hope of securing redress for the residents of Chavez Ravine seemed doomed to failure. It remained to be seen how a new city administration, which came into office as a result of the municipal elections of 1953, would deal with the issue.

L.A. Elects a New Mayor

For those who kept their ears to the ground it was clear well before the 1953 election took place that the business community and its supporters were determined, if they could, to get rid of liberal mayor Fletcher Bowron and his stubborn defense of public housing once and for all. On January 5, L.A. *Times* editor Norman Chandler invited Congressman Norris Poulson to meet with his "downtown group" of advisors to consider running for mayor. Poulson was a shrewd choice. A small-town accountant by training, he was in many ways an ideal conservative candidate for the mayor's job. In Congress he had opposed financial waste, voted for the antilabor Taft Hartley Act, and supported President Truman's Cold War foreign policy.[46]

Although he later denied it, Poulson was quite willing to submit to the tutelage of Chandler's conservative political allies. They included right-wing councilman George Cronk, who served as Poulson's campaign manager; real estate magnate Fritz Burns, who paid for candidate Poulson's public relations firm; and up-and-coming aircraft contractor Howard Hughes, who defrayed the cost of his campaign billboards. Another close advisor was Carleton Williams, city editor of the *Los Angeles Times*, who saw himself as a municipal kingmaker. Rarely had the *Times* and the real estate lobby displayed their political influence so openly.[47]

Before the election campaign began, Mayor Bowron briefly considered withdrawing from the race. He had been in office for fourteen years, and even some of the liberals among his supporters thought it was time for a fresh face. But he was still angry with right-wing efforts to portray him as pro-Communist, and after reviewing other possible candidates, he became convinced that none of them could defend his liberal record as well as he could. Once the campaign began it became obvious that public housing would be the main issue and that red-baiting remained the conservatives' political weapon of choice. "The public housing program brought him [Bowron] to bed with some characters who were dubious indeed," stated an L.A. *Times* editorial, referring to Frank Wilkinson. "And he did not detach himself from them even when he was given evidence of their Red connections."[48] These tactics appeared to work. Poulson won the primary election in April, although not by a large enough margin to avoid a run-off.[49]

Realizing that he was fighting for his political life, Mayor Fletcher Bowron rallied organized labor, former New Dealers, minority voters, and as many other supporters as he could to his side. In a May 5 radio speech he attacked the business elite's political power. The current election, he declared, was an attempt "by a small, immensely wealthy, incredibly powerful group to force you to elect as your mayor a man who will represent them—not you—a man who will do their bidding, not yours."[50] Bowron's campaign also released a cartoon depicting Norris Poulson as a puppet of the *Times*. The cartoon infuriated the Poulson camp. In response,

Figure 16. Mayoral candidate Norris Poulson portrayed as a puppet of the *Los Angeles Times*. Courtesy *Los Angeles Times*.

Councilman George Cronk prevailed on members of the House Committee on Government Operations in Washington to come to Los Angeles just before the election and embarrass Mayor Bowron by publicly interrogating the CHA employees who had been dismissed as a result of the investigations of the Tenney Committee.[51]

These hearings proved disastrous for Mayor Bowron. Police Chief William Parker read from the dossiers of three of the dismissed CHA employees—Sidney Green, Frank Wilkinson, and Adina Williamson—revealing new details of their associations with the Communist Party. Then Bowron himself was called before the committee and grilled as to why he had allowed the City Housing Authority to become "infested with reds."[52] In its efforts to tar the mayor with the brush of radicalism, committee members bullied him, cut him off in the middle of a sentence, and refused to accord him the respect due a city official. Bowron was furious, saying he had "never received such discourteous treatment in my life."[53] But the tactic worked. When the votes were counted on May 26, 1953, Norris Poulson defeated Fletcher Bowron by a margin of 35,000 votes. Poulson's election as mayor swept the liberals from office and inaugurated two decades of conservative municipal rule.[54]

In fact, as suggested earlier, the 1953 mayoral election was a major turning point in Los Angeles history. The social engineering traditions of the New Deal were set aside, municipal politics took a significant step to the right, and the cause of public housing—and with it the hopes of the residents of Chavez Ravine for some sort of redress—was dealt a shattering blow. "For the first time in fifteen years," wrote William G. Bonelli, "special interests took precedence over the public interest in city hall."[55]

Mayor Poulson Goes to Washington

In a parting shot before he left office, Bowron appointed three additional liberals to the City Housing Authority who were sympathetic to his policies in an effort, he said, to prevent the incoming administration from selling land in Chavez Ravine to real estate speculators or private realtors.[56] This was the first mention of an issue that was to bedevil negotiations with baseball magnate Walter O'Malley and the Brooklyn Dodgers in the following years, namely, the liberal desire to ensure that the land made available by the departure of residents from Chavez Ravine was used for a public (as opposed to a private) purpose, including the erection of a privately owned baseball field.

Incoming mayor Poulson resented this effort to influence his new administration's policies. But to the surprise of both liberals and conservatives, after his inauguration he suggested a compromise solution to the public housing question that was more moderate than *L.A. Times* publisher Norman Chandler had expected. He proposed to cut the size of the public housing program in half by eliminating Elysian Park Heights, Rose Hills Court, and several other projects but to keep the rest of it intact. On July 6, 1953, Poulson's plan was adopted by the City Council by a vote of

13–1. The sole dissenting vote was cast by Councilman Edward R. Roybal, who stated that the council should have been given more time to consider the changes.[57]

The key player in negotiating this proposed compromise was the City Housing Authority, which continued to maintain that the city of L.A. had a legal obligation to complete the entire public housing program, as it had agreed to in 1949. But Director Howard Holtzendorff, recognizing that public opinion had now moved to the right, agreed to a scaled-down version of the original arrangement, stating, "We are now willing to abandon part of [the contract], provided it can be done lawfully." On hearing this, according to the left-wing *People's World*, the antihousing city councilmen "bubbled with glee."[58] No apparent consideration was given to restoring title to the original residents in Chavez Ravine or to providing any relief to the remaining holdouts.

As a result of these developments, on July 15, 1953, a large delegation, including Mayor Poulson, Howard Holtzendorff, the L.A. city attorney, and several city councilmen, flew to Washington to negotiate the downsizing of the 1949 agreement. They found Albert Cole and other Federal Housing Administration officials in President Eisenhower's new Republican administration more willing to grant their wishes than Truman administration officials had been. President Eisenhower's conservative housing polices were shown by the fact that he asked Congress to fund only 35,000 new units of public housing during his first term in office; in his second, he requested no new public housing units at all.[59]

There are differing versions of how the Washington negotiations were conducted. In his memoirs Mayor Poulson said that his friend Congressman John Phillips, who had previously served with him on the House Appropriations Committee, placed a rider on an appropriations bill that enabled L.A. to "bail out" of the financial requirements it had earlier agreed to.[60] According to Ronald Lopez, it was Vice President Nixon and California senator William F. Knowland who took the lead.[61] Whichever of the two moved first, the outcome came very close to what the anti–public housing lobby wanted. Congress adopted new legislation permitting the federal government to absorb the difference between the money L.A. had already spent from its 1949 contract and the future sale price of the land from Chavez Ravine. This involved the U.S. government in a loss of several million dollars.[62]

Fifty-seven percent (or 5,649) of the housing units were cut from the original agreement. Chavez Ravine and several other public housing projects were canceled, while the rest were allowed to go forward. The City of

Los Angeles was given six months in which to purchase the land in the ravine rendered vacant by the evictions, an option it exercised in 1954. Significantly, however, this land could only be used "for a public purpose."[63] The revised agreement also left several integrated public housing projects to be completed. But since the public housing program, which had been used by liberals to advance the cause of housing desegregation, was now much smaller, the new dispensation struck a major blow to the efforts of civil rights activists to end discrimination in the Los Angeles housing market. Further progress on that front would have to wait until the 1960s.[64]

Was There a "Baseball Conspiracy" Against Public Housing?

The emasculation of L.A.'s public housing program reinforced the determination of the city's business elite to use large-scale, private development as its main instrument for revitalizing the downtown area and enhancing the city's reputation as a major cultural center.[65] The critical point, however, is that alongside campaigns for a new concert hall and other cultural landmarks went an interest in bringing a Major League Baseball team to the city for the first time. In the fifties L.A. became the third largest city in the country. "It is absurd," said Mayor Poulson, "to envision a population center of this size without Major League Baseball."[66]

Until World War II, virtually all of America's Major League Baseball teams were located on the East Coast. Interest in bringing such a team to L.A. was renewed by the Boston Braves' successful move to Milwaukee, followed by the Giants' transfer from New York to San Francisco. In Los Angeles, there was also talk of approaching the Washington Senators and the Kansas City Athletics. But the first serious expression of interest in the Brooklyn Dodgers came on September 1, 1955, when Councilwoman Rosalind Wyman, supported by County Supervisor Kenneth Hahn, wrote to Dodgers owner Walter O'Malley asking if he was interested in moving his team from Brooklyn to the West Coast. O'Malley, then in the middle of a pennant race, said he was too busy to consider the matter. In his reply, he also added that since L.A. already had two Pacific League baseball teams he did not want to stir up any publicity that "might be . . . detrimental to their franchises."[67]

Despite her youth and inexperience, Councilwoman Rosalind Wyman played an important part in the campaign to persuade O'Malley to move the Dodgers to L.A. This was not because she participated directly in the

Figure 17. Supervisor Kenneth Hahn (third from left) and Councilwoman Rosalind Wyman (in baseball cap) meet with Walter O'Malley (third from right), June 1957. Courtesy *Los Angeles Times*.

contract negotiations. That was left to the men. It was because of her charm, her popularity, and the fact that she was the first woman to be elected to the Los Angeles City Council. Rosalind Wyman had a flair for publicity. She courted O'Malley, urged Mayor Poulson to offer him generous terms, and campaigned vigorously on behalf of Major League Baseball in her own West Side constituency.[68]

It is important to establish September 1, 1955, as the date on which serious interest was first expressed in bringing the Brooklyn Dodgers to Los Angeles. This is because historian Ronald Lopez, among others, has suggested that "there was a conspiracy to defeat public housing in Chavez Ravine *in order to* build a baseball stadium there" (my italics).[69] I find this argument unpersuasive. It is undoubtedly true that the manner in which the residents of Chavez Ravine were initially deprived of their homes was unjust. There is also good evidence to believe that, when the city finally sold some of its land in Chavez Ravine to Walter O'Malley, it deliberately circumvented the requirement of the courts and the federal government that it be used for a public purpose only. We shall review this evidence later on. But it strains credulity to conclude from this that the campaign to terminate public housing in Los Angeles was based on a secret plan to bring the Brooklyn Dodgers to Southern California. For one thing, such a theory suggests that the ideological basis of the anti–public housing movement—that it posed a collectivist threat to the American free enterprise system—was either bogus or secondary to the conspirators' main purpose of bringing the Dodgers to L.A. This idea is inherently implausible.

Several other points Lopez makes in support of his conspiracy theory are also dubious. He argues that Chavez Ravine was first suggested as an appropriate site for a baseball stadium in 1952. This may be true, but it does not advance the argument for a conspiracy. Given the increased Cold War pressures they were subjected to, there is no reason to believe that the councilmen who voted to rescind their support for public housing on December 26, 1951, were not acting sincerely.[70] Lopez also suggests that Mayor Poulson was subjected to increased pressure to bring the Dodgers to L.A. in 1955 and that several of the meetings subsequently held between the city's officials and Walter O'Malley were conducted in secret.[71] Both of these observations are indeed accurate. But, again, neither of them is sufficient to demonstrate the presence of a political conspiracy.

Finally, Lopez contends that no other purpose for Chavez Ravine was ever suggested save that of becoming the site for the Dodgers. This is simply untrue. In his memoirs Mayor Poulson states clearly that during the period from 1953 to 1956 he was unable to find a suitable purchaser for the land. "For three years I tried to get public groups interested in the area—including a zoo enthusiast, a cemetery builder, and an opera house buff."[72] But none of these schemes worked out. If any of them had, the secret conspiracy to bring the Dodgers to L.A.—a conspiracy in which Poulson himself was supposedly involved—would presumably have collapsed.

None of this meant, once the Brooklyn Dodgers became amenable to an offer from the City of Los Angeles, that the downtown business elite did not immediately seize on Chavez Ravine as the best site to offer Walter O'Malley or that they did not offer him too many concessions to ensure his team's move to the West Coast. But as we shall see, O'Malley did not commit himself to moving the Dodgers to Southern California until 1957, or even 1958, several years after sufficient land had become available in Chavez Ravine to build a new baseball stadium there. Even then, the negotiations between the two sides frequently came near to breakdown over financing, how much land was to be sold, and several other aspects of the matter.[73] The time the negotiations took, and their near breakdown on several occasions, renders the conspiracy theory still more implausible.

Using conspiracy theory to explain the demise of public housing and the city's desire to bring the Dodgers out to Los Angeles is also unsatisfactory because it reinforces the misleading notion that the tragedy of Chavez Ravine can be explained primarily as a conflict between greedy white bureaucrats on the one hand and a group of helpless Mexican victims on the other. In the 1950s many of L.A.'s white city employees, like their state and federal counterparts, were indeed indifferent, not to say hostile, to the interests of the Mexican American community, as they were to the interests of the city's African Americans. The year 1954, for example, witnessed "Operation Wetback," a notorious event in which thousands of Mexican immigrants left over from the World War II Bracero Program were swept up off the streets and "sent back" to Mexico, even though some of them were probably U.S. citizens.[74]

But it is misleading to interpret the Chavez Ravine affair simply as an exercise in ethnic cleansing. Both the white and Mexican participants in the affair were themselves divided over the best course to follow. Mexican Americans were split between those who urged the ravine's residents to accept public housing as the best solution to their problems and those who opposed their doing so. In addition, the Mexican American homeowners in Chavez Ravine who resisted eviction can hardly be described as a group of "helpless victims" who lacked the temerity to fight back. The white community was similarly split between those who, like Frank Wilkinson, supported the Elysian Park Heights project; those—like architects Richard Neutra and Robert Alexander—who were skeptical about it; and a much larger population of suburban, middle-class whites who did not care about the housing needs of Mexicans one way or the other.[75]

A better approach is to see the unfolding events of the tragedy for what they really were—a complex and sometimes contradictory mixture of prior planning and opportunism, chicanery and good intentions, and chance developments over which neither side could exert complete control.

PART III

Building Dodger Stadium

CHAPTER FIVE

L.A. Pursues the Brooklyn Dodgers, 1957–1959

"Many saw a Major League Baseball franchise as an economic stimulus and as a prestigious status symbol for modern Los Angeles."

—DON PARSON

"The forcible and highly publicized eviction of the Arechiga family from Chavez Ravine on May 8, 1959, . . . made a powerful and often permanent impression on many of those who saw the newsreels of the event on television."

—RONALD WILLIAM LOPEZ

Negotiating with Walter O'Malley, 1955–1957

The negotiations that ended with a tentative agreement between Walter O'Malley and the City of Los Angeles in 1957 to bring the Brooklyn Dodgers to Southern California involved a wide variety of actors. They ranged from the voters of Los Angeles to the California Supreme Court, from the New York City planning authorities to the nation's baseball authorities, and from baseball fans to team owner Walter O'Malley.

Let us begin with O'Malley and his reasons for wanting to move the Dodgers out of Brooklyn. Born in New York in 1903, Walter F. O'Malley was a bluff, hearty man who cut a congenial figure in company. But he was also a shrewd businessman and wily negotiator who by the 1950s had become one of the most influential figures in American baseball. The issue for him was not how to maintain the prowess of his team, which was already high, but how to deal with the cramped quarters of Ebbets Field in Brooklyn. It was this problem that first prompted his interest in moving the Dodgers to L.A. Ebbets Field only had seating for 25,000, and it could not readily be expanded because of its inner-city location. Seating for 25,000 fans was considered sufficient when Ebbets Field first opened in 1913, but it was inadequate for a modern baseball stadium.[1]

With Jackie Robinson, Roy Campanella, and Don Newcombe on its roster, the Brooklyn Dodgers was one of the best teams in the country. But with women, families, and African Americans attending the games in increasing numbers in the postwar period, the raucous intimacy that had served its male, white supporters well before the war seemed tasteless to an increasing number of fans. Although admired for his skills, Jackie Robinson's role on the team also raised racial hackles in some of Brooklyn's poorer white, ethnic neighborhoods. Ebbets Field's run-down appearance and its many pillars, which obstructed the view from all but the best seats, increased consumer dissatisfaction. The result was that after 1947, when attendance peaked, the number of fans attending the Dodgers' home games fell, sometimes reaching no more than seven or eight thousand. This was far smaller than the large number of fans at rival Yankee Stadium.[2]

Walter O'Malley had long been aware of the space problems at Ebbets Field. They were highlighted by the large crowds the Braves drew when they moved from Boston to Milwaukee in 1953. O'Malley was determined to get hold of a larger stadium. In August 1955 he made his views known to Robert Moses, the powerful head of New York's planning agency who had transformed New York City by reshaping its parks, highways, and overall development plans. Moses's influence as Mayor Robert Wagner's right-hand man was so great that few applications for new building schemes or financial support got through without his consent.[3]

In this case, money was not the immediate issue. O'Malley simply wanted permission to build a large, new, privately funded facility for the Dodgers at the junction of Atlantic and Flatbush avenues in Brooklyn, where several subway lines converged.[4] Unfortunately for him, Robert Moses rejected his request, even though it would only have required a small outlay from New York's treasury. "We have no confidence in Walter O'Malley's scheme to put a Dodger Field at the Brooklyn terminal of the Long Island Railroad," Moses stated. He added that he saw "no prospect of an alternate Dodger location in Brooklyn."[5] Nevertheless, he left the door slightly ajar when he expressed concern that, in the absence of a new stadium, the Dodgers might leave the New York area altogether.[6]

In response to this rejection, O'Malley displayed the negotiating skills that had already made him a man to be reckoned with. On August 16, 1955, he announced that the Dodgers would play several home games in Jersey City in the 1956 season. This did not mean that he had decided to move his team from Brooklyn to New Jersey. It was a tactical maneuver designed to create doubt about his intentions and to pressure New York City authorities into reconsidering his request. For a time the tactic appeared to

Figure 18. Ebbets Field was too small for the Brooklyn Dodgers. Courtesy *Los Angeles Times.*

work. In February 1956 Mayor Robert Wagner sent a bill to the New York state legislature seeking authorization for a new Sports Center Authority, including a provision that would enable it to sell bonds for the construction of a new baseball stadium in Brooklyn. Soon after it reached the state capital in Albany, however, the plan fell through because of disagreements over funding.[7]

Mayor Poulson and the Los Angeles city authorities eagerly followed these developments. They had been impressed by the boost given to the prestige of Milwaukee by the transfer of the Boston Braves to that city. A report by the L.A. Downtown Businessmen's Association (which included Bullocks, Title Insurance and Trust, and other major L.A. firms) noted how "overnight, big league baseball [had] transformed a dull Midwestern city into blazing, dancing, fairy tale headlines."[8] This was just the kind of fillip L.A. needed to revive its downtown and enable it to compete with the more attractive downtown areas of other large American cities.

Capitalizing on this new, optimistic mood, Mayor Poulson flew to New York in the fall of 1956 to attend the World Series and hold informal talks with Walter O'Malley. At approximately the same time County Supervisor Kenneth Hahn was in Washington, DC, checking out the future plans of the Washington Senators. While there, he received a private note from O'Malley urging him not to talk to the Senators because his consultations with Poulson seemed likely to bear fruit. Prospects for a possible Dodger move to L.A. looked even brighter when O'Malley announced on October 31 that he was selling Ebbets Field to a local developer, while retaining the option of leasing it back from him for five years. Once more it seemed that O'Malley was threatening to leave Brooklyn. But once more it turned out to be a tactical move to pressure Mayor Wagner and Commissioner Robert Moses to stop the bureaucratic haggling over the new Sports Center Authority and authorize the construction of a new stadium.[9]

Back in L.A., Mayor Poulson and Supervisor Hahn anxiously awaited the outcome of O'Malley's new maneuver. Meanwhile, Poulson appointed a city commission to study the future of L.A.'s parks and recreational needs, with the unspoken purpose of attracting the Dodgers. The commission recommended that L.A. build a large, modern baseball stadium in Chavez Ravine and that a $2 million appropriation be included in the city's 1957 budget for leveling the necessary land.[10] In November O'Malley held further talks with Supervisor Hahn when the Dodgers came through L.A. on their way to Japan for an exhibition tour. Its city leaders were even more encouraged when, on December 24, 1956, the New York Board of Estimate only authorized $25,000 to be spent on feasibility studies for a new stadium in Brooklyn—an inadequate sum for the task. When Mayor Wagner and Robert Moses let this decision stand, they effectively killed the possibility of a new major league stadium in Brooklyn.[11]

At this point the decision seemed to favor L.A. In February 1957, O'Malley purchased the franchise of the minor league Los Angeles Angels, along with their ballpark at Wrigley Field (not the famous Chicago park). This seemed to confirm his intention to move his team out west. But once again the move turned out to be a tactical maneuver, this time to persuade L.A. to sweeten its offer regarding Chavez Ravine. Mayor Poulson willingly obliged. In the fall of that year he persuaded the City Council to add 115 additional acres to the 185 acres originally promised O'Malley, in return for his agreement to sell Wrigley Field back to the city and build a forty-acre recreation center in Elysian Park.[12]

But then, in May 1957, Los Angeles city attorney Roger Arnebergh called a halt to the whole proceedings. He pointed out that the city of L.A. could not offer the Dodgers 115 additional acres of land in Chavez Ravine because it did not yet own them. Thus the proposed agreement neglected the requirement that whatever land the city sold to the Dodgers must be used for a public purpose, not for the building of a private baseball stadium. The proposed agreement was illegal. It would have to be negotiated all over again.[13]

The Dodgers' Indian Summer at Ebbets Field

The years from 1955 to 1957 were a time of uncertainty both for O'Malley and for the champions of Major League Baseball in L.A. Ironically, however, these were also the years when the Brooklyn Dodgers played some of the best remembered games in U.S. history—games that served to make the team still more desirable in the eyes of Southern California's baseball fans. By 1951 the Dodgers had already amassed an impressive post–World War II record. In September 1951, having fought their way to the top of the National League, they lost a close-fought, end-of-season game to the New York Giants. One commentator called the contest "the greatest pennant scramble in history."[14] In 1952 the Brooklyn team went one better. It won the National League pennant only to lose the World Series to its longtime rival, the New York Yankees. The following years, 1953 and 1954, were less successful. Then in the summer of 1955, with rumors flying that the year might be the team's last at Ebbets Field, the Dodgers pulled off their best season ever.

The setting was once more a Dodgers-Yankees contest in the World Series—except that this time the Dodgers won. When Johnny Podres threw the winning pitch, the scene in Brooklyn was comparable to V-E Day in 1945. Walter O'Malley leapt up and kissed everyone in sight, and his daughter Terry burst into tears. A Yankee usher, mistaking her tears of joy for disappointment, patted her on the back and said, "Don't take it so bad, girlie. I'm a Yankee fan too, but deep down I'm glad those Brooklyn bums finally won!"[15]

The 1956 season did not begin auspiciously. The shadow cast by the possibility of leaving Brooklyn seemed to affect the team's performance, as well as the enthusiasm of its fans. After a brief appearance in first place in April, the Dodgers struggled to stay among the leaders of the National League. But no other team rose to a dominating position, and due in part to Don Newcombe's excellent pitching, the Dodgers once again met the Yankees in the World Series. This time their old rivals were led by Mickey Mantle at the top of his form, and it seemed impossible that they would repeat the triumph of the previous year.

That judgment turned out to be correct, even though the Dodgers were sentimental favorites among many fans. President Eisenhower, campaigning for reelection, attended the first game of the World Series, as did Adlai Stevenson, the Democratic candidate for president. Again the Series was tied up. Newcombe did his best, but the Dodgers' aging hitters let them down, and they lost the last game by a score of 9–1. Nevertheless, it had been a wonderful two years, and many Brooklyn fans asked themselves how, after such a display of heroics, O'Malley could contemplate moving his team to another city.[16]

But O'Malley continued trying to hammer out a deal with L.A., whose negotiating team was led this time by downtown business leader Harold McClellan instead of the overeager Poulson, who later admitted that he had "gotten in over my head."[17] A new draft contract between the Dodgers and the city of L.A. was agreed on, containing many of the same clauses as the old one. It involved spending $2.7 million of Los Angeles' money—an increase of $750,000—to build the access roads to the proposed Chavez Ravine stadium, in return for O'Malley's agreement to pay for a forty-acre recreation center in Elysian Park.[18]

But the public purpose problem once more intruded into the debate. Responding to the objections of L.A. city attorney Roger Arnebergh, the new draft stated that L.A. would initially make over to O'Malley the 185 acres it already owned, then "use its best efforts to acquire . . . and convey additional land, to make a total of 300 acres, more or less."[19] The draft contract tried to get around the public purpose requirement by inserting the following language: "Whereas all of the foregoing is useful and convenient in connection with the city's rights and powers, it was therefore declared to be in the public interest."[20] Later on, this language, too, would fail to pass legal muster.

Despite some who expressed doubts, on October 7, 1957, the Los Angeles City Council voted to approve the revised Dodger contract by a vote of 10-4. On the following day, seemingly a momentous one, Walter O'Malley announced that the Dodgers would move to Los Angeles for the 1958 season, and a jubilant Mayor Poulson declared victory. "At long last we've got the Dodgers!" trumpeted the *Los Angeles Times*.[21] In Brooklyn, by contrast, there were scenes of mourning. In bars, on street comers, and in private homes Walter O'Malley was condemned as a traitor to the city, and New York City authorities were excoriated for their failure to provide enough financial aid to build a new stadium. Some Dodger fans even went to Ebbets Field to hold a wake. Everywhere there was a sense of loss and a feeling that a great tradition had come to an end.[22]

Proposition B and the Dodgers' Elusive Contract, 1958

The scenes of triumph in Los Angeles after the positive City Council vote on the Dodger contract in October 1957 turned out to be a classic case of counting one's chickens before they were hatched. The council debate was bitter, and the minority who opposed the Dodger contract fought hard to reject it. Councilmen John Holland and Pat McGee argued that Chavez Ravine land could not be sold to O'Malley without public bids being entertained, that the $2.7 million that had been set aside for access roads was excessive, and that the contract as a whole amounted to a giveaway. "I'm for the Dodgers," said Councilman Ernest Debs, but the city was offering Walter O'Malley far too much in return for far too little. "First it was 200 [acres], now 350. I shall oppose any deal giving them a tremendous bargain."[23] The battle for Chavez Ravine was far from over.

Much of the L.A. public appeared to agree with him. By December 1, more than enough signatures had been obtained to submit the revised contract to a citywide referendum. It would be placed on the June 3, 1958, ballot in the form of another Proposition B.[24] (This Proposition B campaign should not be confused with the one held in 1952.) A Yes would be a vote for the Dodger contract; a No vote would reject it. To the chagrin of the Poulson administration, L.A.'s voters turned out to be far more divided over the terms of the contract than they had anticipated. A war of words broke out between supporters and opponents that rivaled the worst mudslinging that had occurred over public housing seven years earlier. Walter O'Malley, who had finally burned his bridges by declaring that the Dodgers would move to L.A. for the 1958 season, appeared to backtrack when he described Chavez Ravine as a "wasteland . . . of interest only to goats."[25]

The political campaign in favor of Proposition B, which was supported by the downtown business community, the baseball lobby, and L.A. boosters generally, was coordinated by the Committee on Yes for Baseball, headed by Hollywood comedian Joe E. Brown.[26] Mayor Poulson waxed eloquent on the plans for the new stadium, describing it as part of the modernization process that would help L.A. become a truly great American city. He even compared building the new baseball field to dredging San Pedro Harbor in the 1890s and the opening of the Owens Valley aqueduct in 1913. These landmark events had opened up the city to international trade, brought it a reliable water supply, and led to the development of the San Fernando Valley.[27]

But Proposition B also had many opponents. The question is whether they voted against the contract because they wanted to bring justice to the

Figure 19. Walter O'Malley urges L.A. voters to pass Proposition B. Courtesy *Los Angeles Times*.

evicted residents or whether they were motivated by other considerations. The evidence suggests a mixture of motives, among which concern for the plight of the evictees from Chavez Ravine appears to have been minimal. This despite the fact that, according to public opinion expert Herbert Baus, "there were a lot of surviving political scars" in East L.A., since many voters there "never did swallow this Chavez Ravine matter gracefully."[28]

Other observers suggested that most of the opponents of Proposition B rejected it because they agreed with Ernest Debs and other city councilmen that it gave O'Malley and the Dodgers too much in exchange for too little. Some liberal Democrats and progressives who had earlier supported Mayor Fletcher Bowron also voted against Proposition B because they wanted to punish the *L.A. Times* and the Poulson administration for their use of Red Scare tactics in the 1953 election.[29] The opponents of Proposition B did not, however, point out the obvious hypocrisy in the position its supporters took regarding the use of public money to subsidize the stadium.

During the fight over public housing, the *L.A. Times* and other opponents of public housing had repeatedly denounced the expenditure of public funds on government-subsidized, publicly owned housing as un-American and as a socialist—or even a Communist—threat to U.S. free enterprise. Now, however, business supporters of the Dodger contract appeared willing to spend millions of taxpayers' dollars to subsidize a new baseball stadium, without appearing to recognize the contradiction. A young journalist asked O'Malley how he could justify spending government money on the new stadium while opposing it in other contexts. He replied, without a hint of irony, "Son, look what the government did for the railroads to help develop this country."[30]

None of these considerations, however, spoke directly to the main issue concerning the injustice perpetrated on the survivors of Chavez Ravine. Did any of Proposition B's opponents feel sympathy for the homeowners who had been evicted? The name of one opposition group, the Citizens Committee to Save Chavez Ravine for the People, suggests a grassroots organization formed to benefit the Mexican American homeowners who still lived there. But it was not. The committee was led by T. A. Smith, part owner of the San Diego Padres, a Pacific Coast League team that stood to lose fans if the Dodgers moved to Southern California. Smith never mentioned his real reason for opposing Proposition B. Instead he complained about the "nitwit politicians" who had sold O'Malley too much land and who had failed to mention the presence of (possibly valuable) oil deposits that lay beneath the surface of Chavez Ravine.[31]

The only public official who came near to speaking out on behalf of the ravine's evicted residents was Councilman Edward Roybal, who now took a much livelier interest in the proceedings. His public statement opposing Proposition B is worth quoting in full: "It is not morally or legally right for a governmental agency to condemn private land, take it away from property owners through Eminent Domain proceedings, then turn around and give it to a private person or corporation [meaning O'Malley and the Dodgers] for private gain. This I believe is a gross misuse of Eminent Domain."[32]

This was a powerful statement. It not only cogently restated the argument about public purpose. It also raised the possibility of investigating the behavior of the City Housing Authority to see whether it had misused its power of eminent domain. But no influential persons on the No side of the referendum debate took Roybal's suggestion seriously. They continued to focus on the argument that the city was giving away too much to O'Malley in return for too little. That was also the theme of a two-day hearing held by the state legislature in Sacramento on the subject. On

June 3, a few days before the Proposition B election, the Yes side staged a "Dodger Telethon" in which Hollywood personalities such as George Burns, Groucho Marx, Jack Benny, and Joe E. Brown all urged its passage. When the vote was counted, Proposition B favoring acceptance of the new draft contract passed by a margin of 351,683 votes to 325,898.[33]

The most interesting fact about the Yes vote was the strong support the Dodger contract received in East L.A. and in the neighborhoods surrounding Chavez Ravine itself, which were heavily populated by Mexican Americans. Had they forgotten the eviction scandal, or were they just lovers of baseball? It is also worth asking why the opponents of Proposition B did not take up Edward Roybal's suggestion for an inquiry into the manipulative behavior of city authorities with respect to the use of eminent domain.

Supporters of conspiracy theory would no doubt argue that there was a "conspiracy of silence" on the matter. Again, I find this argument implausible, not because the residents were not ill-treated or because the supporters of Proposition B did not use misleading arguments in their efforts to get the proposition adopted. The fact was that Roybal's argument did not resonate with the Los Angeles public. This was partly because the pro-baseball lobby was persuasive and powerful. Many believed at the time that the acquisition of a Major League Baseball team would alleviate L.A.'s feelings of inferiority vis-à-vis cities like Chicago and New York and that it would help to propel the city into the front rank of American metropolises.[34]

Second, the major reputation the Dodgers would bring with them from Brooklyn to L.A. had by this time caught the public imagination. Third, and most important, the majority of L.A.'s white voters simply did not care enough about the fate of the Mexicans in Chavez Ravine to press for an inquiry into the behavior of the City Housing Authority. If the residents who had been evicted from their homes had been white, one can be sure that Roybal's views would have been taken more seriously.

In addition, a new generation of Mexican Americans was now coming to maturity for whom the eviction scandal of the early fifties had less meaning than it did for the older residents who had lived through it. Thus, aside from the survivors themselves and a group of local activists, the No voters on Proposition B consisted mainly of those who disapproved of the new contract on fiscal grounds or who were suspicious concerning its legality.

After Proposition B passed, there was once more rejoicing in the pro-Dodger camp, and once more it turned out to be premature. Even before Proposition B was adopted, two Los Angeles taxpayers filed suit to invalidate the Dodger agreement on the familiar ground that it improperly used public land to build a privately owned ballpark. Judge Arnold Praeger agreed, and on July 14, 1958, he granted an injunction halting the implementation of the contract. The city promptly appealed his decision to the California Supreme Court, which reversed Judge Praeger's ruling by a majority of 7-1 on the ground that the "restrictions as to public purpose . . . were intended to apply only while the city retained the land."[35]

This was the first time the Dodger contract had been upheld in a court of law, seemingly bringing the arrival of the team in Los Angeles closer to reality. The court decision caught the eye not just of the downtown baseball lobby but also of the Mexican American community in the neighborhoods surrounding Chavez Ravine. How did they react to the possibility of the Dodger move? Dozens of municipal, school, semipro, church, and traveling *beizbol* clubs existed in East L.A., some of them going as far back as the 1920s. So important were these clubs to the social life of the community that local politicians (including Edward Roybal when he was running for reelection) would be sure to attend the games.[36]

But until World War II baseball in Los Angeles was pretty rigidly segregated, as it was elsewhere. Talented Mexican players, unable to play for major league clubs, often went south to Mexico to play in the professional leagues there. So even the 1958 court decision regarding the Dodgers failed to raise much of a stir in East L.A. Until it actually moved to Southern California, the Brooklyn Dodgers remained an elite, white-run club situated on the East Coast. Historian Samuel O. Regalado puts it this way: "If you're living in East L.A. and it's 1953 or 1954 your heroes aren't coming out of the Brooklyn Dodgers. Your heroes are playing in Belvedere Park. Those were the players that meant something to you."[37]

For the small group of powerful, white civic leaders working to ensnare the Dodgers, however, the July 1958 California Supreme Court decision was an exciting development. But victory was snatched from them yet again when the opposition appealed the California decision to the Supreme Court of the United States. Finally, by refusing to hear the case, in the fall of 1959 the Supreme Court allowed the Dodger contract to stand. The *Los Angeles Times*, city authorities, and fans of Major League Baseball had won their long-sought victory. Walter O'Malley breathed a sigh of relief, and Mayor Poulson hailed the glorious days for the city that lay ahead. "One World Series in Los Angeles," he declared, "and every cent invested in this project will be repaid many times over. Progress must not be stopped in Los Angeles!"[38]

Public Drama Accompanies the Final Evictions

But the pro-Dodger camp was not quite out of the woods. Unknown to most of the city's public, there still remained a small group of residents in Chavez Ravine who had refused to leave their homes in the early fifties and were determined to stay. Most notable among them was the extended Arechiga family, who owned several properties in the ravine. The callous manner in which the Arechiga family was treated in the incident that followed took the edge off the Dodgers' impending victory in the Supreme Court and temporarily reignited the public sympathy expressed toward the evictees who had lost their homes seven years earlier.[39]

The houses in which this small group of resisters lived had already been bought by the city of L.A. under its powers of eminent domain. The CHA had suspended eviction procedures against the tenants while litigation over the use of the land was under way. But in the spring of 1959, anticipating victory in the Supreme Court, the Authority decided to reactivate its eviction procedures against the Arechigas and the other residual families so that work on grading the land for Dodger Stadium could begin.

On March 10, 1959, the City Attorney's office informed the Arechiga family and other remaining holdouts that unless they left by May 8, "you and your belongings will be removed by the sheriff."[40] The family refused to leave, so the L.A. County Sheriff's Department, under whose jurisdiction the matter fell, decided to evict them by force. The confrontation that followed sparked the last attempt to secure redress for the residents of Chavez Ravine, and it also raised new questions about the conduct of L.A.'s public officials. The fact that the evictions were recorded on television added to the drama of the event and briefly touched the conscience of the city.[41]

During the weeks preceding these final evictions, Councilmen Roybal and Holland had both tried to postpone the May 8 date, on the ground that the legal challenges to the Dodger contract had not yet been exhausted. But they failed. On the appointed day fourteen sheriffs' deputies, accompanied by moving vans and bulldozers, drove up the winding roads of Chavez Ravine to the home of the Arechiga family. Awaiting them was a crowd of about forty family members and supporters—including councilmen Roybal and Holland. Both of these men tried once more to halt the proceedings, but they were compelled to leave for other appointments before the actual evictions took place.[42]

As the sheriffs approached, the Arechigas locked their front door and barricaded themselves inside the house. Acting quickly, the sheriffs broke down the door, ordered the occupants out, and began removing their furniture and other effects. When Manuel Arechiga (aged seventy) went back inside to retrieve some of his personal belongings he was physically restrained. Tensions rose, dogs barked, and chickens scuttled back and forth across the porch as Manuel Arechiga's wife Avrana (aged sixty-six) shouted out, "Why don't they play ball in [Mayor] Poulson's backyard—not ours!"[43] Refusing to walk down the steps of the house, Aurora Vargas (the Arechigas' younger daughter) was carried down, shouting and struggling. In her frustration, when she got to the bottom of the stairs she slapped a deputy sheriff and was booked on suspicion of battery.[44]

Two other women—including the Arechigas' older daughter Victoria Angustain, who had a baby in her arms—were also arrested for refusing to leave peaceably. Mrs. Alice Martin, who had returned to her house after its illegal seizure in 1951, and several other holdout families were similarly evicted.[45] With the homes now empty and the stunned crowd still watching, the bulldozers knocked down all of the remaining residences, easily crushing the flimsy wooden structures. That evening, following a prearranged plan, the Arechigas and several other evicted families set up a tented encampment on the site of their former homes, vowing never to leave what they still called "their land."[46] That same evening Councilman Edward Roybal went back up to Chavez Ravine to offer the evicted families comfort and advice. He was the only public official to do so.

As already noted, all of this activity was captured on film by KTLA Channel 11, and later broadcast on the evening news, bringing highly charged commentary to radio, television, and the press. Letters critical of the sheriffs' behavior arrived from all over the country, providing new insights into public attitudes toward the Chavez Ravine affair. Alice Ingersoll of Denver, Colorado, wrote to Councilman Roybal commending him for his supportive behavior: "What a scene to be on t v—screaming children, women yelling and crying. Police carrying a woman down the front steps by her arms and legs to a police car. We all sat there speechless. Free America . . . something like this makes you wonder!"[47]

Several other commentators also emphasized the police brutality argument, describing both the evictions and the Elysian Park Heights public housing scheme of 1951 as manifestations of excessive state power. This brought back memories of the Red Scare. "The events at Chavez Ravine," wrote P. M. Seldon, who ran the small, L.A.-based Civic Research Action Group, "are a fitting climax to the illegal and unconstitutional procedures which have been taking place in the area ever since the first socialistic scheme of public housing was hatched by power-hungry local politicians.

Figure 20. Aurora Vargas forcibly removed from her home. Courtesy UCLA Special Collections.

When our City Government begins to think that it—the City Council—is empowered to use Iron Curtain tactics on American citizens, it is time for . . . citizens to awaken—and ACT."[48]

Francis Middleton of Patterson, New Jersey, agreed with Seldon. He likened the behavior of L.A.'s city sheriffs to "the Nazi Gestapo." But he added an East Coast twist to the story when he commended the New York authorities for refusing to build a new baseball stadium in Brooklyn, which would have displaced the homeowners living near Ebbets Field. "The city of New York had brains enough not to put people out of their homes to build a ball park, and that is more than I can say about Los Angeles."[49]

Equally interesting were the comments of those who pointed to the class aspects of the affair. Several letters sent to the Los Angeles City Council criticizing the evictions lamented the persecution of the "little fellow" by "big business" or by "those rich bastards" who stood to benefit from the coming of the Dodgers and the redevelopment of downtown Los Angeles. Attacking the business elite, O. J. Temple of the Federated Labor Council of California commended Councilman Roybal for being "one of the very few in the city council that takes any interest in the taxpayers and the workingman—just let that Walter O'Malley defend himself as this man's greed knows no bounds; with the cooperation of the Mayor he will own city hall next."[50]

A number of progressive L.A. unions, including Local 123 of the Furniture Workers and Upholsterers, whose membership was heavily Mexican, also protested the May 8 evictions. On the other hand, some of the city's biggest unions, such as the white-dominated Carpenters and Electricians, which stood to gain because of the large number of new construction jobs that building the new Dodger Stadium would provide, endorsed the eviction of the Arechigas and the other remaining residents from Chavez Ravine. Historians Eric Avila and Don Parson also point out, correctly, that on this issue much of organized labor, which in the 1930s and 1940s had been stalwart supporters of minority rights and the progressive policies of the New Deal, were now beginning a drift to the right.[51]

Finally, there were those who saw the final evictions from Chavez Ravine in overtly racial terms. Mexican American spokespersons such as Elisa Garcia, who was L.A.'s only female Spanish-language newscaster at the time, openly criticized the evictions on the air. She compared them to the brutal treatment of African Americans in the South, where the civil rights movement was just getting into high gear. On the other side of the racial divide, however, these positive voices were canceled out by the usual mixture of white indifference and even contempt. The day after the evictions, for example, Mrs. Lota Bairett of Altadena wrote a particularly nasty letter to Edward Roybal: "Those poor, poor Mexican people," she said, referring sarcastically to the removal of the Arechiga family. "Being hot-blooded they had to go out feet first. What a touching sight. No one but a Mexican would think of that!"[52]

Councilman Edward Roybal Fights a Rearguard Action

By visiting the Arechigas' encampment on the night of the final evictions, Councilman Edward Roybal identified himself with the grievances of Chavez Ravine's residents more closely than ever before. On the Monday following the evictions, he raised the issue in the City Council and invited the surviving residents and their supporters to air their grievances. The result was a confused and raucous debate that rivaled the one over public housing seven years earlier.[53]

Figure 21. Councilman Roybal comforts the Arechiga family. Courtesy UCLA Special Collections.

Outside city hall, pro-Arechiga demonstrators marched up and down with placards stating "We Refuse to Be Cheated of Our Land!" and "Let's Get More Elected Officials Like Ed Roybal!"[54] Inside the council chambers the residents' supporters, including Mrs. Arechiga's daughter Victoria Angustain and her cousin Paulino Cabral, denounced the Sheriff's Department for the brutal way it had carried out the evictions. Alvilla Jackson, a friend of the Arechiga family, presented a petition with 1,122 signatures demanding compensation from the city for the personal property the bulldozers had destroyed during the evictions, including beds and other household items.[55]

But then two speakers broke new ground. Henry "Hank" Lopez—also an attorney and a prominent Mexican American civic leader—urged the renegotiation of the Dodger contract, although he did not specify how it should be done. Margaret Wheeler Hess of the Small Property Owners Association went even further. She suggested that when Mayor Poulson canceled the city's public housing contract with the federal government, the houses that had been condemned by the City Housing Authority "should have been returned to their original owners."[56]

It was immediately apparent that Margaret Hess's proposal to return the condemned property in Chavez Ravine to its owners was impractical because by the time Mayor Poulson canceled the Elysian Parks Heights public housing project early in 1954 most of the condemned houses had already been demolished. Henry Lopez's suggestion about renegotiating the Dodger contract, on the other hand, was more realistic. After all, the Dodger contract had been renegotiated several times already. But the only way such a renegotiation could have provided the evicted residents of Chavez Ravine with real help would have been if the new version offered them financial compensation for their losses. But in the conservative climate of the 1950s it would have been politically difficult, if not impossible, to get such a proposal through the City Council.

It is true that, for a brief time after the Arechiga evictions, the level of public sympathy for the Chavez Ravine survivors was higher than it had been at any time since the early 1950s, owing to the brutal way in which the May 8 removals had been carried out. But not only would Mayor Poulson's administration, L.A.'s business and civic elite, and (in all probability) most of the public have opposed the revision of the Dodger contract along these lines, so, too, would the City Housing Authority, on the grounds that the residents had already been paid by the city for their property when they were first evicted. It seems likely, as I pointed out in Chapter 3, that in 1951–1952 some of the CHA's agents had paid the residents less for their property than it was worth. But, if challenged, these agents would undoubtedly have claimed that they had paid market value. By 1959 the only realistic way that the residents of Chavez Ravine could have obtained financial compensation would have been to take their cases to court—a move that few of them could afford. Even then, their chances of winning would have been remote. Nevertheless, Councilman Edward Roybal was now faced with a choice—perhaps even a moment of truth. A year earlier, during the debate over Proposition B, he had raised (but had not followed up on) the question of whether the city had misused its power of eminent domain during the initial eviction process. Now he was faced with a similar choice. Should he pursue Henry Lopez's suggestion to renegotiate the Dodger contract and try to get an official inquiry into CHA malfeasance? Or should he undertake some lesser course of action?

Roybal may well have thought his options had narrowed after the strong defense city officials put up regarding the recent evictions. City attorney Roger Arnebergh assured the City Council that the evictions had followed the proper legal procedures.[57] Sheriff Pitchess claimed that only minimal force had been used to evict the Arechigas. And CHA director Howard

Holtzendorff told the City Council that he had offered the Arechigas temporary accommodations in the Ramona Gardens public housing facility to ease their exit from Chavez Ravine. But the most damaging evidence, from the Arechigas' point of view, was given by Mayor Norris Poulson himself. At a special press conference on May 16 he revealed for the first time that, far from being rendered homeless by their eviction, the Arechigas owned several other properties outside Chavez Ravine that, taken together, were worth $75,000. Poulson showed photos of the other properties to back up his statement.[58]

This news was flashed over the airways, and within hours it had undermined public sympathy for the Arechigas. The *Los Angeles Times* blasted the Arechiga family for what it called their "phony claims of destitution."[59] Even *La Opinion*, the city's premier Spanish-language newspaper, expressed doubts. The revelation that the family owned other properties, the paper said, "deflated the impression that was given to the public that the Arechiga family was poor."[60]

Faced with these revelations, and with a sudden and dramatic loss of public support, Roybal chose a lesser course of action. He condemned the evictions as callous and inhumane, but he did not challenge their legality: "The eviction in itself is legal," he said in a public statement, "but the manner in which it was carried out was certainly not. This is the type of action that occurred during the Spanish inquisition and Hitler's Germany. But never have I heard of anything like this taking place in this city."[61]

To give him his due, Councilman Roybal did not stop there. He defended the Arechigas' right to keep control over the land their house had been built on in Chavez Ravine, even though they no longer held title to it. For him, however, the question of land ownership was no longer the central issue. The two main matters requiring resolution were the brutality and unfairness of the evictions and the fact that the Arechigas and other residents of Chavez Ravine had not been paid fair market value for their property—a question he urged be reconsidered.[62] But Roybal did not press for the renegotiation of the Dodger contract, nor did he call for an official inquiry into the conduct of city officials or challenge the legality of the CHA's use of eminent domain.

Roybal's failure to call for stronger action did not necessarily mean that he lacked the courage to adopt an unpopular stance. Earlier, he had championed minority complaints about police brutality in the City Council, and he had defended the idea of a citywide Fair Employment Practices Commission even when it was unpopular. It is also true that, before public sympathy for the Arechigas collapsed, there was still a significant body of white opinion that disapproved of the Dodger contract. But the leaders of white, liberal opinion were dissatisfied with the contract because they believed L.A. had concluded a bad financial deal with Walter O'Malley, not because they were concerned about the injustices done to Chavez Ravine's Mexican American residents.[63]

This point is confirmed by two developments that occurred shortly after the City Council debate took place, which showed the different priorities of the Anglo and minority communities. On June 1, 1959, the *Torch Reporter* published an editorial on behalf of Chavez Ravine's survivors stating that the Mexican American community had been angered by the Arechigas' eviction not only because of its brutality but also because for years the residents of the ravine as a whole "had been lied to, cheated out of their property, and treated like second-class citizens."[64] Four days later, a Chavez Ravine Appeal Committee was established by Councilman John C. Holland and three leading Anglo attorneys. Its stated purpose was to raise money in order to prove in court that the sale of Chavez Ravine land to Walter O'Malley was illegal, on the familiar ground that the land had been intended for a public not a private purpose. The Appeal Committee's literature said nothing about whether the evictions had been improper or about the property rights of the former Mexican American residents.[65]

This evidence of a racial divide was unfortunate, but it was not surprising. In the late 1950s it was still true that, with the exception of the Communists and a relatively small group of civil rights activists, most mainstream liberals were unwilling to call city hall to account on behalf of a tiny band of evicted Mexican Americans who had almost no political power and who had a dubious case in law. Six or seven years later, after the Watts uprising had occurred and the civil rights movement had developed increased traction, they might have been willing to do so. But in 1959 they were not.

To put it another way, once popular sympathy for the Arechigas collapsed, there was virtually no chance that any new attempt to cancel the Dodger contract, or renegotiate it in some fundamental way, could have succeeded. This point was driven home by the failure of a last-ditch effort by Phil Silver, the Arechigas' family attorney, to challenge city authorities on the eminent domain issue. On May 21, 1959, Silver filed a complaint in Los Angeles Superior Court arguing that when the Arechigas' house in Chavez Ravine was condemned in February 1953, the CHA already knew that the Elysian Park Heights public housing project would never be built.[66]

The implication of Silver's complaint was that the CHA should not have used its power of eminent domain to evict the residents because it was already aware that the alternative housing they had been promised would not be forthcoming. However, Silver's complaint was set aside on the ground that the L.A. court could not rule on it until the U.S. Supreme Court had made its own decision on the matter. In October 1959 the Supreme Court refused to hear the appeal from the lower courts, thereby granting victory to the supporters of the Dodger contract. Silver's complaint was allowed to lapse.

Walter O'Malley Wins the Last Round

After a long, confused, and exhausting battle, the Mexican American residents of Chavez Ravine and their friends and supporters had finally lost their struggle for legal and financial redress. Walter O'Malley, Mayor Poulson, the *Los Angeles Times*, and all those who wanted to bring the Dodgers to L.A. had finally come out on top.

On May 18, 1959, with Councilman Roybal on hand to console them, the Arechigas and their friends took down their tent in Chavez Ravine and left, never to return. A few days later the City Council, anticipating victory in the Supreme Court, gave its final approval to the long-stalled contract between the Dodgers and the City of Los Angeles.[67] The building of Dodger Stadium could now begin.

CHAPTER SIX

Dodger Success and the History of Minority Displacement in Los Angeles, 1870–1970

"They're breaking ground today for a structure of the greatest importance for the future of Los Angeles—Dodger Stadium."

—LOS ANGELES HERALD (SEPTEMBER 17, 1959)

"All Los Angeles, after all, had been seized from Mexico in 1846; and the sense of displacement felt by the evicted families remains an element in the Mexican imagination as it contemplates the lost Mexico north of the Rio Grande."

—KEVIN STARR

L.A. Dodgers Success Story

Shortly after 1 p.m. on Saturday April 10, 1962, before a large and festive crowd, Eddie Kasko of the Cincinnati Reds drove in a single off pitcher Johnny Podres, one of Walter O'Malley's holdovers from Ebbets Field. Before fifty thousand spectators, the Reds went on to win the first scheduled Major League Baseball game played in the new stadium by a score of six to three. Of course, the fans would have preferred it if the Dodgers had won. Nevertheless, first-class baseball in Los Angeles was off to an excellent start.[1]

L.A. Times sportswriter Jim Murray, writing up the game after that brilliant opening day, went overboard in his description of the new stadium and all that it promised the citizens of Los Angeles after so many years of delay. He called it "not just any baseball park but the Taj Mahal, the Parthenon, and Westminster Abbey of baseball."[2] For several years afterward the new stadium, with its excellent sight lines, beautiful landscaping, and bused transportation from the parking lots, won praise from sports commentators all over the country as America's most modern and exciting baseball park.[3] How did it achieve that status?

Building Dodger Stadium was not easy. A groundbreaking ceremony was held in September 1959. But Walter O'Malley and his staff had to go through almost three more years of legal and financial wrangling before the ballpark was finally ready. One problem was the terrain. Chavez Ravine was covered by a dense network of woods, gullies, and gulches interlaced with steep hills and twisting roads. More than eight million yards of earth had to be moved in order to lower and reshape the hilltop. This task was both difficult and expensive, and it took considerably longer than had been anticipated. The demolition of once-familiar buildings, including a school and a church in La Loma, caused additional pain to many former Mexican American residents, who wrote up the process of the stadium's construction in the columns of the *Torch Reporter*.[4]

Many kinds of building permits had to be obtained from the City of Los Angeles to develop the huge site, as well as to prepare new recreation facilities in surrounding Elysian Park. In the end, the Dodgers never completed the forty-acre recreation center the team had promised. An additional delay was caused by torrential rains in the winter of 1961, which almost threatened Walter O'Malley's target date for the season's opening day. It took ten days for the ground to dry out, and 150 square feet of new sod had to be added before the field was ready. But the finished playing surface was worth waiting for. Dodger shortstop Maury Wills called the new infield perfect. "It's nice and firm and true. It's bound to get better too. They've done a wonderful job on it."[5]

Given the legendary reputation the Dodgers brought with them from Brooklyn, Southern California's baseball fans had high expectations of their new team. They were not disappointed. Because of the large number of attendees, the staff managed to keep ticket prices low. Ticket prices ranged from 75 cents to $3.50 per person, a level maintained for eighteen years. A slump at the end of the first season meant that the Dodgers lost the National League pennant race to the San Francisco Giants in the fall of 1962. But with Sandy Koufax and Don Drysdale on the mound and hitters like Tommy Davis, Willie Davis, and Maury Wills at bat, the next season they provided some of the best entertainment baseball had to offer. The L.A. Dodgers won the World Series in 1963, taking four straight games from the New York Yankees, and again in 1965, when they beat the Minnesota Twins.[6]

In the seventies the baton was passed on to a new generation of stars, when the famous infield of Steve Garvey, Davey Lopes, Bill Russell, and

Figure 22. Grading land for Dodger Stadium, 1959. Courtesy UCLA Special Collections.

Ron Cey—all of them raised in the Dodger nursery—guided the team to another decade of brilliant success. In 1970 Walter O'Malley, long recognized as the grand old man of American baseball, finally retired and was succeeded by his son Peter. Before he quit, however, O'Malley recognized the importance of cultivating a multiracial fan base in increasingly polyglot Los Angeles. Vin Scully kept English-speaking fans glued to their radios. But by 1965 the Dodgers' coaching staff also included African American Jim Gilliam and Cuban-born Preston Gomez. The popular Spanish-language commentator Jaime Jarrin, who has been broadcasting the games in Spanish since 1959, continues to do so.[7]

For L.A.'s Mexican American baseball fans, the most exciting development occurred in 1981 when the Dodgers signed the brilliant left-handed pitcher Fernando Valenzuela, who swiftly became a baseball hero of legendary stature. Born in a tiny village in the northern Mexican state of Sonora, Valenzuela's rise to fame was meteoric. He began playing as a teenager in the Mexican League and soon mastered the difficult art of the screwball (a ball that breaks from right to left), which later proved to be his most deadly pitching weapon. In September 1980, the Dodgers brought

Figure 23. Dodger pitching star Fernando Valenzuela. Courtesy *Los Angeles Times*.

him in to help out with their aging pitching staff. Barely twenty years old, in his first game Valenzuela stunned both Dodger management and the Chavez Ravine crowd by refusing to concede a single run, meanwhile striking out sixteen batters. In 1981, he was given a lucrative contract similar to those of the best white players on the field.[8]

It was Valenzuela's dramatic success that drew in large numbers of Mexican Americans to watch the Dodgers. In the barrios of East L.A. Valenzuela's rise carried a social significance that went beyond the fame of just another baseball star. For years Latinos' love of baseball, which became an avenue of upward mobility, had rarely gone beyond the small, poorly financed clubs of northern Mexico or Puerto Rico. Now, with Valenzuela's front-rank status, L.A.'s Latino population had a hero who was just as respected in the white world as he was in their own. "Can you imagine what it means to the whole country of Mexico and to the immigrants here?" asked Dodger boss Tommy Lasorda. "Here's a kid from an obscure little village in Mexico. . . . Now they can say 'Look at Fernando—he's a hero and he's one of us.'"[9]

Ravine Evictions Still Rankled

At a time when racial tensions were rising as a result of the unprecedented flow of undocumented immigrants into L.A., Valenzuela's dazzling performance simultaneously raised the self-confidence of the city's resident Mexican American community and reinforced the ties between recent Mexican immigrants and their homeland. By hiring African American, Mexican, and even some Asian players Walter O'Malley and his successors changed the image of the Dodgers from that of an Anglo-run, East Coast import to one of a popular Los Angeles institution that drew in thousands of new fans. They ranged from Anglo suburbanites in Pasadena to black families from Watts, from Filipinos in Macarthur Park to working-class Mexican Americans in Boyle Heights, and from baseball aficionados on the South Side to white professionals in Santa Monica.[10]

During the course of its campaign to lure the Brooklyn Dodgers to Chavez Ravine, the *L.A. Times* had expressed the hope that mass attendance at the ball games would help dispel the image of L.A. as a "group of neighborhoods without common aims, with nothing to hold them together but the mountains." It predicted, instead, that enthusiasm for the Dodgers would "bind the neighborhoods together with a sort of communal glue."[11] In 1962 the Dodgers set a major league record for attendance, with 2,755,184 seats sold, and in 1978 they drew no fewer than three million fans.[12] With attendance figures like this, the *Times*' prediction seemed to be justified.

Nevertheless, the Dodgers' popularity among L.A.'s Mexican community failed to assuage the anger and resentment that many survivors of the evictions in Chavez Ravine still felt toward the ball club. Even after the evictions of the 1950s had receded from public memory, several hundred former residents, together with their supporters and friends, met sporadically to reminisce and keep the memory of the episode alive. In 1983 they established a group called Los Desterrados (the Uprooted) that met on the third Saturday of every July for a picnic in Elysian Park near where the three subbarrios had formerly existed. The group was led by Luis Santillan, a former Chavez Ravine resident whose family lived in Solano Canyon. The group continues to meet for its annual picnic to this day.[13]

Southern California's journalists and radio interviewers also returned frequently to the debacle surrounding the fifties evictions. Some of the interviewees who participated in these call-ins responded to questions in the same way the early survivors did. But others raised new issues. "The Dodgers do have an incredible following," said one interviewee in 1979. "But I wonder how many Dodger players and fans actually know what happened there?"[14] Other respondents tried to disentangle the legal ramifications of the affair. In a 1984 radio show a caller from Terre Haute, Indiana, posed a series of questions about the former homeowners in the ravine—whether they paid taxes, how much money they had received for their houses, and how and why the city had acquired the Chavez Ravine land. "The answers to these questions," he said, "would serve to better validate the claims of either side."[15]

But the most interesting group of respondents were those who continued to express hostility toward Dodger management. Some members of this group even suggested that L.A.'s Mexican American community should organize a formal boycott of the team. "With the recent movement over immigration," stated Victor Cortez—referring to the revival of anti-Mexican sentiment that surrounded the passage of the 1986 Immigration Control and Reform Act—"I would only wonder what we could accomplish if we banded together and stopped supporting Dodger games. Do you think us Mexicans could make a difference?"[16] Other interviewees rejected the boycott idea but agreed that some sort of action against the Dodgers was still needed. One Echo Park resident put it this way: "The city of Los Angeles needs to publicly apologize to the families that suffered and to all Angelenos for misleading them. . . . Eminent domain, indeed! How un-American! Shame on the Supreme Court for their ruling. Makes me sick."[17]

This drumbeat of criticism alarmed the Dodger management. On July 17, 1986, the team's public relations spokesperson defended Walter O'Malley's original negotiations with the city and summarized the controversy from the Dodgers' point of view. "The ball club had not even known about the dispute over public housing in the mid and early 1950s," he said. "At that time, the city still had not addressed the few remaining residents in Chavez Ravine who were living there illegally and were not paying property taxes. The land lay dormant for seven years, while elected officials decided what to do with it."[18]

The spokesperson went on to cite the expenses the Dodgers had incurred in building the stadium, noted the support the public had provided when it voted for Proposition B, and pointed to the favorable decisions regarding the Dodger contract that had been made by the California Supreme Court and the U.S. Supreme Court in Washington, DC. "The public acceptance of Dodger Stadium is reflected in the attendance of more than 80 million since it opened on April 10, 1962," he added.[19] In May 1985, the *Los Angeles Business Journal* included Dodger Stadium in an article featuring the "Ten Transactions" that had transformed L.A.'s rise into a world-class city.[20]

But even these justifications failed to silence the tenacious minority of survivors who felt that the city's planning authorities had betrayed them. On July 14, 1988, when television station KTTV broadcast a program on the history of the stadium, Vin Scully referred to Chavez Ravine in the pre-Dodger era as a "dump or wasteland." "How dare you call Chavez Ravine a wasteland or a dump," Natalie Ramirez wrote to Scully after watching the program. "Maybe it wasn't Beverly Hills, but it was home to a lot of people, my family included. Doesn't anyone want to acknowledge us because we are Mexicans?"[21]

Twelve years later, the Dodgers tried again to put an end to the lingering controversy. By this time the number of survivors from the original evictions had dwindled to a few hundred scattered throughout Southern California. But quite a few of them still lived near the ravine, especially in the Solano subcanyon area, which had escaped demolition at the hands of the CHA. The leader of this group was Alicia Brown, a former schoolteacher who had helped to preserve the local community and the Elysian Park area that adjoined it. She was particularly supportive of Solano Elementary School, which had lost students following the evictions but had recovered with financial help from Dodger management. The Dodgers sent players to visit the school, paid for children to receive coaching from Dodger staff, and gave the school financial support—all in an effort to improve the club's standing in the East L.A. community.[22]

In October 2000, Alicia Brown convened a "reconciliation meeting" at San Conrado Church in Solano Canyon at which a bust was unveiled of the late Father Tomas Matin, who had served as priest in Chavez Ravine many years earlier.[23] Dodgers President Bob Graziano also attended this meeting. After the dedication ceremony, Virginia Pinedo-Bye, a survivor from La Loma, distributed olive branches among the crowd. "It's time to heal," she said. "We want to move forward." In reply, Bob Graziano made a conciliatory speech and ended it by thanking the community for "not forgetting, but forgiving the past."[24]

Most of the residents in the crowd accepted Graziano's remarks as a genuine gesture of reconciliation. But others remained skeptical, and a few repudiated his remarks altogether. "What kind of crap is that—giving you an olive branch!" said an angry Carol Jacques. She dismissed the meeting as a hypocritical exercise in public relations. Even then the issue would not go away. After the beating of San Francisco Giants fan Bryan Stow on the opening day of the 2011 season, Buddy Carver of Solano Canyon told the *L.A. Times* that the Dodgers were "terrible, terrible neighbors. It's a love-hate thing that goes back to the stadium being built. They are loved because they are L.A., but they are hated for their disregard for the communities that surround them."[25]

Reasons for Continuing Discontent

What explains the continuing strength of these protests and the survivors' ability to arouse public sympathy concerning an event that had taken place more than sixty years earlier? Three developments during the intervening years helped keep it alive: the rise of the Chicano civil rights movement, the growing political clout of L.A.'s Mexican American community, and the recognition that similar racial displacement policies had been carried out in other southwestern cities besides L.A.[26]

None of these developments bore a direct relationship to the injustices suffered by those who had lost their homes in Chavez Ravine. But all of them, in one way or another, reminded the Los Angeles public of the long record of condescension, neglect, and contempt for the interests of Mexican Americans that the city's authorities had built up over the years. This racist record gave the remaining survivors a new incentive for keeping the memory of the evictions alive.

The Chicano cultural movement of the 1960s also sparked a literary renaissance within the community in which Latino students and scholars began to write their own interpretation of Mexican American history for the first time. They offered an interpretation of Anglo conquest in the pre–Civil War period that differed markedly from the triumphalist version of Manifest Destiny narrated by white historians. New and more radical views of the Chavez Ravine affair naturally earned a place in this new scholarship.[27]

But the most potent explanation for the continuing appeal of Chavez Ravine as a symbol of racial injustice was revealed in an apparently trivial remark made by a caller from Tucson in a Talkback radio program about the evictions broadcast over PBS radio in June 2008. The expulsion of the Mexican American homeowners from the ravine, the caller said, reminded him of "so many other times in history when the [white] majority in this country simply stripped Latinos of their land for no other reason than they could."[28] No other comment could have brought into sharper focus the root cause of the anger and resentment that, in greater or lesser degree, had affected every generation of Mexicans who had lived in Southern California, whether as immigrants or as American citizens, since the Mexican-American War of 1846 to 1848.[29]

Each one of these generations, beginning with the mestizo Indians who lost their land to Anglo settlers who came to California before the Civil War, suffered humiliation, displacement, and the loss of property and status at the hands of the dominant, Anglo-American ruling class.[30] Translated into the twentieth-century world of large-scale Mexican immigration, slum clearance, and urban renewal, it was the psychic wounds inflicted by this historical experience, more than anything else, that enabled the fifties evictions to retain their emotional appeal.

L.A.'s Mexican American population was not the only minority group in the city to suffer from the consequences, however well meant, of slum clearance and urban renewal. Beginning with the 1931 decision to build Union Station on part of old Chinatown, most of the city's three thousand Chinese Americans were forced to leave their original shops and homes and move either into a new area called China City or settle farther north in the Mexican neighborhood once known as Sonoratown. For some of the Chinese, this was a positive experience, but for many others it was not. Commenting on a pageant held to celebrate the transition in September 1934, the *L.A. Times* contrasted the "bright eyes and laughing faces of the children" at the pageant with the "wistful expressions worn by many of the old Chinese."[31]

As is well known, in World War II L.A.'s Japanese Americans were forced to leave their long-established neighborhood in Little Tokyo to be interned in concentration camps scattered across the country. Little Tokyo was renamed "Bronzeville" for the duration of the war, because the overflow of blacks from the South looking for war jobs occupied most of the homes belonging to the former Japanese American residents. To its credit,

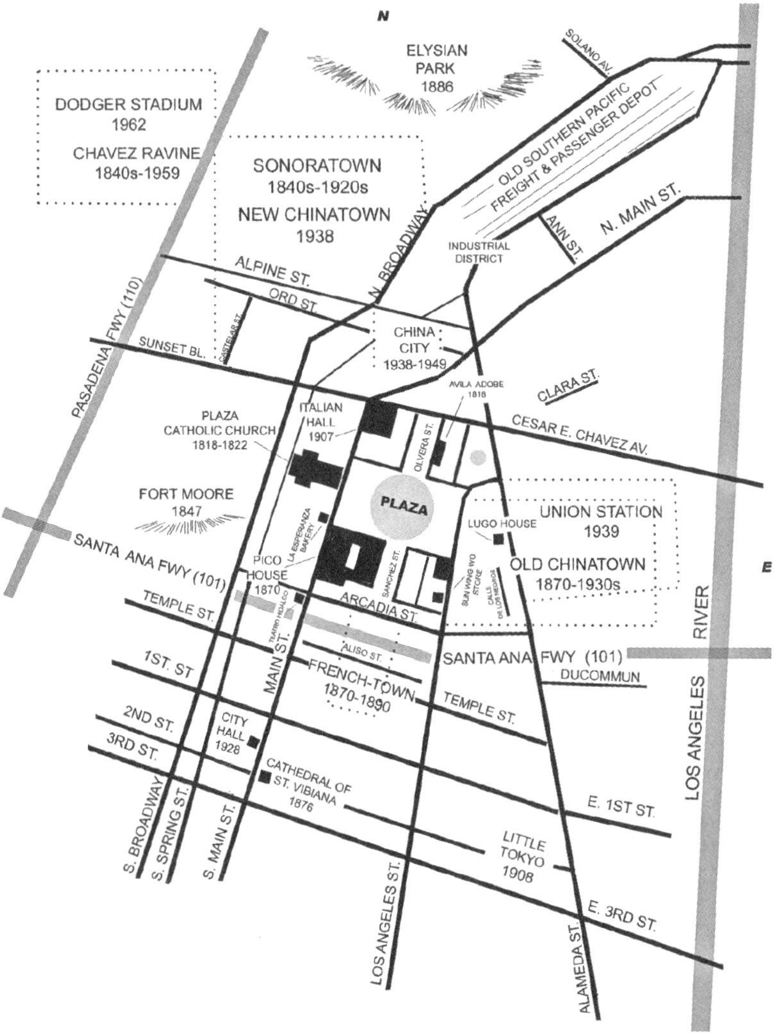

Figure 24. Displacement of ethnic minorities in downtown Los Angeles. Courtesy University of Texas Press. William David Estrada, *The Los Angeles Plaza: Sacred and Contested Space* (Austin: University of Texas Press, 2008).

after 1945 the *California Eagle* (L.A.'s premier African American newspaper) abandoned its anti-Japanese stance and supported the efforts of the returning internees to reclaim their property. But most of them were too traumatized by their wartime experiences to move back into Little Tokyo itself. Instead, many of them lived out the remainder of their lives in war relocation camps or in isolated trailer parks.[32]

Although in World War II L.A.'s Japanese Americans were forced to leave, there can be no doubt that the city's Latino community, as an indigenous group who preceded the white settlers downtown and had once enjoyed virtually undisputed control over the entire area, suffered more than any other minority group from the establishment of Anglo-American hegemony. As Raul Homero Villa puts it, "Once the city's dominant growth coalition set the course of modern metropolitan expansion in the late 1800s," its success ensured that the negative effects of that expansion would be "felt most fully and most swiftly by the *mexicanos* who, as workers, were essential to [the city's] construction and maintenance and who, as residents, were in the path of its ceaseless restructuring."[33]

Viewing L.A.'s racial history in this way makes us see that the eviction of Chavez Ravine's homeowners in the 1950s was not a single, fortuitous, or unlucky event. It was one episode among many in a long and continuous narrative of Latino displacement—political, cultural, and spatial—that had been going on for more than a hundred years. This view of the matter puts a significantly different complexion on the Chavez Ravine affair, one that merits deeper exploration.

Chavez Ravine and the History of Contested Space

The pressures placed on Mexican Americans to move from their original places of settlement in Los Angeles began in the late nineteenth century, after Anglo control over the city's administration had been assured. At first, the movement of Mexicans eastward across the Los Angeles River from Sonoratown and the Plaza area to Belvedere and Boyle Heights was a voluntary process, not one of enforced displacement. Mexicans who moved east sought more recently settled neighborhoods where the price of land and housing were cheaper than they were downtown. By 1920 many Japanese, Jewish, and other European settlers had also moved into Boyle Heights. At the same time, however, a relatively prosperous middle class of Mexican homeowners, shopkeepers, and cultural leaders had emerged in the area that enabled them to hold their own against the newcomers.[34]

The unincorporated neighborhood of Belvedere, by contrast, was heavily Latino, and it included many residents who had been forced out of downtown by rising house prices or by the imposition of racially restrictive housing covenants. By the late 1920s Belvedere had become the fifth largest area of Mexican settlement in the United States. Local property developers, noticing the influx of Jewish and other white entrepreneurs into the neighborhood, proposed to the Los Angeles county commissioners that Belvedere be incorporated into the city of L.A. They hoped to gentrify the area in such a way as to shift political control from the hands of the Mexicans into those of the white minority. As real estate prices rose, Mexican homeowners would be forced to sell their homes and move elsewhere, enabling real estate developers to resell their properties to incoming middle-class whites—a pattern of development becoming increasingly common in the western parts of the city. But Belvedere's Latinos gathered enough signatures to force a referendum on the issue, and the incorporation proposal was turned down.[35]

Since the first days of Anglo dominance, city officials had been concerned about the dilapidated state of the Plaza—the core area of Mexican settlement—and its role as a historic gathering place for transients, job seekers, and political activists who defended the traditions of free speech. Three developments, in particular, increased tensions between the white community and the minority elements who lived around the Plaza. The first was the Christmas Day riots involving Mexican American members of the IWW, who supported the Magonistas. On December 25, 1913, an LAPD squad used violence to break up an IWW meeting in the Plaza. The resulting melee resulted in one death, in efforts by the City Council to restrict the right of free speech in the Plaza, and in the imprisonment of several rioters who were assumed to be Mexican immigrants but were actually U.S. citizens. At a deeper level, the Christmas Day riots symbolized the white community's unwillingness to continue honoring the spatial rights of the city's preexisting Mexican American population.[36]

A more direct threat to the Plaza as a traditional "Mexican space" was posed by the establishment of white commercial enterprises in the surrounding streets. The resulting rise in property values forced many Mexican families to abandon their homes and move to cheaper neighborhoods. Some of these former Plaza residents even ended up in Chavez Ravine. The third source of tension was cultural and political rather than spatial. By World War I very few Mexican American candidates stood for political office anymore, English was the required language for all business transactions, and most of the isolated barrios had taken on their modern shape. In the 1930s a well-meaning—but in reality somewhat demeaning—effort to revive the Plaza and nearby Olvera Street was undertaken by philanthropist Christine Sterling and backed by Harry Chandler of the L.A. *Times* and a number of progressive reformers.[37]

Christine Sterling and her supporters intended to stimulate tourist and commercial activity in the Plaza. But by installing a statue of a Mexican campesino with his eyes closed leaning against a tree, white preservationists reinforced the prevailing stereotype of the "lazy Mexican." And by displaying scenes of old Mexico in nearby Olvera Street, they betrayed a characteristic Anglo-American desire to portray native cultures as romantic and "quaint"—as if by doing so they could divert attention away from the contemporary world of racial conflict.[38]

The 1940s and 1950s witnessed a dramatic escalation in the process of Mexican community displacement, of which the evictions from Chavez Ravine was only the most notorious example. Rising traffic congestion resulted in the realignment of Broadway and in the construction of three new freeways (the Santa Ana, the Golden State, and the Harbor) that sliced through East L.A.'s established barrios without regard to the needs and desires of the local residents. Thousands of Mexican families were forced to leave their old homes, usually with no more than lip service being paid to providing alternative accommodation. "The constant moving," wrote one observer, "divided families, broke up churches and school ties, and ended the incentive of homeowners to invest in barrio businesses."[39] The expansion of the freeway network also undermined the profitability of the Red Car streetcar system, which many minority workers used to commute to their jobs. In 1958 Mexicans and African Americans of South Central L.A. protested the extension of the Harbor Freeway, only to be told by city authorities that Southern Californians "will just have to make up their minds that . . . freeways will help some property owners, hurt others, and remove a lot of residents from their present homes."[40]

This callous statement, coupled with the empowering effects of the 1960s civil rights movement, sparked the emergence of a new generation of Mexican American critics who challenged the redevelopment plans of city authorities with greater vehemence and authority than before. Their leaders included Ernesto Galarza of UC San Diego, Guillermo Flores, who coauthored *A Study of Unincorporated East Los Angeles* (one of the first research papers on the subject to be published without the aid of whites), and Rosalio Munoz, who helped organize the Chicano Moratorium Committee against the Vietnam War.[41]

Another destructive consequence of the expansion of the freeway system was the isolation of the downtown barrios one from another and the erection of physical barriers in the path of their further expansion and growth. At UCLA, *Aztlan* (newsletter of the Movimiento Estudiantil de Aztlan, or MEChA) condemned the Golden State Freeway for erecting a virtual wall between the East Side and downtown. It also criticized the Santa Monica Freeway for preventing the northward movement of African

Americans from the city's South Side. Both freeways were seen by Chicano and African American radicals not so much as traffic facilitators but as defensive barriers behind which the white, middle-class inhabitants of the West Side sheltered themselves against the threats of an angry and vengeful East Side populace.[42]

In 1973 Guillermo Flores went even further and linked the city's displacement policies to a neo-Marxist theory of domestic colonialism through which the white ruling class extracted wealth from the Chicano working class and used it for its own aggrandizement. Implicit in his analysis was the threat of a "neo-colonial revolt." But the worst long-range consequence of the corporate modernist philosophy remained the forced removal of the downtown Mexican population, either through slum clearance or as a result of new commercial developments. The role of the city's Planning and Highway Commissions, Guillermo Flores wrote, was to "destroy the barrio section by section for 'progress,' while the white sections continue to expand. As the white middle class flee to the suburbs, the inner cities are being 'redeveloped' as commercial centers with an impoverished Mexican proletariat as its labor force."[43]

Some of the more radical assertions of these critics should be taken with a pinch of salt. For example, however insensitive it appeared in retrospect, even the 1950 decision of the City Housing Authority to demolish the houses in Chavez Ravine was not motivated by a desire to destroy the barrio as such. It was prompted by a well-meant (but naïve) intention to replace existing slum dwellings by a public housing complex that would enable the residents to return to their former neighborhood under more salubrious conditions. But the *effect*, if not the *intention*, of the evictions proved disastrous for those who lost their homes only to be left, as a result of the City Council's change of heart, without any accommodations at all.

Bunker Hill as the Crown Jewel of Downtown Redevelopment

None of these academic research studies, nor even the Chicano radicals' implied threat of urban revolt, deterred L.A.'s city planners from continuing their racially blinkered redevelopment plans. To the contrary, in March 1959—even as the Sheriff's Department's plans to evict the Arechiga family from Chavez Ravine were being developed—the Community Redevelopment Agency, and subsequently the City Council, approved the biggest slum clearance plan of them all: bulldozing thousands of old

Figure 25. Bunker Hill and Chavez Ravine. Courtesy Alexander Ortenberg.

houses and businesses on Bunker Hill in the center of downtown to make room for modern high-rise commercial buildings, stores, and entertainment centers.[44]

Bunker Hill was not primarily a Mexican barrio. It was home to more than 12,000 mostly white pensioners, transients, and single men who occupied one- or two-room apartments in the subdivided Victorian mansions that had dominated the hilly area during the Edwardian era. Once, wrote Raymond Chandler in *The High Window*, Bunker Hill had been "the choicest residential district of the city. But now in the tall rooms haggard landladies bicker with shifty tenants. On the wide, cool front porches, reaching their cracked shoes into the sun, sit the old men with faces like ghosts."[45] Because Bunker Hill's residents were largely white, the protests that subsequently arose over the replacement scheme were therefore based more on class, on the desire of low-income residents to continue living in cheap quarters downtown, than on arguments between city hall and any single racial or ethnic group.

Nevertheless, according to the 1950 population census, Mexicans constituted the largest minority group among the numerous Japanese, African American, and other poor families of color who lived on Bunker Hill. As in Chavez Ravine, a significant number of the condemned buildings lacked private bathrooms, toilets, and running water. But (again as in Chavez Ravine) many of these old mansions could probably have been rehabilitated if more moderate councils had prevailed.[46] However, these rehabilitation arguments were once again dismissed, and the bulldozers were unleashed. The result—for many years—was a barren wasteland in the very center of downtown, so that by 1965, Los Angeles, which once had a stock of beautiful Victorian and Edwardian houses to rival those of Oakland or even San Francisco, had hardly any of these houses left.

Some staff members at the Community Redevelopment Agency (CRA) suggested that there were enough vacant apartments in the adjacent area, or in the preexisting public housing projects scattered throughout the downtown area, to accommodate all of the 12,000 residents who were forced to move. But most of these alternatives were too expensive for Bunker Hill's poor residents, and this exaggerated estimate, coupled with other anticipated sources of opposition, persuaded city planners to secure a $33 million loan from the federal government, intending some of the money to be used to rehouse the former residents of Bunker Hill. By 1954, however, President Truman's 1949 Housing Act, which had provided the money for Chavez Ravine's proposed public housing project, had been revised under President Eisenhower to permit new land acquired under eminent domain to be resold to private developers. As a result, new apartments on Bunker Hill were offered at rents ranging from $65 to $110 per month—sums beyond the means of most of its low-income residents.[47]

Opposition to the Bunker Hill plan did indeed develop. The Downtown Community Association enlisted Councilman Roybal to fight the scheme in the City Council, and groups of demonstrators picketed city hall. One of their banners declared that "thousands of the poor and aged will be forcibly dispossessed to provide mansions and gaming rooms for the rich."[48] In the end, however, the Bunker Hill redevelopment project became so large and unwieldy, and was influenced by so many competing interests, that it remained tied up in revisions and lawsuits throughout much of the 1960s and 1970s. Much of it has since been completed, but parts of it remained unfinished at the end of the century.[49]

Although it forced more whites than Mexican Americans and others to relocate, the policies pursued by L.A.'s Community Redevelopment Agency on Bunker Hill followed a pattern similar to the one used at Chavez Ravine. Wedded to the idea of razing below-standard homes and to a downtown devoted almost entirely to administrative and commercial interests, L.A.'s top-down city planners essentially cut Bunker Hill off from its previous working-class connections and turned it over to private housing and entertainment developers. "Along the base of California Plaza," wrote Mike Davis in 1990, "Hill Street [became] a local Berlin Wall separating the publicly subsidized luxury of Bunker Hill from the lifeworld of Broadway, now reclaimed by Latino immigrants as their primary shopping and entertainment area."[50] By 1970, most poor residents of color had effectively been forced to leave downtown. Some of them ended up in a drug-infested skid row notorious for its crime rate and inhumanity, which the city is still dealing with today.[51]

The Tide Begins to Turn in Boyle Heights

Propelled by a new progressive coalition consisting of black voters, Jews, and liberals from the West Side, in 1973 L.A. elected Tom Bradley as its first African American mayor. In his election campaign Bradley promised to inject new funds into the Latino and black neighborhoods of East and South Central L.A. But after expanding the role of minorities on city commissions and increasing the number of minority white-collar employees in civil service jobs, Bradley largely turned his back on the ghetto communities that had helped to elect him. Instead, he bought into the business elite's master plan for corporate modernism. It was not until housing policy changed at the state and federal level, and L.A.'s Latinos began electing their own representatives to city and county offices, that the CRA modified its policies and began putting forward plans to reinvigorate the barrios instead of undermining them.[52]

One positive result of this change occurred in Boyle Heights, which had suffered severely from freeway construction in the forties and fifties. In 1993 City Councilman Richard Alatorre persuaded the CRA to invest $93 million in the so-called Adelante Eastside Project, which promised new schools, low-interest loans for small businesses, and the upgrading of

Boyle Heights' derelict industrial zone. Modifying the CRA's earlier top-down methods, a thirty-member citizens committee—most of whom were Latino—was selected to consult on the Adelante project. However, several older members of the committee remained so suspicious of the CRA that they found it hard to believe it would actually upgrade the barrio without further damage to its residents' interests. "The thing I think about is Chavez Ravine," committee member Don Lippman told the *L.A. Times* in August 1997, "when they went into that Hispanic community and literally took them out of their homes."[53]

Despite this negative comment, many of the reforms promised in the Adelante Eastside Project were implemented.[54] Nevertheless, Los Angeles continued, and still continues, to suffer from an atomized downtown and a chronic shortage of affordable housing. Between 1970 and the turn of the century the city of L.A. adopted a variety of laws, rules, and ordinances that reinforced legislation passed at the state and federal level calling for neighborhood rehabilitation rather than wholesale demolition and requiring the inclusion of affordable housing as a standard element in the redevelopment of any given neighborhood. But the new rules did not necessarily benefit those who had earlier been evicted from their homes. So far, for example, most of the new apartments and lofts the city has helped fund in the downtown area have been sold to white-collar professionals or artisans seeking space for artistic experimentation, not to families of modest means.

To what extent did the successes of the civil rights movement in the 1960s and 1970s and the massive influx of Mexican immigrants in the 1980s persuade L.A. city authorities to adopt a more humane, community-oriented philosophy of slum clearance and urban redevelopment? What did that philosophy consist of? Has it really been implemented? These questions are taken up during a final review of the material legacy of Chavez Ravine in the next chapter.

PART IV

Chavez Ravine in the Light of Subsequent History

CHAPTER SEVEN

Have L.A.'s Urban Renewal Policies Been Successfully Reformed?

"The legislature further finds and declares that a fundamental purpose of redevelopment is to expand the supply of low and moderate income housing."

—CALIFORNIA REDEVELOPMENT LAW

"Community development corporations . . . continue to work with poor and unemployed neighbors, demand fair lending and equitable public services, and otherwise press business and government in their neighborhoods' interest. But the levers they seek to pull are nowadays more likely those of the market than of power politics or official charity."

—PAUL S. GROGAN AND TONY PROSCIO

Introduction

At first glance, it seems reasonable to suppose the furor that resulted from the eviction of Chavez Ravine's residents could have been prevented if the Los Angeles City Council had only stuck to the promise it made to provide them with alternative housing. In one of the mea culpas that Frank Wilkinson later voiced, he stated: "If our wishes had been honored, we could have rehoused all the residents comfortably."[1]

A cynic might even claim that, because the City Housing Authority purchased the homes of the residents legally, no real scandal had occurred. It is true that the City Council changed its mind about public housing in December 1951. But it often changed its mind about policy issues. The CHA had acted within the law, had it not? So why all the fuss?

L.A.'s City Council was, of course, entitled to change its mind about the CHA's proposal for public housing, although many of its critics argued that it did so because it feared being tarred with the brush of socialism, not because it had seriously reconsidered the city's housing needs. In the midst of the furor over Chavez Ravine the public housing lobby published a strong defense of its views, arguing that because it was tied to the profit motive, private industry could never satisfy the city's need for low-income housing.[2]

But to blame the Chavez Ravine scandal solely on the insensitivity of the CHA, or on the political cowardice of the City Council in the face of the Red Scare, is to avoid the deeper questions raised by the affair, including questions about the philosophy of urban renewal itself. Why, for example, did the CHA make no attempt to ascertain the wishes of Chavez Ravine's residents before proceeding with its plans? And why, when it became clear that the residents were strongly opposed to moving, did it decide to tear down the entire barrio without considering some alternative course of action?

Some of the answers to these questions are already clear. Support for the bulldozing tactics of the CHA stemmed partly from a belief that the only effective answer to the slum problem was to demolish all of the blighted buildings—even those that were redeemable—and build from the ground up.

But it also arose from the blinkered attitude of the city's planning authorities, who believed implicitly in the superiority of their demolition policies—without considering the human costs involved. Their complacency also resulted from the fact that they were appointed by the mayor, not elected by the voters.[3] The CHA's leaders were architects, lawyers, bankers, and businessmen, all of whom were members of the city's Anglo-American elite. Not being responsible to the voters, they had little incentive to take seriously the opinions of those who disagreed with them.

Equally important was the fact that the CHA's members were exclusively white, middle-class, and male. No housewives, working-class men, or people of color sat among them. Hence it is hardly surprising that, in the conservative 1950s, most of L.A.'s city planners shared the same racist attitudes toward Mexicans, blacks, and other poor people of color as the rest of the city's Anglo population. To confirm this, one has only to recall the callous way in which Sheriff's Department officers evicted the Arechigas from their home in May 1959.

The High Tide of Neighborhood Demolition and Its First Serious Critic

The demolition school of neighborhood clearance remained dominant throughout the 1950s, when America's love affair with the suburbs was in full force and when L.A.'s white, business-oriented government vowed to refashion the downtown area to its own specifications. It would be ten years or more before any large body of opinion would openly challenge the CHA's grandiose commitment to freeway building, bulldozing slum areas, and moving "undesirable populations" (i.e., poor people of color) out of the city's "desirable" neighborhoods.[4] Why did these policies prove so difficult to change?

Part of the problem was that the CHA's destructive bulldozing policies were reinforced by federally sanctioned programs designed to move ghetto residents out of crowded downtown city centers and rebuild decaying industrial neighborhoods all over the country. According to one estimate, from 1949 to 1973 a combination of federal, state, and municipal urban renewal programs "bulldozed 2,500 neighborhoods in 993 cities."[5] They displaced more than one million people in the industrial cities of the Midwest, many of them African Americans from the South who had come north during and after World War II to take jobs in domestic work, service industries, and heavy industrial plants.[6]

To make matters worse, federal and state laws permitted local planning authorities to define words like *slum, blighted,* and *ghetto* in exceedingly broad terms. Applicants for state funding in New Jersey, for example, could designate buildings as blighted—and hence subject to demolition—if they were "dilapidated [or] obsolescent"; if they showed evidence of "overcrowding, faulty arrangement or design," or if they had an "obsolete layout."[7] These broad definitions enabled the Newark Housing Authority to propose a giant urban renewal scheme intended to clear nearly half of that city's land area. Had it been put fully into effect, it would have displaced one in seven of Newark's residents, virtually all of them African Americans. Plans similar to these were drawn up and implemented in Pittsburgh, Philadelphia, and a dozen other industrial cities.[8]

These sweeping displacement schemes did not go unchallenged, even in the early days. In 1953, the California State Highway Commission proposed to drive the Golden State Freeway through the Boyle Heights section of Los Angeles, severing it from the adjacent East Side community of Hollenbeck Heights. Both areas lay within Councilman Edward Roybal's Ninth municipal district. He helped to set up a protest committee, backed by local residents and the *Eastside Sun*, a supportive East L.A. newspaper, to persuade the State Highway Commission (another unelected body) to reroute the freeway. The committee failed in its efforts, and the freeway remained where it was. This was one of several unsuccessful early attempts to modify L.A.'s sweeping urban redevelopment program.[9] Similar freeway building schemes, which were seen by city planners as "essential to progress," were also challenged in Chicago, New York, and other large cities.[10]

In response to this groundswell of protest, architectural experts and academic planners began for the first time to examine the negative aspects of the nation's urban renewal program. The most influential early critic of the bulldozing approach was not a planning specialist but a feisty female journalist named Jane Jacobs, who in 1961 published *The Death and Life of Great American Cities*. Despite her lack of professional qualifications, Jacobs rejected the central premise of most urban planners at the time, which was to divide cities up spatially according to function. Residential housing would be placed in one area, commerce and industry in another, and stores and places of entertainment in still a third. Jacobs labeled this idea "nonsense, dangerous nonsense."[11] Why? Because such divisions artificially separated from each other the many urban functions essential to maintaining the lifeblood of a living community.

Instead, Jacobs advocated economically integrated neighborhoods, each of which would provide all (or most) of the urban functions citizens needed, within easy reach of each other. This idea ran counter to orthodox planning opinion, especially in a city like Los Angeles where the city government was determined to consign most residential housing to the suburbs. Jacobs also rejected the idea of demolishing slum properties wholesale, advocating instead for what she called "spot renewal." By this she meant "seeing how many old buildings can be left standing and the area still converted into a passable version" of a well-planned city.[12]

Jacobs also shocked architectural opinion by opposing the building of huge, tower-like apartment blocks, like the ones proposed for Elysian Park Heights by Richard Neutra and Robert Alexander. Virtually all city planners in the fifties accepted high-rises as the best way to rehouse slum dwellers. Jacobs agreed that razing old neighborhoods and replacing them with giant tower blocks may have been the most rational and cost-efficient way of dealing with slum housing. But she argued that the destruction of such neighborhoods cut residents off from the corner bars, movie houses, park benches, and all the other small conveniences—which she labeled "the endless intricacy of life"—that made living in a city worthwhile.[13]

Jane Jacobs especially deplored the effects of razing old neighborhoods on the people who lived in them, a message that would surely have resonated with the former residents of Chavez Ravine. Residents who were ousted from their traditional communities, she said, were treated by urban planning departments like "the subjects of a conquering power."[14] Instead, Jacobs championed the idea of "deslumming" old neighborhoods by saving as many old buildings as possible, preserving a mix of different kinds of housing, and introducing new people and new services into dilapidated areas to restore them to health. On these matters Jacobs was ahead of her time.

The Death and Life of Great American Cities infuriated city planners and housing experts nationwide. They dismissed Jacobs as a crackpot, ignorant housewife who didn't know what she was talking about.[15] But her book, especially those parts that criticized the arrogance of professional urban planners like those in L.A., struck a chord in many underprivileged areas.

The Fight for Urban Planning Reform in Los Angeles

Today, now that the grandiose bulldozing schemes of urban renewal in its immediate post–World War II phase have mostly been abandoned, much of what Jane Jacobs said in *The Death and Life of American Cities* seems like common sense. But Jacobs was a New Yorker, and at first her influence was largely confined to the East Coast. In Southern California it was not so much her ideas as the anger generated among minorities and inner-city dwellers by the urban riots of the 1960s that first precipitated a slowdown, then a slow process of reform, in the bulldozing policies pursued by local city planners. In L.A., minority demands for change grew rapidly after the Watts uprising of August 1965. They grew still louder when serious rioting broke out in Detroit, Cleveland, and dozens of other cities in the years that followed.[16]

Nearly everywhere civil rights activists marched during the inner-city riots of the 1960s, blue-collar jobs were moving to the suburbs, African Americans were demanding greater access to political power, and the number of low-income housing units being built was far fewer than the number being demolished. "Virtually all of the riot areas," wrote one observer, "were sites of major renewal efforts: quite frequently struggles over the nature of renewal lurked behind the riots as an implicit issue, as in the case of Newark's planned new medical school."[17]

Another source of the militancy that prompted criticism of L.A.'s divisive urban renewal policies was the "internal colony" model of minority oppression developed by French racial theorist Frantz Fanon. Fanon's American followers argued that the position of racial minorities in the United States resembled that of native peoples in the third world countries colonized by western Europe. Esteban Torres, a former auto worker important in Chicano politics during this period, argued that "East Los Angeles, like other Mexican-American communities, is but a colony dependent on outside forces that control the ownership and flow of economic resources. Given the ability to own and control their own economic resources, the community can then reverse the situation by attaining political power."[18]

Building on this desire for neighborhood autonomy, in April 1961 the Citizens Committee to Incorporate East Los Angeles placed a proposition declaring the area an independent city on the Los Angeles city ballot. Despite significant grassroots support, it was defeated by a coalition led by the local Property Owners Association, which raised the specter of the increased taxes that would be required to sustain a newly independent city.[19]

These grassroots demands for local autonomy were reinforced, at least temporarily, by an experiment in community democracy undertaken by the federal government as part of President Johnson's War on Poverty. In 1964 the federal Office of Economic Opportunity established a series of Community Action Agencies all over the country to enable poor peoples' organizations to administer federal antipoverty aid themselves, instead of channeling it through the municipal authorities. Local antipoverty groups immediately clamored for representation on the city boards that distributed the funds. This federal initiative alarmed the bureaucrats at Los Angeles' city hall, as it did those in other cities. Mayor Sam Yorty had to struggle hard to keep control over the program in his own hands.[20]

But the most important new players on the local scene were the newly empowered pressure groups that had been thrown together by the Watts Riots of 1965. These minority activists were suspicious of, and in some cases flatly opposed to, the top-down policies pursued by L.A.'s CRA. As a result of changes in the law, this new body had been put in charge of most of the city's redevelopment projects. One of the largest and most important of these projects involved the creation of the Watts Labor Community Action Committee (WLCAC), which was established just before the Watts uprising occurred. Its equivalent in the Mexican American community was the East Los Angeles Community Union (TELACU), a neighborhood-based organization that sponsored low-income businesses and housing projects in Boyle Heights, Belvedere, and other East L.A. barrios.[21]

The late 1950s and early 1960s are now remembered as a confusing period in which various state, federal, and municipal agencies struggled to reformulate the nation's urban renewal plans. Opposing factions favoring demolition, rehabilitation, and a variety of other solutions vied for control. The federal Department of Housing and Urban Development (HUD), which came into being in 1965, also became an important player. HUD approved the razing of blighted areas, but it also provided large sums of money for big urban renewal projects such as Bunker Hill.[22]

The Southern California real estate industry tried to channel as much of the increased flow of public money as it could into private, commercial ventures. In 1959, for example, it successfully lobbied Congress to increase the proportion of federal funds used for nonresidential construction from 10 percent to 35 percent.[23] But minority lobbyists who opposed L.A.'s wholesale demolition policies also made several breakthroughs. The Temple-Beaudry urban renewal project was shelved, Lincoln Heights and Monterey Hills had their clearance plans voided, and the demolition plans for Mount Pleasant were also put off. In South Central, the WLCAC received statutory authority to apply for federal and local funds in order to build or rehabilitate substandard housing.[24]

Faced with these contradictory pressures, the CRA was almost overwhelmed by the pressure of work. By September 1967, it was responsible for administering an investment program worth $500 million in federal, state, and local funds in more than sixty urban renewal projects. But the rapid turnover of personnel, the shortage of experienced planners, and the sheer complexity of the projects the agency was responsible for put many of its projects behind schedule. In September 1967 the *L.A. Times* complained that "virtually no headway has been made in responding to a HUD suggestion to . . . handle the mounting workload brought on by greater activity in the Bunker Hill, Hoover, and Watts areas."[25]

Bunker Hill was downtown L.A.'s largest and most complex rebuilding scheme. More than a square mile in extent, it necessitated the leveling of many large, old apartment buildings inhabited by poor residents of the city. In November 1965, a special task force was created to cut through red tape and speed up the Watts reconstruction project, which at that point was the most important redevelopment plan in the city. But the Watts task force made little headway. "More than two years after the Watts riots," the *L.A. Times* noted in January 1969, "the type of results the community has been waiting for—a new pedestrian mall, shopping centers, a residential complex, and new industries—may still be many years away."[26] Delays in getting the Hoover-USC project off the ground also illustrated the difficulties the CRA faced in securing adequate funds, overcoming local opposition, and reconciling federal, state, and local planning criteria. This

Figure 26. L.A.'s giant Bunker Hill redevelopment project, circa 1967. Courtesy UCLA Special Collections.

166-acre project south of downtown, in which Coliseum sports authorities, the University of Southern California, and local residents all had an interest, was approved by the L.A. City Council in January 1966. But three years later it still had not gotten off the ground.[27]

As a result, advanced deterioration hit the already blighted area, neighborhood crime increased, and local merchants—uncertain how long they would be able to remain open—complained that their volume of business had declined by 80 percent. "The uncertainty creates a certain panic," one Vermont Avenue shopkeeper declared. "No one wants to invest or improve his business until we know what is going to happen."[28] Anger and resentment among the local inhabitants continued to grow. Mrs. Woodell, who lived on Hoover Avenue, was openly contemptuous of the Hoover-USC redevelopment plan. "I've seen the misery it does to people. The people living here now, those who will be pushed out, will never get back. Furthermore, the urban renewal people say we'll get the right price for our property. But we all know it's pretty unlikely we'll ever get it."[29] It seemed like Chavez Ravine all over again.

Disappointing Results of Reform

By the early 1970s there was a growing national consensus that the financial, social, and emotional costs paid by slum dwellers for the old bulldozing approach to urban renewal were too high to justify continuing it on a large scale. Alternative methods of revitalizing blighted areas began coming into use. They included rehabilitation, the preservation of mixed residential and commercial neighborhoods, and the rigorous enforcement of existing building codes to avoid the necessity of demolition. At the same time, in response to growing anger at the grassroots level, serious efforts were made to include local residents in the decision-making process.[30]

The first major step toward revising Southern California's urban redevelopment code was taken in 1976, when the California legislature redefined the responsibilities of City Redevelopment Corporations, or CDCs. These local agencies, which provided the institutional framework for implementing the CRA's development plans, retained their power to designate blighted areas and to implement redevelopment projects through the power of eminent domain. They also kept their authority to borrow money, issue bonds, and use tax increment financing as a means of paying for their schemes.[31]

But new restrictions were placed on the CDCs' powers to prevent them from acting arbitrarily and to subject them, to some extent at least, to community control. First, municipal ordinances that authorized the implementation of redevelopment projects were made "subject to a referendum determining that there is a need for such an agency."[32] Second, no scheme requiring the demolition of houses could be implemented "prior to the development of a plan for the relocation of the affected residents."[33] And third, all new and rehabilitated buildings in a redevelopment area had to "contain set percentages of low and moderate income housing."[34] Had these rules been in place in the 1950s, many of the problems that resulted in the eviction of Mexican Americans from Chavez Ravine might have been avoided.

Other reforms were enacted. The revised guidelines mandated the creation of Project Area Committees, to consist of local citizens and business leaders whose function was to cooperate with Community Redevelopment Agencies in the planning and review of local rebuilding projects. Their members were either appointed by city hall or elected by the local community.[35] This meant that the residents of East L.A. now possessed, for the first time, a direct means of shaping and responding to urban renewal projects proposed for their barrios.

On paper these changes in the law promised a marked improvement over the insensitive policies pursued in the 1950s. In some respects, the situation did indeed improve. The refusal of Chicano militants and neighborhood activists to collaborate with city hall declined, as the realization sank in that self-determination for local communities in an economically interdependent metropolis was impossible to achieve. As confidence in the role of the Project Area Committees grew, several new urban renewal projects were successfully completed, even though they sometimes took even longer to finish than they had before owing to the need for grassroots consultation.[36]

Nevertheless, huge problems remained. In the seventies and eighties the income gap between L.A.'s white, suburban residents and its poor, inner-city families widened dramatically. The number of minority households with incomes below the poverty line increased by 43,000, while the quantity of housing units they could afford to buy (or rent) fell by 62,000. By 1989, three-quarters of L.A.'s inner-city residents spent more than half of their income on rent.[37] Most alarming of all, a 1996 report on housing conditions stated that the city's barrios and ghettos contained "a population of more than half a million living precariously, in housing conditions little better than those of the Third World."[38]

Not all of these problems could be blamed on the CRA. The most important reasons for the city's growing number of poor, minority residents—and hence for their inability to afford decent housing—were political and economic forces over which the city's planning authorities had little or no control. They included the loss of high-paying jobs in mass production industry, the decline in federal housing subsidies, and—most serious of all—the influx into L.A. of hundreds of thousands of poor immigrant families from Mexico and Central America. By 1985 overcrowding in the downtown area was rife, and regional housing prices had risen 55 percent above the national average. Apartment rents also continued to escalate.[39]

Nonetheless, other problems emerged that *did* reflect negatively on the operation of the city's urban renewal policies. From 1970 to 1989 not only did L.A.'s overall housing stock grow at less than half the national rate, its supply of low-cost housing effectively shrank. In 1974, low-cost units made up 35 percent of the total housing stock. By 1985, that proportion had shrunk to 16 percent. During the same period the proportion of higher-rent units (at $500 per month and up) rose from 14 percent to 45 percent of the total housing stock.[40] Why did this happen?

Various reasons can be cited. One was inflation. The cost of most kinds of accommodation, especially newly fashionable condominiums, rose without a significant number of cheaper units being added to the housing stock. As a result, from 1974 to 1985 the number of homes and apartments in the city that rented for less than $300 a month fell by 42 percent, forcing increasing numbers of poor, minority householders to stay in their densely packed, substandard premises; occupy fewer rooms; or move in with relatives. During the Reagan administration the amount of state and federal money made available for affordable housing was cut substantially. Even more dismaying was the fact that, despite all of the rhetoric about rehabilitation instead of destruction, the housing demolition rate in Los Angeles County in the 1980s actually rose instead of declining, especially among the oldest—and hence the most affordable—categories of accommodation.[41]

In addition, only twenty-one out of the seventy-two new housing projects the CRA undertook in the 1980s were completed, while the number of new and restored houses that became available, either to rehouse evicted tenants or to sell at subsidized prices, was extremely small. The 1983 CRA report stated that only 1,849 low-income housing units had been completed that year—a drop in the bucket compared to the need.[42] The report added that, of the 107 projects the CRA currently had in hand, no fewer than thirty-one involved the construction of suburban shopping malls, many of which were located a considerable distance away from the areas where the residents lived.[43] It seems likely that some kind of business boondoggle was involved here.

The CRA's rehabilitation projects were sometimes so expensive that only a minority of former tenants could afford to move back into their old buildings. The city's building code enforcement program, under which grants were made to homeowners to bring their houses up to standard, also produced ambiguous results. For example, when a code enforcement program was begun in the Sawtelle area of West Los Angeles, many local homeowners either sold their properties instead of repairing them or else failed to repair them sufficiently to bring them up to code. The result was that the number of buildings in the area that had to be demolished almost equaled the number restored.[44]

Gentrification and the Problem of Local Control

Other contentious issues continued to fester. The most explosive concerned the proper definition of urban blight and how it was to be corrected. In principle, this issue remained the same as it had been in the case of Chavez Ravine, more than twenty years before. As in that case, the most fiercely contested point was whether the axe should be withheld from a blighted area in light of what the local residents considered to be the vital interests of their community, as they—not outside experts—saw them. As one of the participants in a symposium held on the topic in 1975 put it, L.A. planners still ignore the fact that "redevelopment areas, although defined by the planners as blighted, are seen by their inhabitants as still viable, even if flawed, for reasons which never occur to outsiders."[45]

Arguments also arose over which local residents should be appointed, or elected, to the newly established Project Area Committees. In theory, everyone agreed that a representative sample of local citizens should be permitted to stand. But the question remained as to how city planners were to reconcile the differing requirements of participatory democracy with those of rational management and professional expertise. The complexity of many planning projects indicated that outside experts should make most of the critical decisions. When that happened, however, Project Area Committee members complained that they could not understand the language used by the experts and consequently refused to vote for redevelopment plans they did not understand.[46] On the other hand, denying ordinary citizens the chance to participate in the planning process also generated anger and noncooperation and threatened to restore some of the same top-down procedures the reforms of the 1970s and 1980s were designed to eliminate. As one observer put it, "The process of improvement is not likely to strike very deep unless the target people themselves are part of it."[47]

By the end of the century, moreover, a problem that had first appeared in Southern California in the 1970s also became widespread: gentrification, or the process by which developers and white, middle-class professionals moved into former minority, working-class neighborhoods intending to "rehabilitate" them.[48] The arrival of affluent residents changed the culture of low-income neighborhoods. It increased rents and real estate prices, forcing out poor residents who could no longer afford to pay them. Despite this, most municipal governments—including those in Southern California—approved of gentrification. This was because it diminished wear and tear on the urban infrastructure and increased city revenues as a result of the higher property taxes paid by newcomers who upgraded the local housing stock.[49]

The process of gentrification also tended to lower crime rates, improve the quality of local schools, and rescue declining neighborhoods without spending a great deal of extra public money. This was because of the private funds spent by incoming residents to refurbish their dilapidated houses. These were positive developments. But there was also a significant downside. Besides forcing poor and minority homeowners to move elsewhere, the process of gentrification led to cultural conflicts between poor residents and affluent ones whose way of life was different. It also led to the closing of minority businesses and to the loss of jobs. Most serious of all, rising rents and increasing home prices often resulted in the loss of affordable housing.

Ironically, the areas in L.A. most adversely affected by gentrification included Silverlake, Echo Park, and Lincoln Heights near Dodger Stadium, areas many barrio residents had moved into in the 1950s after they were evicted from Chavez Ravine. "Echo Park is in the grips of a venomous dispute over gentrification and the future of the . . . neighborhood," reported the *L.A. Times* in June 2008.[50] Here, as elsewhere, rising housing costs, which many of these former evictees could no longer afford, were a major bone of contention. Thus, having lost their homes once to a public housing plan that never materialized, some Chavez Ravine survivors were forced to move a second—or, in some cases, even a third—time.

The prospect of gentrification could even threaten to replay history in still more gruesome ways. In 2005, an organization called the Committee for a New America sought to speed up the gentrification of L.A.'s downtown, which remained uneasily balanced between wealth and squalor. To secure control of the land around Broadway and other streets where Mexicans still lived and shopped, the proposal called for "the resettlement of the poor"—as if poor people were merely pawns in the hands of city planners to be shuffled about at the whim of those with political power.[51] Luckily this scheme, an obvious throwback to the racist policies of the 1950s, never got off the ground. But if any of the surviving victims of the Chavez Ravine scandal got wind of it, their blood must have run cold.

Are Urban Renewal Programs Still Worthwhile?

Given these mixed results, it seems obvious, at least as far as Los Angeles is concerned, that the efforts to reform the urban redevelopment process instituted in the 1970s and 1980s have not succeeded in correcting all of the evils that led to the ousting of Mexican Americans from Chavez Ravine half a century ago.

This does not mean that these reforms have not yielded any positive results. For example, the election of local citizens to Project Area Committees, despite their controversial electoral procedures, is a distinct improvement over the undemocratic policies followed by the old City Housing Authority. In recent years the federal government has severely reduced the scale and extent of its urban renewal programs, as a result of the conservative social policies first introduced by President Ronald Reagan. Nevertheless, some of those that still exist, such as the housing subsidies provided under Title 8 of the 1937 Housing Act, have worked quite well.[52] A good case can also be made that the advantages brought about by gentrification outweigh the disadvantages.

Nationwide, in fact, according to census figures published in 1998 by housing expert Peter D. Salins, the overall housing situation in America has improved greatly since World War II. Salins states that in 1940, "more than 20 percent of U.S. dwellings were overcrowded (those occupied by more than one person per room). Fewer than 5 percent are today. In 1940, 18 percent of all dwellings were severely deteriorated physically. Only 2 percent are today."[53] We should also remember that urban renewal schemes were never supposed to fill all the gaps in the nation's housing supply. They were only intended to redevelop blighted areas and to provide assistance to those who could not otherwise afford housing for themselves, such as the very poor, the elderly, and the disabled.

Nevertheless, the record of government-sponsored urban renewal programs, of whatever kind, is undoubtedly mixed. Given this fact, should the nation turn its back on the modern urban renewal movement originally inspired by the New Deal? My answer is an unequivocal no. The main reason for this is the fact that many, if not most, of America's major industrial cities, and many smaller ones, still suffer from a serious shortage of affordable housing, which urban renewal schemes—if they are intelligently applied—can help to alleviate. State intervention is also necessary to monitor redevelopment procedures so that catastrophic blunders of the kind that led to the tragedy at Chavez Ravine are not repeated.[54]

In Los Angeles, which has experienced a massive influx of Mexican and Asian immigrants and where, in the year 2000, 63 percent of the residents were renters, the shortage of low-income housing is particularly serious. It became even more chronic following Governor Brown's ill-judged decision in 2012 to abolish all the state's Community Redevelopment Agencies, which for years had been the main supplier of affordable housing. According to a February 2013 report, rents in Southern California had increased by nearly 30 percent over the preceding twenty years. By contrast, the income of average renters, adjusted for inflation, fell by 6 percent. The result was that "only thirty-seven affordable units were available for every one hundred would-be renters."[55]

It also appears that, despite promises made to citizens in neighborhoods subject to redevelopment that alternative accommodations would be made available to them, fears persist that such promises will not be kept. In August 2013, the long-standing plan of L.A. authorities to rehabilitate the notoriously run-down Jordan Downs public housing project in Watts took a new step forward. At that point funding seemed likely to become available to build an "urban village" of shops, town houses, and gardens on the huge site. However, no mention was made in the report as to whether the town house component in the plan would contain any low-income housing. As so often in the past, uncertainty on this point prompted anxiety on the part of Jordan Downs' poorest residents that once the old public housing had been removed, they would be left homeless. "I'm scared my family will be pushed out," wrote one Jordan Downs resident.[56]

It is also obvious that L.A.'s housing stock, like that of any other city, will continue to decay, as it has in the past. Hence, even if slums in the classic sense are now rare, a need to deal with urban blight will be present in the years to come, just as it was in years past. As in former years, too, the city's changing needs with respect to land use, transportation facilities, industrial development, and environmental policy will inevitably necessitate the destruction of some portion of its housing stock before the end of its useful life has been reached. The private construction industry will no doubt continue to fill some of these gaps. But, given the ongoing problem of urban poverty, some of L.A.'s inner-city poor (including, especially, poor people of color) will continue to need low-income housing, or some other form of subsidized accommodation, to keep them afloat. Driven as it is by the profit motive, the private construction industry has no incentive to build such houses unless it is required to do so.

For these reasons it is unrealistic to suppose that urban renewal programs geared toward low-income housing will become any less necessary in the future than they were in the past, especially at a time when rising income inequality makes working-class families less and less able to purchase anything but the cheapest form of accommodation. No instant formula will enable America to solve this difficult problem. But a number of suggestions can be made to enhance and preserve a higher proportion of the nation's stock of affordable housing.

Some of these suggestions have been made before but never tried on a large scale.[57] The first priority should be to restore California's state-mandated Community Redevelopment Agencies, which should again become the main source of L.A.'s affordable housing supply. If a neighborhood deteriorates to a point at which some demolition is unavoidable, it should be limited to those buildings that are beyond repair. In order to keep the lifeblood of existing communities flowing, displaced residents should also be offered relocation housing within the remaining portions of the same neighborhood, instead of scattering them throughout the city.

It might also make sense to adopt a policy of slow but continuous rebuilding within a problem area, with as many new houses built as are removed—the point again being to avoid reducing the total sum of available homes. Such a policy would avoid razing entire neighborhoods, while at the same time preserving their core values. In addition, new houses of differing types (some low-cost, others more expensive and elaborate) should be gradually introduced into problem areas to increase the overall housing supply, widen residential choices for those with rising incomes, and prevent affluent residents from fleeing the neighborhood. To discourage flight from problem neighborhoods, increased attention should also be paid to beautifying neighborhoods' surroundings and to making sure they are supplied with sufficient parks, schools, and medical facilities.[58]

None of these proposed solutions to the problem of urban blight is comprehensive, and none of them is cheap. Only the richest cities can afford to rehabilitate problem neighborhoods completely. Admittedly, too, many of these policies would be slow to mature. But the gradual introduction of more sophisticated urban renewal policies, coupled with an attempt to fit them more closely to the needs of individual communities, instead of pursuing a failed policy of "one size fits all," makes far more sense than abandoning the idea of state-mandated urban renewal altogether.

One of the marks of a civilized society is how much of its resources it is willing to devote to provide its poorer citizens with access to affordable and decent low-income housing. In this respect, as in its treatment of old people, the United States still lags way behind the most enlightened nations in western Europe and elsewhere. In the future, as in the past, a creative mix of private and public investment, oversight, and control will remain necessary if tragedies such as Chavez Ravine are to be avoided and the progress of the last two generations is to be maintained.

CHAPTER EIGHT

Chavez Ravine's Cultural Legacy

"Noting that the 'Battle for Chavez Ravine' served as a precursor for the Chicana/o Movement of the 1960s and 1970s, Culture Clash asserts that the displaced Mexican American families of the Ravine cultivated a legacy of resistance against social injustice, and that such 'memory cannot be flattened.'"

—DAVID GUMARIO GARCIA

"Most of us, inmates or not, live in self-imposed prisons. Poetry created a world of freedom beyond the walls of my heart and mind. Plus, it filled the void left by my lost life."

—MANAZAR GAMBOA

Introduction

The long drawn-out coda to the evictions from Chavez Ravine, with its stories of weeping women, sheriffs' beatings, bureaucratic double dealing, and down-to-the-wire negotiations with Walter O'Malley, suggests that the fifties displacements became deeply etched in the historical memory of L.A.'s Mexican American community. The importance of those stories was affirmed by young Chicanos during the following decades, even as the community was undergoing a process of renewal and empowerment. The memory of the evictions was also kept alive by members of the older generation at the annual picnics of Los Desterrados in Elysian Park and by other former residents scattered throughout the city.

It comes as no surprise, therefore, to find that the tragedy at Chavez Ravine spawned a rich cultural legacy, including plays, poetry, fiction, and musical performances that still resonate with the L.A. public today. That legacy drew on a history of artistic protest against Anglo dominance among Indians, Mexican writers, and other indigenous artists that goes back to the nineteenth century. In 1850, for example, Francisco Ramirez denounced the land stealing practices of Anglo settlers arriving from the East in a Los Angeles newspaper called *El Clamor Publico*.[1] Fifteen years later, in 1865, L.A. landowner Mariano Vallejo, angered by the way Anglo writers blamed the downfall of the Californios (the state's indigenous landowners) on their "idleness and passivity," wrote a "true history" of the region to show that Southern California's early inhabitants were not "indigents or a band of beasts" but an "illustrious race of people."[2]

The next year Helen Hunt Jackson published *Century of Dishonor*, followed in 1884 by her best selling novel *Ramona*, which excoriated white settlers for repressing California's Indians. Unfortunately, *Ramona* became better known for its romantic love story than for its critique of native displacement. The aim of the Women's National Indian Association, which Helen Hunt Jackson supported, focused most of its attention on bringing Christianity to the Indians and on teaching Victorian domesticity and submissiveness among their wives.[3] As historian Douglas Monroy puts it, the "disordered sense of narcissism" of the white ruling class helps to explain "their alternation between pastoral and derogatory views of Hispanics; and their remarkable lack of compassion for people who suffered the consequences of their newly introduced capitalist system."[4]

Between 1890 and World War II numerous other Mexican American writers expressed their disapproval of the racist policies pursued by Anglo-American settlers in Southern California. After the Chicano nationalist movement emerged in the 1960s, the rhetorical battle heated up once again. In his poem "Cuervos," poet and journalist Victor Valle criticized the historical usurpations of the Anglo "landed gentry," beginning with *L.A. Times* founder General Harrison Gray Otis, whose support for modern industry had undermined Southern California's pastoral traditions and threatened its indigenous population. As a child in Whittier, Valle's backyard had bordered on

> "A still wild river,
> home for *palomas, coyote, carrizales*,
> the green smell of moss outside my window."

But by the time of his adolescence,

> "We were barricaded
> by boulevards, freeways,
> clouds of high octane smoke
> and a ceaseless roar."[5]

Despite their sentimentality, some of Victor Valle's other works, especially his essay "To the Students of Hollenbeck Junior High" (1979), were directed toward the same ends that Manazar Gamboa would later pursue during his visits to schools and reformatories for minority detainees, using creative writing to empower underprivileged Mexican youths.[6]

In the 1970s Southern California's artists and writers began using the evictions from Chavez Ravine as a major source of inspiration. In 1976, when Judy Baca painted her celebrated mural *The Great Wall of Los Angeles* on the side of the Tujunga Wash Greenway in the San Fernando Valley, she included several panels displaying the 1950s evictions.[7] The year before that Ron Arias published his fantasy novel *The Road to Tamazunchale*, which carried numerous echoes of the tragedy at Chavez Ravine.

In his novel, Arias portrays Los Angeles as a degraded, urban jungle, in contrast to the scenic splendors of the Andes—the mythical birthplace of the Aztec people—and the rural tranquility of Elysian Park.[8] At the turn of the new century Ry Cooder recorded a series of popular songs about the events in Chavez Ravine, while in 2003 a team of three writers calling themselves the Culture Clash wrote a play about the evictions. It received rave reviews when first performed at the Mark Taper Forum in downtown Los Angeles.[9]

Finally, Manazar Gamboa, who was born in Chavez Ravine in 1934, wrote many poems, plays, and short stories about his life in the ravine, only a few of which have been published. Gamboa's work is important because of its literary merit and also because it offers, more directly than that of any other artist, a personal view of the barrio's history and way of life drawn from the author's own experience.[10]

These works did not emerge out of a cultural vacuum. They formed part of a wide-ranging literary and artistic renaissance among Chicano and Chicana writers and poets that emerged during the 1960s and 1970s. Their cultural productions drew on a wide variety of Mexican and Indian artistic traditions, including *corridos* (satirical ballads), *teatro campesino* (improvisational theater), and the annual celebration of Dia de los Muertos (Day of the Dead), whose rituals pervade *The Road to Tamazunchale*. The variety of approaches the authors employed sometimes prompted criticism. For example, was it better to portray Chavez Ravine's evicted families as victims of greedy white bureaucrats or as heroic defenders of the barrio? Each interpretation has its defenders.[11]

Ron Arias's *The Road to Tamazunchale* came out of a long tradition of Mexican and Indian fiction that imagined the modern leaders of the Chicano/a movement as descendants of the elite Aztec and Mayan princes, warriors, and princesses who once ruled Latin America. The celebration of pre-Columbian heroes such as Don Fausto Tejeda in *The Road to Tamazunchale* was also influenced by figures such as Emiliano Zapata and Francisco "Pancho" Villa in the 1910 Mexican Revolution.[12] Each of these traditions enabled L.A.'s contemporary writers and artists to cultivate a new sense of pride among Mexican Americans in their pre-Anglo past and provided them with inspiration for their present-day political and economic struggles.

Judy Baca's Chavez Ravine Mural

Judy Baca was, and is, a much admired Chicana artist who grew up not in East L.A. but in Watts. At first, her efforts were limited by public disapproval and by the practical problems of executing murals outdoors. To encourage herself and her sister artists, Baca wrote a practical, illustrated guide called *A Woman's Manual: How to Assemble Scaffolding*. But her work was also influenced by the growth of feminist ideas in the 1960s and by the example set by women's art collectives such as the Mujeres Muralistas in San Francisco.[13]

Judy completed her first mural, *Mi Abuelita* (*My Grandmother*), on the side of a building in Hollenbeck Park. That work made it clear that Baca intended to dedicate her art—as Manazar Gamboa later did with his poetry—to helping underprivileged minority youths heal their psychic wounds. *Mi Abuelita* depicts an aging Mexican American grandmother with outstretched arms, as if about to hug the residents of her deprived community. This portrayal recognized the primary position of women in the Mexican family. The grandmother's outstretched arms also symbolized one of Baca's long-range goals: to persuade the warring gangs in notoriously violent Hollenbeck Park to reconcile their differences. She even invited members of local gangs to help her paint her mural.[14]

The LAPD, fearing violence, did not approve of Baca's bringing in rival gang members to help her. On one occasion some gang members who had not been invited to join her team did in fact vandalize the mural site. But Baca persisted and after *Mi Abuelita* was finished was delighted when the local community took it into their hearts. "Everybody related to it," she stated. "For 12 years people put flowers at the base of the grandmother image."[15]

After this success Baca accepted an official position as head of a new citywide mural painting program, which over time executed more than

Figure 27. Dodger Stadium descends on Chavez Ravine in Judy Baca's *Great Wall of Los Angeles*. Courtesy Social and Public Art Resource Center.

five hundred wall paintings throughout East L.A. and in other Spanish-speaking parts of the city. Hence when she began *The Great Wall of Los Angeles* in1976, she was already an experienced artist with a clear vision of the message she wanted to convey. On a twelve-foot-high wall hundreds of yards long, she portrayed the life struggles—some of them fantasized, others not—not just of Mexicans but of all the city's oppressed groups. *The Great Wall* depicted Dust Bowlers from the 1930s, Japanese American internees from World War II, Zoot Suit rioters from 1943 to 1944, and Freedom Bus Riders of the 1960s from the southern civil rights movement.[16]

The segment of the wall depicting the residents from Chavez Ravine took up only a small portion of its length. But the commonality of the minority experience was enhanced by the residents being placed alongside not just L.A.'s Mexican Americans but other downtrodden groups who struggled to find a place in the Southland. On the left side of the Chavez Ravine panel a Chicano family is shown divided by encircling freeways separating the family into two groups. On the right side, beneath the summit of Chavez Ravine itself, a Mexican woman is portrayed being manhandled by a police officer. This probably refers to the eviction of Mrs. Arechiga from her home in 1959.

Above the human figures Dodger Stadium is depicted as an alien, threatening invader hovering over the scene, as if about to crash down on the people below. It is hard to imagine a more graphic visualization of the paralyzing effect that slum clearance, freeway building, and the eviction of Chavez Ravine's residents had on L.A.'s minority communities.[17]

Ry Cooder's Chavez Ravine Album

At the turn of the twenty-first century, the story of Chavez Ravine attracted the attention of veteran folk musician Ry Cooder, whose previous work encompassed blues, Tex-Mex, soul, gospel, and rock. Cooder's national reputation meant that his *Chavez Ravine* album probably sparked more interest in the tragedy among young people than any other demographic group. Three years in the making, the blood-red cover of the album depicts a bulldozer crushing the residents' homes, while a UFO hovering over the scene—much like Dodger Stadium in Judy Baca's mural—illuminates the chaotic scene below.[18]

The album's fifteen songs offer an eclectic mix of *corridos*, Afro-Cuban tunes, Costa Rican melodies, and riotous, good-time Pachuco boogie-woogie. They evoke the spirit of Chavez Ravine, which Cooder affectionately labels "a place you don't know, up a road you don't go, where the sidewalk ends," in many ways.[19] "Onda Callejera" recalls the Zoot Suit Riots with its story of conflict between locally stationed navy personnel and Pachucos. "Corrido de Boxeo" champions the prowess of Chavez Ravine's celebrated young boxers. In "3rd Base, Dodger Stadium," longtime Cooder collaborator James Bla Pahinui plays the part of a stadium car parker lamenting the fact that his home has disappeared under thousands of tons of dirt.

Most fun is "Chinito Chinito," a playful strut through a fifties tune by Felguerez Diaz, whose casual racism—the Spanish lyrics poke fun at a Chinese laundryman—contrasts with the singer's innocent exuberance. "Poor Man's Shangri-La," by contrast, celebrates the comradeship between Chavez Ravine's residents that connected one subbarrio with another:

"La Loma boys will run with you,
Do anything that you want them to,
If you need a friend 'cause you're feeling blue
Palo Verde girls never let you down."[20]

Figure 28. Ry Cooder. Courtesy Dani Canto.

The most political song on Ry Cooder's album is "Don't Call Me Red," which satirizes Frank Wilkinson's insensitivity in the eviction scandal, while at the same time celebrating his victory against HUAC in later years. In one verse Wilkinson urges barrio residents to accept public housing, while pleading with them not to reject him because he is a Communist:

"Don't call me red, don't turn me down, I've got a plan.
Richard Neutra is my friend, and he's the man.
He's been to school and can see what's best for all of you.
Please trust me, my name is Frank, don't turn me down.
Don't call me red."[21]

In the next verse, Wilkinson joyfully records his release from prison after being jailed for pleading the Fifth Amendment:

"We survived those dark days full of danger,
In the end fate has been good to me.
Fritz Burns, Chief Parker, and J. Edgar
I outlived those bastards after all!"[22]

Given the determination of newly aroused Chicano writers to repossess their own history, white artists such as Ry Cooder sometimes came in for criticism. For example, one critic, reviewing the *Chavez Ravine* album, contended that his songs reflected a "colonial, anthropological, and folkloric effort . . . to use the cultures of aggrieved groups for white uplift, insight, and emotional renewal."[23] This criticism is unfair. Cooder goes out of his way to include a variety of Mexican and Cuban musical traditions among his songs. Track nine of his album, "El U.F.O. Cayo," celebrates the departure of an alien space invader and expresses the hope that the residents of the ravine will be able to reclaim the land and heritage of their "Poor Man's Shangri-La."[24]

Ron Arias's Fantasy Novel *The Road to Tamazunchale*

In *The Road to Tamazunchale* Ron Arias uses a different kind of satire to get his point across, even though part of his purpose—like that of Ry Cooder—is to restore respect for the campesino life-style of the Mexican immigrants who crossed the border into the United States in earlier decades. The novel describes the deathbed adventures of Don Fausto Tejeda, an old man living in "Frog Town" near the Los Angeles River. No actual mention is made of Chavez Ravine, but several of its most important episodes, most notably the encounter between Don Fausto and an LAPD trainee at the police academy, take place near Chavez Ravine in Elysian Park. Arias, a Los Angeles native who taught at UC Riverside, was honored by having his novel named "one of the founding texts in Contemporary Chicano/a Literature."[25] Earlier in his life he had served in Peru as a Peace Corps volunteer, an experience also reflected in the pages of the book.

The story opens with Fausto lying in bed in his dingy apartment, oppressed by L.A.'s downtown smog and by "the eerie cries of rusty freight car wheels" that rumble through the nearby railroad yards.[26] Determined to enjoy his last few days on earth, Fausto walks out of his apartment and is immediately transported by train to "a giant white peak" in Peru—"the very soul of Inca greatness."[27] The train descends to the River Amazon, where "fountains of tangled vines and broad, lustrous leaves pushed from both sides. Passing quickly beneath Machu Picchu, Don Fausto gazed up at the rock-hewn terraces and for a moment forgot the arthritic jab in his limbs."[28] The journey momentarily restores his youthful vigor.

This travel scene introduces a recurring theme in the novel, one that contrasts the decay of Fausto's body—and the social ills of the East L.A. barrio—with the pristine beauty of the mountains and countryside in an area of the world where the mighty Incas, putative ancestors of the Latino

Figure 29. Don Fausto gazes up at Machu Picchu in the Andes Mountains. Courtesy Ron Arias.

people, once ruled. At a more immediate level, the juxtaposition recalls the contrast between the bucolic images of early life in Chavez Ravine and the barrenness of the razed hillsides created by the construction of Dodger Stadium.

This urban-rural contrast is developed further when Fausto meets Marcelino, a Peruvian shepherd (complete with flute) who angers the LAPD by guiding his flock of alpacas onto an entry ramp of the Pasadena Freeway. Having escaped from this dilemma—as well as from a coffin into which he is prematurely placed in Forest Lawn Mortuary—Fausto is driven in a stolen car up to Elysian Park by Mario, an urchin boy, in search of Marcelino.[29]

Here Fausto and Mario encounter the threatening figure of Mr. America. While not actually identified as a member of the LAPD, the proximity of the police academy marks Mr. America as a symbol of white, gringo power. His satirical nickname also reflects the long-standing fear undocumented Mexican immigrants felt—and still feel today—toward mainstream American authority, especially the INS. Mario, fearful of being arrested for having stolen the car (shades of Manazar Gamboa in his youth) wants to flee the park:

> "Vamonos."
>
> "Wait . . . just a few more minutes. Somebody has to help him [Marcelino]. You know, he came all the way from Peru."
>
> "I don't care if he came from China. You ain't gonna help nobody if some cop sees us. Them 'vatos' train their dogs around here. Man, them dogs'll rip you up so bad you'll look like chorizo."[30]

Later, the novel depicts Fausto in the role of guide, or "coyote," who brings hundreds of undocumented Mexican farmworkers across the U.S.-Mexican border at Tijuana. Many of these *mojados* end up wandering, destitute, in the bed of the Los Angeles River. The story ends when Fausto leads a procession of cars through downtown Los Angeles, once more ending up in Elysian Park. Don Fausto, sinking fast, is given last rites by a Catholic priest. But at the end of the novel he and his companions enter the park in triumph, claiming it as a rural paradise (an Elysian field), and they celebrate together with an outdoor picnic.[31] This ending seems to represent the symbolic reclamation of Chavez Ravine by its former residents.

Culture Clash's "Reality Play" *Chavez Ravine*

Of all the cultural productions reviewed here, this play provides the most direct commentary on the evictions from Chavez Ravine because it deals openly with the events that occurred there fifty years before. By 2003, when *Chavez Ravine* was first performed at the Mark Taper Forum in downtown L.A., Culture Clash's three authors—Richard Montoya, Herbert Siguenza, and Ric Salinas—had already written and performed dozens of plays at other prestigious regional theaters throughout the country. Their previous productions, all of which featured their trademark sarcasm, included *The Mission* (1988), which satirized the proposed canonization of the founder of California's eighteenth-century missions, Father Junipero Serra, and *Radio Mambo: Culture Clash Invades Miami* (1994).[32]

In *Chavez Ravine*, the Culture Clash trio sets out to bring the voices of racially marginalized groups to the attention of a wider, largely white, American audience. Although the interpretation is original for the late 1990s, most of the scenes in *Chavez Ravine* were based on newspaper reports and other published accounts of the evictions from the ravine, the building of Dodger Stadium, and the role of Fernando Valenzuela in popularizing baseball among L.A.'s Mexican population. Consistent with the traditions of Luis Valdez, *carpa*, and Mexican tent shows, the authors include slapstick, music, and dance episodes in the performance. While the play is arguably a resistance narrative that symbolizes the opposition of all Chicanos to white oppression, it avoids romanticizing the plight of the Chavez Ravine residents themselves. As coauthor Richard Montoya explained, "The Taper stage certainly isn't a classroom, but we feel a great responsibility with this piece to get the facts right, because the collective memory of a community is a precious thing."[33]

As the play opens, a number of houses symbolizing the homes razed in Chavez Ravine are lowered onto the stage. This enables the set to fulfill a dual role as Dodger Stadium and as a platform for the community's residents to voice their protests. The audience becomes both a group of baseball fans and a group of L.A. citizens encouraged to think critically about the events taking place in their city. The most startling image is the appearance of Manazar Gamboa as the play's narrator. He speaks directly to the audience and introduces the remainder of the action. "Now, I am going to bring out some professional actors to help dramatize these events," Manazar tells the audience. In order to preserve his artistic detachment, however, he adds that the other actors will not be able to hear him. "Only you, the audience, can see and hear me."[34]

By 2003, when the play was first performed, Gamboa had been dead for three years. But employing him as narrator both reflected his fame as a Chicano poet and—because he was born in the ravine—reinforced the authors' claim to verisimilitude. Reminiscing about Chavez Ravine in his introductory speech (delivered in Spanglish), Gamboa remains faithful to our image of him as a small boy. Recalling the tamales his friend next door cooked for him when he visited her on the day of his sister Lina's death, he remembers how "on holidays, pura aroma de tamal of menudo, y los compadres tocando la guitarra till late at night. That was our community; that's something you can never erase from your cabeza."[35]

The play's other leading characters, Senora Ruiz and her son Henry and daughter Maria, are modeled on members of the Arechiga family. Their appearance on stage is followed by that of Frank Wilkinson and Richard Neutra (represented by actors), who reprise their real-life roles by proposing the public housing complex of Elysian Park Heights as an alternative to the slum housing of Chavez Ravine. While Wilkinson is treated benignly, Neutra is satirized (perhaps unfairly) as a condescending white bureaucrat when, having announced that his housing plan will include cul-de-sacs, a down-to-earth Mexican resident asks him, "What the hell are culo-sacs?"[36]

This exchange sets the scene for the play's main theme: to contrast the Mexican community's determination to preserve its land, which Maria calls "sacred space," against the "profane" displacement of the residents threatened by the City Housing Authority's plans for slum clearance. In the play's most significant exchange, Henry Ruiz angers his mother and sister by deciding to accept the CHA's monetary offer for his house and move away from the ravine:

> SENORA RUIZ: "Hank, do what you have to do, you have your own familia now. Your sister and I are staying put. But do me a favor, si vendes tu casa, if you dare to sell that little house that your father built with his hands and sweat and blood, don't look back mijo, because you will never ever set foot in this house, me entiendes?"[37]

This speech precisely echoes the family divisions over whether to accept the CHA's eminent domain policies of 1951–1952 chronicled earlier. Just as her real-life predecessors had once done, Maria then sets about fighting city hall by establishing the Palo Verde Home Owners Protective Society. She holds fund-raisers and forums where the community formulates strategy and confronts city officials. Through Maria, Culture Clash illuminates the resilience and resistance of L.A.'s Mexican American community. More broadly, Maria symbolizes the important role that Mexican American women in Los Angeles—from Dolores Huerta to Maria Elena Durazo—have always played in the struggles against social injustice.

To broaden the drama and show its relevance to other civil rights struggles, the play also introduces renowned folk singer Pete Seeger singing Woody Guthrie's famous song "This Land Is Your Land." In an epilogue addressed directly to the audience, Maria reflects on some of the barriers her predominantly Mexican community faced in their struggle to save their homes. She broadens the relevance of the drama still further by

Figure 30. Pete Seeger character supporting protesters in *Chavez Ravine*. Photo by Craig Schwartz ©2014.

linking it to other civil rights struggles of the 1960s. In saying what she does, Maria draws perhaps the most important lesson that any commentator, either before or since, has extracted from the evictions that took place at Chavez Ravine:

> MARIA: "It's true we lost, but what's more important is that we helped create a culture of resistance. The struggle for Chavez Ravine prepared me for Civil Rights, the Farmworkers Union, my labor work with Bert Corona, and the Chicana Movement. Chavez Ravine was huge for me. It made me the person I am today. So do me a favor, remember Chavez Ravine, eh?"[38]

In addition to its success as a play, Culture Clash's *Chavez Ravine* gave fresh impetus to critical race theory, which was introduced by a number of minority writers and activists to explain the significance of the evictions at Chavez Ravine and their place in the canon of Chicano literature. Seeking to dispel notions of racial inferiority, these writers challenge the assumption that because of their material poverty Chicanos are culturally impoverished. To the contrary, they argue that the play's heroes possess a "multi-faceted portfolio" of cultural assets, including what they call linguistic, familial, and aspirational cultural capital—meaning they all aspire to a better life-style than the one they currently enjoy. If these cultural assets are properly recognized, they suggest, it becomes possible to construct a sympathetic historical narrative about the lives of the residents of Chavez Ravine, instead of seeing their eviction simply as a humiliating defeat.[39]

Yet the authors' treatment of other issues raises doubts about their claim to artistic detachment. The most obvious problem with *Chavez Ravine* is that it distorts the motives that prompted the residents to oppose the CHA's offer of public housing to replace their privately owned homes. In the play, a Russian sheepherder named Uri playfully offers Maria the works of Karl Marx as an appropriate source of inspiration for someone who opposes racial oppression. When challenged, Uri jokingly replaces the name of Marx with that of Mexican revolutionary leader Emiliano Zapata, who supported the collectivist politics Maria espouses.[40]

In reality, however, the residents criticized the CHA's demolition plans not because they accepted the offer of public housing but because they opposed it. In contrast to the play's pro-socialist residents, Manuel Cerda and the other Chavez Ravine residents who spoke at the condemnation hearings on behalf of the community expressed conservative, American values—not radical ones—by verbalizing their desire to retain their existing private homes. They did not favor moving into collectively owned housing. As we saw, by refusing to do so the Chavez Ravine residents also publicly opposed left-wing Mexican civic organizations such as the Asociacion Nacional Mexico-Americana.[41]

The play's treatment of Fernando Valenzuela, and baseball in general, is also somewhat misleading. Late in the play, Maria attempts to persuade some Chavez Ravine old-timers to vote against the pending referendum to ratify the Brooklyn Dodgers' move to Los Angeles, saying, "You guys don't want a baseball stadium up here, do ya?" The old-timers respond by stating they had frequently played baseball in the ravine and had particularly enjoyed beating the local white kids' teams. They imply that, indeed, they did want the Brooklyn Dodgers to move to Southern California. Maria persists in opposing the Dodgers' arrival, only to be told she is missing the point. "Fight or no fight," a character named Lencho tells her, "we all loved baseball."[42]

This exchange does not fully answer lingering questions about to what extent Fernando Valenzuela's arrival in Los Angeles in 1980, and his status as a Mexican hero, helped persuade members of the Mexican community in the Elysian Park area to abandon their hostility toward the Dodgers and to attend games in the stadium. But it does remind us that, with the passage of time, the majority of East L.A.'s Mexican Americans became ardent fans of the team.

Manazar Gamboa's Cultural Legacy

I previously described the early life of Manazar Gamboa in Chavez Ravine, including the childhood pranks that led him into serious crime. In 1954 he was given the first of a series of prison sentences that kept him incarcerated, on and off, for the next seventeen years.[43] The focus here is on his literary legacy.

After he was sent to prison Manazar Gamboa spent the first year or two in the same mood of anger, bitterness, and despair that most of his cellmates shared. Indeed, he might never have written a word if one of his cellmates had not brought a copy of Shakespeare back to his cell from the prison library. Manazar had never shown any aptitude for reading or writing before. But he had always had a lively imagination, and he was afraid that if he remained idle in prison he might be tempted to commit suicide. He also became intrigued by the personalities of some of Shakespeare's macho heroes such as Henry V.

So once he had mastered the intricacies of Shakespeare's Elizabethan language, Gamboa began—slowly and painfully—to write poetry for himself. Much more significant (and also much rarer) he learned how to write both prose and poetry well. After one of his poems was accepted for publication by the editor of a poetry magazine at the University of Colorado, he went from strength to strength. Influenced by Shakespeare's love poetry, Manazar also allowed his humanitarian feelings to surface. He began to express compassion for the empty lives of the prisoners around him:

> "I am one of the lucky ones;
> my mind has wings to fly,
> and I will not wallow in the valley of woe.
> But what of those
> institutionalized men
> walking around inside wasted lives
> acting tough and bad
> because that's what they are told they are."[44]

It was insights such as this that persuaded Gamboa to devote his postprison life to helping minority youth avoid a life of crime by teaching them how to write.

But Manazar's road to moral and intellectual redemption was not without setbacks. In 1971, when he was temporarily out of jail, he and a woman named Roberta, whom he met on Santa Monica Beach, went to a motel together and got high on heroin. The girl overdosed and died in his arms, precipitating the worst crisis in his life. Gamboa panicked, went on a crime spree, and ended up in Soledad Prison, this time with a sentence of ten years to life.[45]

But this crisis not only convinced Manazar to quit drugs for good, it also inspired one of his best poems. "Roberta" offers a chilling look into the deadly consequences of drug addiction. The ordeal he describes also serves as a stand-in for the anguish other Chicano drug addicts from East L.A., including some from Chavez Ravine, felt when beset by similar disasters:

"The needle pierced our arms
dropping liquid snow
in our hungry veins.
Everything went black.
At midnight I woke up.
Roberta was sitting next to me,
her nails deeply buried in my arms,
her eyes as hard as ivory.
I thought I heard the devil laughing
as I shook her stiff body.
I tried to get her to walk,
laid her in a tub with ice.
But she wouldn't come back."[46]

In 1977 Manazar Gamboa was finally released from prison, determined to build a new life for himself. Returning to Los Angeles, he first began working for Beyond Baroque, a small literary institution on the West Side. By now, the Chicano/a literary renaissance was in full swing. After becoming editor of Beyond Baroque's literary magazine, he changed its name to *Obras* (*Works*) and transformed it into a multicultural journal by publishing poems not just by mainstream white authors but by Mexican, African American, and other minority writers.

The mostly white board of editors of Beyond Baroque disliked the new material Gamboa printed in *Obras*, calling it "nothing but street poetry." Manazar refused to back down, so he was fired. But this did not stop him from writing. He moved back to Echo Park and continued to produce poems, plays, and short stories in profusion. He also began visiting schools, juvenile halls, and prisons to give creative writing lessons to disaffected young Chicano/as. Unlike most teachers, he understood the sources of alienation that had driven many of them to shun school. He managed to persuade at least some of them to think about a better future by writing about their hopes and fears, instead of compromising their lives through violence and petty crime.

Gamboa's writing workshops were a success, even as they also helped him to improve his own writing skills. One of his short stories provides such a vivid portrait of his boyhood experiences in Chavez Ravine that it is worth analyzing with some care. In taut and vivid prose, "Ponchi" describes a quarrel that occurred in 1942 over whether the inhabitants of the Bishops Road community should be allowed to break away from the larger barrio of Palo Verde and form a subbarrio of their own. The issue was settled by a fist fight between the chosen champions of each side. As the story proceeds, we learn much that is new about how neighborhood loyalties were established in Chavez Ravine, about the impact of Pachuco culture, and about the role of gender in the barrio.

"Ponchi" opens with Gamboa's alter ego, eight-year-old Meno, eagerly watching the two sides gather near his house on Bishops Road as they wait for the impending contest:

> Today's the day!! I jumped out of bed, grabbed a tortilla from the ice box, and ran down the street as fast as my eight-year-old legs could carry me. . . . Ponchi, a quiet young man of seventeen [who supported the new Bishop subbarrio] stood in the middle of the crowd looking up at Effie Street, where the gente from Palo Verde would be coming down. Everyone on our street—even those who were not on the corner—were standing in front of their homes: older men in work clothes; older women wearing aprons; young women holding babies; and little kids forced to stay close to their mothers.[47]

The military language Gamboa uses to describe how the two sides faced off against each other reminds one of Greeks and Trojans drawn up opposite each other on the plain outside Troy—or, perhaps more aptly, of two street gangs confronting each other in an East L.A. public park. On both sides there is honor to be satisfied. Both male Pachucos and female Pachucas are on the scene, wearing their special garb. So, too, is Ponchi's beautiful girlfriend (Helen of Troy?) who stands to one side, ready to back up her man. Tensions rise as the crowds gather and as each side surveys the other across the physical divide:

> The gente from Bishops Road were lined up in ranks. Our fighters stood up in front: ages 13 to 20. Pachucos, with their long black hair slicked down, ending in tails. Shirts immaculately cleaned and pressed, flair-out drapes pegged tightly at the ankles, and double-soled, cordovan colored shoes. Behind them stood the girls, same age range: pachucas wearing sky-scraper pompadours, thin blouses, mid-thigh skirts or drapes, and sandals strapped over the calf, ancient Greek style. They were ready for anything. Behind them stood the adult males, age twenty to forty. They were the mentors, the veteranos, battle-scarred fighters whose faces showed no quarter. They were entrenched like solid, immovable, granite rocks. Behind them, at their flanks, and, roving about, were us boys, close, but not too close, with dogs sniffing the nervous smell of sweat-stained armpits. Ponchi's girlfriend, Aurora, was there too. Long brown hair, combed down the side of her face. Brown eyes; slender grace: an inner beauty reflecting her gliding movements. She stood a small distance from the others. I couldn't keep my eyes off Ponchi; calm in the midst of it all. Average build, deep, dark, penetrating eyes. An Aztec warrior: a Pachuco Cuautemoc, pinnacle of dignity and honor.

Palo Verde's representatives enter the scene from across the nearby hill, dressed just like their opponents. Each side chooses a fighter to represent it in the coming struggle, incidentally revealing that one of the reasons for the quarrel was the condescending attitude of Palo Verde's *gente* toward the residents of Bishops Road:

> The gente from Palo Verde soon came over the ridge—a whole mob of them. Cocky, sure of their superior numbers, and humorously impressed by the audacity of the people on our street. They formed a semicircle, near the bottom of Effie Street; their ranks formed exactly like ours, but more menacing because their numbers were much greater.
>
> Not addressing anyone in particular, Ralphie, a slender 20-year-old man from Palo Verde with midnight hair and fair complexion, yelled out, "So you vatos want to start your own barrio, huh?"

"That's right," Ponchi answered.

"Are you vatos from Bishop gonna take us all on?" Ralphie asked Ponchi, smiling, turning around, surveying all the gente behind him.

"Sure, Why not?" Ponchi smiled back.

Big Tony from Palo Verde, a dark-complexioned bulk of a young man—wearing his battle uniform: blue mechanic's overalls—stood next to Ralphie.

"Look, man," Big Tony addressed our people, "We don't want you vatos from Bishop to break away. After all, lots of us are primos, familia: it just don't make any sense."

"We thought of all that," Augustin from Bishop, a tall, easy going guy, answered, "But you vatos always act as if you're better than us."

"Well, I don't think it should be all-out war," Big Tony responded.

Because he was respected, not only as a brawler, but as a practical thinker, everyone listened. "Why don't we do this," he yelled out, "You vatos from Bishop pick your champion, and we'll pick ours. If you win, you get your own barrio; if you lose, you still belong to Palo Verde."

"We'll go for that," Augustin replied. The gente from Bishop nodded their heads in agreement.

The Bishops Road crowd chooses Ponchi as their champion; Jaime, Ralphie's younger brother, is chosen to represent Palo Verde. Then the fight, a bare-knuckled affair fought in the dirt on the side of the road, begins. This was no polite boxing match; it was a prolonged and bloody struggle lasting more than half an hour. Emotions peak as Ponchi, having knocked Jaime to the ground several times, is finally declared the winner:

Both fighters stumbled against each other with every punch they threw, but their blows were still damaging.

My small fists were clenched so tightly that my fingernails hurt. Jaime connected two right hooks to the gashes over Ponchi's left eye. Ponchi staggered, but refused to go down. Jaime pounded away relentlessly. Ponchi, bended over from the pain, turned his face away, trying to protect his left eye. Then, with a blow that came all the way from his waist, Ponchi threw a left cross that twisted as it landed on Jaime's jaw. The bone cracked loudly, and Jaime went down, a surprised look on his face.

The crowd screamed in a single, deafening roar! I couldn't even hear my own voice. Suddenly, Ralphie and Big Tony jumped in between them.

"Ya 'stuvo, ese! It's all over," they yelled at Jaime. Jaime stuck out his hand, offering to shake with Ponchi. Ponchi took his hand, and shook it with respect. The crowd let out a deep sigh; they of disappointment; we, of relief."

Honor satisfied, the supporters of each side separate and drift back to their homes. Eight-year-old Meno is delighted at the outcome: "I felt a pride I had never felt before."[48]

During his prison years Manazar had been starved of an emotional life. As "Ponchi" shows, after he was released he turned to, and repeatedly re-examined, his childhood experiences in Chavez Ravine. Their life-giving nourishment remained the main source of his inspiration throughout the rest of his life.

Conclusion

Nostalgia, neighborhood defiance, sentimentality, distortions of reality, and political propaganda were present in most of the artistic productions discussed in this chapter. But all of them, in their different ways, helped preserve the memory of the tragedy at Chavez Ravine for future generations. By using a familiar Chicano vernacular, Mexican American writers also infused the history of the ravine, the evictions, and their long-term consequences with poetic symbols and literary devices that "domesticated" its history with audiences in ways that non-Latino writers were never quite able to do.[49]

Epilogue

What, then, should we make of the hidden history of Chavez Ravine? Some readers may be tempted to conclude, like Frank Wilkinson, that the tragedy could have been avoided if the Los Angeles City Council had kept its promise to build public housing for the residents who had lost their homes. As Wilkinson put it in his memoirs, "If our wishes had been honored, we could have rehoused all the residents comfortably."[1] To reach this conclusion, however, is to indulge in wishful thinking. By late 1951, with the Red Scare at its peak, fear and hatred of anything that smacked of socialism—which was the main reason why the City Council changed its mind about building the Elysian Park project—was too great to permit any such outcome.

Should we, then, blame the great 1950s Red Scare for the tragedy? This argument contains a measure of plausibility. It seems clear that when, on December 26, 1951, the City Council reversed its vote on public housing, it did so not because the housing was any less needed than it had been six months earlier but because continuing to support public housing at a time when it was being repudiated all over the country would have been to commit political suicide.

But as I pointed out earlier, to put the main blame for the sad outcome of the Chavez Ravine affair on the pressures exerted by the Red Scare would be just as misleading as it would be to blame it solely on the political cowardice of L.A.'s city councilmen. In a limited sense, both factors did play a role. But focusing on them alone would be to ignore the other culprits in the affair. Those culprits included the arrogant, top-down behavior of CHA officials, the misguided "expert" belief that razing entire slum neighborhoods was the best way to deal with urban decay, and the blatantly racist attitudes toward poor people of color held by city government and most of L.A.'s white population.

In retrospect, it would clearly have been preferable to destroy only those homes in Chavez Ravine that were beyond repair and to rehabilitate the rest. But such an approach would have been more expensive, more complex, and more difficult to arrange than the existing demolition policy. For most urban planners in the 1950s, including those in Los Angeles, the more limited and humane urban renewal policies that have since been adopted were not yet in the cards. To assume that they were is to read history backward.

Given the greater cost of alternative slum clearance methods, and the rigid thinking of most city planners at the time, the sad fact is that the eviction of the Mexican American residents from Chavez Ravine in the early 1950s was probably inevitable. This is not, of course, to say that the evictions were morally justified. But it is probably the most realistic conclusion that can be reached.

* * *

Whether the events that followed the evictions were also inevitable is more problematic. The decision of the Brooklyn Dodgers to move out west was certainly not inevitable. Walter O'Malley waited until October 7, 1957, the day on which the City Council approved the contract with him, before he made a firm commitment to move his team to Southern California. Even then it took five years and numerous additional setbacks until the Dodgers played their first game at Chavez Ravine.

The role of the courts in the affair was also ambiguous. In his July 1957 decision to reject the Dodger contract, Superior Court Judge Praeger ruled that the city could not justify using public funds to buy land in Chavez Ravine and then donate it to the Dodgers "for the operation of private business." The California Supreme Court reversed that decision. The fact that the contract's provisions "may be of benefit only to the [privately owned] baseball club is immaterial," the justices ruled, "provided that the city receives the benefits which serve legitimate public purposes."[2]

But this ruling ignored the profits that Walter O'Malley was collecting as the private owner of public land. Although the Los Angeles city treasury undoubtedly benefited from the taxes and other fees the Dodgers paid, the profits O'Malley made out of owning Dodger Stadium and selling baseball tickets still accrued to him as the owner of a private business. They remained private assets that he could keep, spend, or reinvest as he thought fit. The ambiguous language the California Supreme Court used in ruling on the public/private issue has never been satisfactorily explained.

When the United States Supreme Court allowed the California court's ruling in favor of the Dodgers to stand, there was no further appeal available. For those who had lost their homes, the only remaining recourse was to sue the City of Los Angeles for the misuse of its power of eminent domain. But, as Councilman Edward G. Roybal pointed out, it was difficult, if not impossible, to see how such a case could have been won.

* * *

What has happened since to those who survived the destruction of the Chavez Ravine barrio and to the politicians and city planners involved in the affair?

First-generation survivors from the 1950s are now few and far between. For some years now, most of those who attend the annual July picnic in Elysian Park to commemorate the tragedy have come from the second or even third generation among the survivors. Nevertheless, there were enough first-generation survivors present at the picnic I attended in July 2012 to make a decent showing. Their leader was seventy-nine-year-old Luis Santillan, who founded Los Desterrados in 1983. Unwilling to forget the fact that his parents were only paid $7,500 for their two houses when he was convinced they were worth a good deal more, Santillan refused to attend baseball games in Dodger Stadium for the rest of his life.[3]

As the sun pierced the morning clouds on the day of the 2012 picnic, Santillan's two sons, Eddie and Louis, greeted their friends and gazed out over the ravine. Unlike their father (but like most of their own generation) they had long since abandoned the family taboo about attending Dodger games. But when they bought tickets they sat as near as they could to third base out of respect for their dad. Their old home still lies beneath it, covered by thousands of tons of dirt.[4]

Occasionally, first-generation survivors from the East contact their family members on the day of the picnic to express solidarity with their former compadres. In July 2012 Oscar Efrente, who grew up in La Loma, phoned his relatives from New York. Oscar ended up in Brooklyn, where the Dodgers once held sway. "When you go to a Dodger game," he reminded the picnickers, "remember, people got uprooted here in Brooklyn, too. They had their souls ripped out."[5]

But most of the oldsters from that era live close by. Alicia Brown, one of the first-generation survivors I interviewed for this book, has lived in Solano Canyon on the eastern edge of Chavez Ravine for more than fifty years. Still trim at seventy-six, Alicia keeps a proprietorial eye on Solano

Canyon Elementary School. The school lost students in the wake of the evictions, but it recovered owing—ironically—to the help it received from Dodger management. Standing in her doorway on a recent afternoon, Alicia glanced up the street to the Catholic church where many of the barrio's Italian minority once worshiped. She told me that the Italians were even angrier about the evictions than the Mexican Americans were.[6]

Another first-generation survivor, Carol Jacques, lives in Mount Washington. Carol is feisty and has devoted her whole life to community activism. Hurting from the loss of her Chavez Ravine home and her seven-year-old brother both at once, in 1970 she channeled her anger into political activism. Carol organized food caravans in support of striking farmworkers in Delano and later took part in the establishment of the Los Angeles County Chicano Employees Association. As chairperson of the Los Angeles Health Alliance advocating for women's health, she also helped overturn the medical establishment's horrendous practice of forcibly sterilizing Latino immigrant women.[7]

* * *

What happened to Howard Holtzendorff, director of the City Housing Authority, and to Frank Wilkinson, his eager young aide who once eyed Chavez Ravine's homeowners uncomprehendingly from the other side of the class divide? For a time after the CHA's notice requiring the residents to move in June 1950, the two men remained friends. Although he was a Republican, Holtzendorff even kept quiet for a time about Wilkinson's Communist connections, calling him a "trustworthy, reliable, and loyal employee."[8]

But after Frank's Communist Party membership was revealed and he was deluged with abuse, Holtzendorff, like many anti-Communist liberals at the time, abandoned his friend to the tender mercies of Senator Tenney's California Un-American Affairs Committee. Holtzendorff's career remained uneventful until 1966, when he was fired for embezzling city funds.[9]

Like thousands of other Red Scare victims, after he lost his job Wilkinson was hounded for years by the FBI. He spent nine months in prison in 1958 for refusing to reveal his political beliefs to the House Un-American Activities Committee. But then he had a lucky break. After his release from jail, Frank crisscrossed the country lecturing to students, liberal activists, and supporters of the First Amendment about the dangers to democracy posed by the suppression of free speech. Thanks partly to Wilkinson's work as a lobbyist, HUAC was abolished by Congress in 1975.[10]

Like many radicals who become respectable in old age, Frank received numerous awards for his civil liberties work, including the Roger Baldwin

Medal of Liberty. When he died at the ripe old age of ninety-one, hundreds of admirers attended his memorial, I among them. "Until his death," stated an obituary, "Frank Wilkinson dedicated his energy and brilliance to defending our basic rights, including challenging the federal government's right to spy on private citizens."[11]

* * *

Long-suffering mayor Fletcher Bowron, who bore the brunt of City Council attacks on public housing during the Red Scare, withdrew from L.A. politics after he lost the 1953 election to Norris Poulson. His defeat signaled the end of the liberal coalition that had ruled the city ever since 1938. It inaugurated a new conservative era at city hall that lasted until African American Tom Bradley was elected mayor of Los Angeles in 1973.

Bowron was not universally admired. Indeed, he was labeled "a little man in a terribly big job" by one of his left-wing critics.[12] But he was an honest politician (something to be proud of at a time when L.A. politics was often scarred by corruption), and he initiated many progressive reforms. Leaving office at age sixty-seven, Bowron briefly resumed his career as a superior court judge, then took up journalism. He died of a heart attack at the Hollywood Receiving Hospital at age eighty-nine.[13]

What about Norris Poulson, Bowron's victorious opponent in the 1953 mayoral election? Poulson was a less sophisticated—and less scrupulous—politician than Bowron. In his memoirs he confessed that in 1956, when negotiations with Walter O'Malley were going badly, "there were strings that . . . had to be pulled."[14] Among the strings he pulled was securing a secret loan from aircraft manufacturer Howard Hughes. Poulson used it in 1957 to prepare an unofficial (and grossly inflated) survey of the land in Chavez Ravine, which he hoped would remove O'Malley's doubts about moving the Dodgers to L.A.

As for Walter O'Malley himself, he had every reason to be satisfied with his decision to move his beloved baseball team from Brooklyn to Southern California. Before he took a backseat to his son Peter in 1970, the Dodgers once more reached the heights of fame and success. Their victory in the 1963 World Series did much to quiet the misgivings that many fiscal conservatives, among them the editor of the *Los Angeles Times*, initially felt about the bargain. On the opening day of the 1965 season the paper proudly asked its readers a rhetorical question: "Can anyone now doubt that we did the right thing in bringing major league baseball to our town?"[15]

* * *

Morally speaking, it was city councilman Edward G. Roybal who came out of the Chavez Ravine affair with the most credit. Roybal can perhaps be faulted for failing to press for a full-scale investigation into the CHA's abuse of its powers of eminent domain. But he emerged from the 1950s with by far the best record of any Los Angeles politician on such issues as minority displacement, police brutality, and opposition to anti-Communist witch-hunting.

In 1962, with his career on the City Council at an end, Roybal was elected to Congress for L.A.'s Twenty-Fifth Congressional District. The first "modern" Mexican American congressman, he worked for immigration reform, championed the interests of Latinos and other racial minorities, and helped to pass the historic Civil Rights Act of 1964. Roybal's East L.A. district included Boyle Heights where, starting in 1949, he helped build the multiracial coalition of Latinos, Jews, and other minority voters that still influences L.A. politics today. Roybal died, a respected elder statesman, in 1999.[16]

* * *

If anyone emerged from the tragedy of Chavez Ravine as a hero, it was poet and writer Manazar Gamboa. In his early years nothing could have seemed more unlikely. Arrested for dealing drugs and stealing cars at the age of fourteen, he ended up spending seventeen years in jail. But as we saw, when in prison Manazar performed the difficult task of conquering his drug addiction without outside help. He also adopted a new moral compass. Released in 1977, Gamboa never broke the law again. Instead, he devoted the rest of his life to helping ex–gang members and minority youth face down their demons by writing about them, instead of manifesting them in violent and risky behavior.

The esteem in which Manazar was held is reflected in the numerous letters of thanks he received from his former students, many of which are preserved in his private papers. Ferdinand Diaz, a forty-one-year-old ex-gangbanger who attended Manazar's writing workshop at the Homeland Cultural Center in Long Beach in 1994, said that he gave up petty crime and became a literature teacher because of what Gamboa taught him. Linda Delmar went further. She said that she only managed to keep her sanity, after her brother was murdered in a gang fight, because of Manazar's classes. "He restored my soul, and gave me a safe place to explore my creativity."[17] In 2010, the building where Gamboa held his classes in Long Beach was renamed in his honor.[18]

In addition to several classrooms, the building contains a performance space where young people and recovering social misfits perform their own plays, read their own poetry, and offer joyful evidence of their artistic creativity.

Figure 31. Manazar Gamboa Community Theater at the Homeland Cultural Center, Long Beach, California. Courtesy Jose Martinez and City of Long Beach.

By the late 1990s, Gamboa's body was showing signs of the heavy toll taken by his former drug habit and his long years in prison. A video of him in his later years shows him climbing up into Chavez Ravine looking in vain for the foundations of his old family home on Bishops Road. Remarkably, as he lay dying in a hospice in Long Beach at the end of the century, he was cared for by two of his former students—Liz Thomas, a nurse who had once attended his poetry workshop, and Carlos Alcanter, a maintenance worker with whom he wrote a short play. Manazar Gamboa died of heart and liver failure on December 13, 2000.[19]

* * *

A final, ironic reminder of the struggle over Chavez Ravine surfaced a couple of weeks after Manazar Gamboa's death. Early in 2001 Linda Delmar, Dixie Swift (Manazar's former boss), and other old friends decided to bury his ashes as near as they could to his childhood home in the defunct subbarrio of Bishop. As they climbed up the same dirt road where, nearly a hundred years earlier, Gamboa's immigrant parents unloaded the possessions they had brought with them from Mexico, they encountered the barbed wire fence that now surrounds the flattened grounds of Dodger Stadium.

Sneaking under the fence, the funeral party was buzzed by an LAPD helicopter. Defying the pilot's angry warnings that they were trespassing on private property, they buried Gamboa's ashes where they had intended.[20] It was a fitting valedictory for a man who, although remembered today by very few save admirers of his poetry, transcended the tragedy of Chavez Ravine by ministering to those who—like his erstwhile self—had once fallen by the wayside.

Notes

Prologue

1. I posed the questions that precede the following excerpts, but the answers are drawn from material authored either by Don Normark or Manazar Gamboa.

Chapter 1

1. Manazar Gamboa, *Memories Around a Bulldozed Barrio* (Los Angeles: Copies Unlimited, 1996), 29.
2. For the tradition of mutualism responsible for shaping this cooperative tradition, see Rosendo Rojas Coria, *Tratado de cooperativismo mexicano* (Mexico: Fondo de Cultura National, 1962).
3. Gamboa, *Memories*, 31–35.
4. For information on Boyle Heights, see George J. Sanchez, "'What's Good for Boyle Heights Is Good for the Jews': Creating Multiculturalism on the Eastside During the 1950s," *American Quarterly* 56, no. 3 (September 2004): 633–62.
5. Don Normark, *Chavez Ravine, 1949: A Los Angeles Story* (San Francisco: Chronicle Books, 1999), 112.
6. Carol Jacques, *Memoirs*, "Carol #3" (March 2013, in author's possession), 1–2.
7. Jacques, *Memoirs*, "Carol #1," 2–3.
8. Leonard Leader, "Los Angeles and the Great Depression" (PhD thesis, UCLA, 1955), 41–44.
9. Normark, *Chavez Ravine*, 43–44.
10. Ibid., 81.
11. Anthony Macias, *Mexican American Mojo: Popular Music, Dance, and Urban Culture in Los Angeles, 1935–1968* (Durham, NC: Duke University Press, 2008), 17.
12. Charlotte Rebecca Negrete White, "Power vs. the People of Chavez Ravine: A Study of Their Determination and Fortitude" (PhD thesis, Claremont Graduate School, 2008), 54–55.

13. Richard Griswold del Castillo, *La Familia, Chicano Families in the Urban Southwest: 1848 to the Present* (South Bend, IN: University of Notre Dame Press, 1984), 100.
14. Gamboa, *Memories*, 47–54.
15. Jacques, *Memoirs*, "Carol #4," 3.
16. Joseph J. La Barbera, "Señor Chavez and His Ravine," *Westways* 54, no. 4 (April 1962): 10.
17. Ibid.
18. Jennifer Palmer-Lacy, "A History of Elysian Park, 'This Delightful Place' Among the Trees and the River" (MA thesis, California State University, Dominguez Hills, 2006), 12.
19. La Barbera, "Señor Chavez," 10–11.
20. Palmer-Lacy, "A History of Elysian Park," 14.
21. William David Estrada, *The Los Angeles Plaza, Sacred and Contested Space* (Austin: University of Texas Press, 2008), 252.
22. Gamboa, *Memories*, 19–21.
23. Jacques, *Memoirs*, "Carol #1," 2–3.
24. George Sanchez, *Becoming Mexican American: Ethnicity, Culture, and Identity in Chicano Los Angeles, 1900–1945* (New York: Oxford University Press, 1993), 65.
25. Mario T. Garcia, *Desert Immigrant: The Mexicans of El Paso, 1880–1920* (New Haven, CT: Yale University Press, 1981), 175–77. See also Charles H. Harris and Louis R. Sadler, "The 'Underside' of the Mexican Revolution: El Paso, 1912," in *The Border and the Revolution*, ed. Harris and Sadler (Los Cruces: New Mexico State University, 1988), 53–70.
26. Gamboa, *Memories*, 19–20.
27. Normark, *Chavez Ravine*, 133.
28. Errol Wayne Stevens, *Radical L.A.: From Coxey's Army to the Watts Riots, 1884–1965* (Norman: University of Oklahoma Press, 2009), chap. 6; Mark Wild, *Street Meeting: Multi-Ethnic Neighborhoods in Early Twentieth Century Los Angeles* (Berkeley: University of California Press, 2005), 154–78.
29. Jacques, *Memoirs*, "Carol #4," 2–3.
30. For the role of the Magonistas in Los Angeles, see W. Dirk Raat, *Revoltosos: Mexico's Rebels in the United States, 1903–1923* (College Station: Texas A&M Press, 2008); and Edward J. Escobar, *Race, Police, and the Making of a Political Identity: Mexican Americans and the Los Angeles Police Department, 1900–1945* (Berkeley: University of California Press, 1999), chap. 4.
31. For the Brown Scare of 1915 to 1917, see Escobar, *Race, Police, and the Making*, 72–76.
32. Lawrence A. Cardozo, *Mexican Emigration to the United States, 1897–1931: Socio-economic Patterns* (Tucson: University of Arizona Press, 1980), chap. 5.
33. Jacques, *Memoirs*, "Carol #3," 4.
34. Ibid.
35. Negrete White, "Power vs. the People," 56.
36. Ibid., 55.
37. Normark, *Chavez Ravine*, 71; Negrete White, "Power vs. the People," 50–51; Eduardo Obregon Pagan, *Murder at the Sleepy Lagoon: Zoot Suits, Race and Riot in Wartime L.A.* (Chapel Hill: University of North Carolina Press, 2003), 149.

38. Sanchez, *Becoming Mexican American*, 110.
39. Edward J. Escobar, *Race, Police, and the Making*, 169.
40. Ibid., 169–70.
41. Gamboa, *Memories*, 31.
42. Kate Braverman, "Poetry, Politics, and the New Chicano: An Interview with Manazar Gamboa," 1988, in Michelle Kholos Brooks Collection of Manazar Gamboa's Papers, Collection 88 (Chicano Studies Research Center, UCLA), box 1, folder 29.
43. Negrete White, "Power vs. the People," 59.
44. William Deverell, *Whitewashed Adobe: The Rise of Los Angeles and the Remaking of Its Mexican Past* (Berkeley: University of California Press, 2004), 148.
45. Ibid., 150. See also Dan L. Mosier, "California Bricks," 2001, http://calbricks.metfirms.com/index.html.
46. Adapted from "1942, to Market," Brooks Collection (Chicano Studies Research Center, UCLA), box 5, folder 3.
47. James Thorpe, *Henry Edwards Huntington: A Biography* (Berkeley: University of California Press, 1994), 186–87.
48. Normark, *Chavez Ravine*, 72.
49. Ricardo Romo, "Mexican Workers in the City: Los Angeles, 1915–1930" (PhD thesis, UCLA, 1975), 141–42.
50. For general studies of Mexicans in Southern California who participated in the harvesting process, see Mark Reisler, *By the Sweat of Their Brow: Mexican Immigrant Labor in the United States, 1900–1940* (Westport, CT: Greenwood Press, 1977), chap. 4; and Cletus E. Daniel, *Bitter Harvest: A History of California Farmworkers, 1870–1941* (Berkeley: University of California Press, 1981).
51. Normark, *Chavez Ravine*, 62.
52. Ibid.
53. Brooks Collection (Chicano Studies Research Center, UCLA), box 4, folder 2.
54. Sanchez, *Becoming Mexican American*, 124–25.
55. Escobar, *Race, Police, and the Making*, 191.
56. Arthur C. Verge, *Paradise Transformed: Los Angeles During the Second World War* (Dubuque, IA: Kendall/Hunt, 1993), chap. 3.
57. Normark, *Chavez Ravine*, 85.
58. Ibid.
59. Ibid., 86–87.
60. Brooks Collection (Chicano Studies Research Center, UCLA), box 4, folder 2.
61. Ibid.
62. John Laslett and Mary Tyler, *The ILGWU in Los Angeles, 1907–1988* (Inglewood, CA: Ten Star Press, 1989), 84–92.
63. Sanchez, *Becoming Mexican American*, 182–93.
64. Jacques, *Memoirs*, "Carol #2," 2–3.
65. Negrete White, "Power vs. the People," 60.
66. Sanchez, *Becoming Mexican American*.
67. *La Opinion*, September 4, 1928, p. 7.
68. Ibid.
69. Ibid.
70. Ibid.
71. *Chavez Ravine Again*, PBS Talkback, April 4, 2010.

Chapter 2

1. William H. Mullins, *The Depression and the West Coast, 1929–1933* (Bloomington: Indiana University Press, 1991), 123–24.
2. George J. Sanchez, *Becoming Mexican American: Ethnicity, Culture and Identity in Chicano Los Angeles, 1900–1945* (New York: Oxford University Press, 1993), 213; Zaragosa Vargas, *Labor Rights Are Civil Rights: Mexican Workers in Twentieth Century America* (Princeton, NJ: Princeton University Press, 2005), 40–45.
3. Sanchez, *Becoming Mexican American*, 211.
4. *Echo Park Advertiser*, March 12, 1934, held in archives of Echo Park Historical Society, Los Angeles.
5. Ibid.
6. Ibid.
7. Ibid., 212.
8. Charlotte Rebecca Negrete White, "Power vs. the People of Chavez Ravine: A Study of Their Determination and Fortitude" (PhD thesis, Claremont Graduate University, 2008), 70.
9. Ibid.
10. Adapted from Manazar Gamboa, "1942, to Market," in Michelle Kholos Brooks Collection of Manazar Gamboa Papers, Collection 88 (Chicano Studies Research Center, UCLA), box 5, folder 3.
11. Ibid.
12. Manazar Gamboa, *Memories Around a Bulldozed Barrio* (Los Angeles: Copies Unlimited, 1996), 36–37.
13. Edward J. Escobar, *Race, Police, and the Making of a Political Identity: Mexican Americans and the Los Angeles Police Department, 1900–1945* (Berkeley: University of California Press, 1999), 89.
14. Sanchez, *Becoming Mexican American*, 89. See also Abraham Hoffman, *Unwanted Mexican Americans in the Great Depression: Repatriation Pressures, 1929–1939* (Tucson: University of Arizona Press, 1974).
15. Negrete White, "Power vs. the People," 69.
16. Ibid.
17. *Echo Park Advertiser*, September 9, 1932.
18. Hoffman, *Unwanted Mexican Americans*, chap. 3.
19. Sanchez, *Becoming Mexican American*, 89.
20. Adapted from Manazar Gamboa, "Downtown L.A., 1942," Brooks Collection (Chicano Studies Research Center, UCLA), box 5, folder 3.
21. Eduardo Obregon Pagan, *Murder at the Sleepy Lagoon: Zoot Suits, Race and Riot in Wartime L.A.* (Chapel Hill: University of North Carolina Press, 2003), 153.
22. Paul Morin, *Among the Valiant: Mexican-Americans in WWII and Korea* (Los Angeles: Borden, 1963), 24.
23. Gamboa, "Notes from the L.A. Barrio: 1942 Armed Forces" (Brooks Collection), box 5, folder 3.
24. Ibid.
25. Escobar, *Race, Police, and the Making*, 200–2.
26. Ibid.
27. Hoffman, *Unwanted Mexican Americans*, 41–44.

28. Don Parson, *Making a Better World: Public Housing, the Red Scare, and the Direction of Modern Los Angeles* (Minneapolis: University of Minnesota Press, 2005), 75–84.

29. Negrete White, "Power vs. the People," 73.

30. Vargas, *Labor Rights Are Civil Rights*, 204–5. In her essay "Rosita the Riveter," in Maggie Rivas-Rodriquez's edited volume on the role of Mexican Americans in World War II, Naomi Quinones examines the lives of ten Mexican American women who worked in the aircraft industry during the war. She describes their role in much the same optimistic and forward-looking terms that Sherna Gluck used in her earlier book, *Rosie the Riveter Revisited* (1987). None of the women Quinones examined, however, came from Chavez Ravine. See Naomi Quinones, "Rosita the Riveter, Welding Tradition with Wartime Transformations," in *Mexicans and World War II*, ed. Rivas-Rodriguez (Austin: University of Texas Press, 2005), chap. 10.

31. Negrete White, "Power vs. the People," 73.

32. Ibid.

33. U.S. Bureau of the Census, *Sixteenth Census of U.S. Population and Housing (Tract 67)* (Washington, DC: Government Printing Office, 1942), 4, 15.

34. Pagan, *Murder at the Sleepy Lagoon*, 6–12, 147–48.

35. Pagan, *Murder at the Sleepy Lagoon*, chap. 3. See also Alice McGrath, "The Education of Alice McGrath" (oral history transcript, interview by Michael Balter, 1987, Charles Young Research Library, UCLA). See also Luis J. Alvarez, *The Power of the Zoot: Youth Culture and Resistance During World War II* (Berkeley: University of California Press, 2008).

36. Eduardo Obregon Pagan, "Los Angeles Politics and the Zoot Suit Riots, 1943," *Social Science History* 24, no. 1 (Spring 2000): 233.

37. Ibid., 176–77.

38. Pagan, *Murder at the Sleepy Lagoon*, 119–20.

39. Ibid.

40. Adapted from Gamboa, "D2 Downtown LA: 1943" (Brooks Collection), box 5, folder 1.

41. Pagan, *Murder at the Sleepy Lagoon*, 119–20.

42. Parson, *Making a Better World*, 9–10.

43. Ibid.

44. Ibid.

45. Norman Klein, *The History of Forgetting: Los Angeles and the Erasure of Memory* (London: Verso, 2008), 27.

46. Parson, *Making a Better World*, 18, 26.

47. Ibid., 144 (italics added).

48. Ibid.

49. Ibid.

50. Ibid.

51. Ibid., 39.

52. Charles B. Spaulding, "Housing Problems of Minority Groups in Los Angeles County," *Annals of Political and Social Science* 248 (November, 1946), 14–18.

53. California Reconstruction Commission (California State Printing Office, 1946), 81.

54. Ronald William Lopez, "The Battle for Chavez Ravine: Public Policy and Chicano Community Resistance in Post War Los Angeles, 1945–1962" (PhD thesis, University of California at Berkeley, 1999), 59–61.
55. Parson, *Making a Better World*, 79.
56. Ibid., 85.
57. Ibid.
58. Ibid., 87–88.
59. Ibid., 90–91.
60. James Thomas Keen, *Fritz Burns and the Development of Los Angeles: The Biography of a Community Developer and Philanthropist* (Los Angeles: Loyola Marymount University, 2001), chaps. 4–5.
61. Parson, *Making a Better World*, 92.
62. Ibid., 98–102. See also Marlin C. Davies, *Housing Reform During the Truman Administration* (New York: Russell Sage Foundation, 1951) and Alexander von Hoffman, "A Study in Contradictions: The Origins and Legacy of the Housing Act of 1949," *Housing Policy Debate* 2, no. 2 (Washington DC: Fannie May Foundation, 2000): 299–326.
63. Parson, *Making a Better World*, 100.
64. Ibid.
65. Ibid. See also Tom Sitton, *Los Angeles Transformed: Fletcher Bowron's Urban Reform Revival l, 1938–1950* (Albuquerque: University of New Mexico Press, 2005), chap. 5.

Chapter 3

1. Robert Alexander and Drayton S. Bryant, *Rebuilding a City: A Study of Redevelopment Problems in Los Angeles* (Los Angeles: Haynes Foundation, 1951), vii, 47–54; Don Parson, *Making a Better World: Public Housing, the Red Scare, and the Direction of Modern Los Angeles* (Minneapolis: University of Minnesota Press, 2005), 165–67.
2. Parson, *Making a Better World*, 167.
3. Ibid., 165.
4. Eugene J. Grigsby, *An Assessment of Fifty Years of Redevelopment in Los Angeles* (Los Angeles: UCLA Advanced Policy Institute, 1998), 14–15.
5. Ronald W. Lopez, "Community Resistance and Conditional Patriotism in Cold War Los Angeles: The Battle for Chavez Ravine," *Latino Studies* 7, no. 4 (2009): 165.
6. Parson, *Making a Better World*, 166.
7. Alexander and Bryant, *Rebuilding a City*, 60.
8. Parson, *Making a Better World*, 168–69.
9. Robert E. Alexander, "Oral History," 1964, Special Collections, Charles Young Research Library, UCLA, 334–35; Thomas Hines, "Housing, Baseball, and Creeping Socialism: The Battle of Chavez Ravine, 1949–1959," *Journal of Urban History* 8, no. 2 (February 1982): 130–37.
10. Raymond A. Mohl, "Shifting Patterns of American Urban Policy Since 1900," in *Urban Policy in Twentieth Century America*, ed. Arnold R. Hirsch and Raymond Mohl (New Brunswick, NJ: Rutgers University Press, 1993), 31–32. See also Jeanne R. Lowe,

Cities in a Race with Time: Progress and Poverty in America's Renewing Cities (New York: Random House, 1957), chap. 7.

11. Alexander, "Oral History," 336.

12. Parson, *Making a Better World*, 168.

13. Hines, "Housing, Baseball, and Creeping Socialism," 130. See also Jane Jacobs, *The Death and Life of American Cities* (New York: Random House, 1993), 354.

14. "Mosier M. Meyer et al v. Housing Authority of the City of Los Angeles," 1952, Frank Wilkinson Collection, Southern California Library for Social Studies and Research, series 3, box 1, folder 3, 487.

15. Ibid., 485.

16. Ibid.

17. Charlotte Negrete White, "Power vs. the People of Chavez Ravine: A Study of Their Determination and Fortitude" (PhD thesis, Claremont Graduate University, 2008), 106.

18. Frank Wilkinson, "Oral History," Special Collections, Charles Young Research Library, UCLA, 827.

19. Ronald William Lopez, "The Battle for Chavez Ravine: Public Policy and Community Response in Postwar Los Angeles, 1945–1962" (PhD thesis, University of California, Berkeley, 1999), 73.

20. Wilkinson, "Oral History," 821.

21. Carol Jacques, *Memoirs*, "Carol #4" (March 2013, in author's possession), 2.

22. Wilkinson, "Oral History," 780–816.

23. Ibid.

24. Lopez, "Battle for Chavez Ravine," 74–79.

25. Negrete White, "Power vs. the People," 104.

26. Ibid.

27. Robert Sherrill, *First Amendment Felon: The Story of Frank Wilkinson* (New York: Nation Books, 2005), 74.

28. Wilkinson, "Oral History," 828–29.

29. The fact that sources do not show the presence of Communist Party members in Chavez Ravine in the early 1950s does not mean there were none, merely that their presence has not yet been definitively established. In her recent memoir, Carol Jacques mentions a story she heard from her stepfather to the effect that Magdaleno Contreras, who was a friend of her grandfather, once interrupted a sermon being preached by Father Tomas in Santo Nino Church about the evils of communism by announcing that he was himself a Communist. This secondhand anecdote is not conclusive, but it suggests that more research needs to be done into the matter. It is possible, also, that some of the survivors of the Edendale Commune, which ran for two years from 1914 to 1916 in Silverlake and was established by Mexican radicals who supported the Magon brothers (leaders of the Partido Liberal Mexicano), later became members of the Communist Party in Chavez Ravine. See Jacques, "Carol #5," 2; Daniel Hurewitz, *Bohemian Los Angeles and the Making of Modern Politics* (Berkeley: University of California Press, 2007), 154–77, 203–25; Miguel Velasco, *Del Magonismo de la fundacion de la CTM: Apuntes de un Militante del Movimiento Obrero* (Mexico City: Ediotiones de Cultura Popular, 1990); http://en.wikipedia.org/wiki/Edendale_Los_Angeles.

30. For the role of Alice McGrath and the Sleepy Lagoon Defense Committee, see Eduardo Obregon Pagan, *Murder at the Sleepy Lagoon: Zoot Suits, Race, and Riot in Wartime L.A.* (Chapel Hill: University of North Carolina Press, 2003), chap. 9.
31. Michelle Kholos Brooks Collection of Manazar Gamboa Papers, Collection 88 (Chicano Studies Research Center, UCLA), box 1, folder 1.
32. Ibid.
33. Don Normark, *Chavez Ravine, 1949: A Los Angeles Story* (San Francisco: Chronicle Books, 1999), 133.
34. Ibid.
35. Lopez, "Community Resistance," 461.
36. Tom Sitton, *Los Angeles Transformed: Fletcher Bowron's Urban Reform Revival, 1938–1953* (Albuquerque: University of New Mexico Press, 2005), 148–57.
37. Don Parson, "Organized Labor and the Housing Question: Public Policy, Suburbanization, and Urban Renewal," *Science and Society* 1 (1984), 75–76.
38. Sitton, *Los Angeles Transformed*, 166; Wilkinson, "Oral History," 861–62.
39. Lopez, "Community Resistance," 461; James Thomas Keane, *Fritz Burns and the Development of Los Angeles* (Los Angeles: Historical Society of Southern California, 2001), 174–75.
40. Lopez, "Community Resistance," 464.
41. Ibid., 464–65.
42. Ibid., 465.
43. Ibid., 461.
44. Emilio Consuelo, *The Evolution of the Mexican State* (Austin: University of Texas Press, 1996), chap. 2.
45. Mario T. Garcia, *Mexican Americans: Leadership, Ideology, & Identity, 1930–1950* (New Haven, CT: Yale University Press, 1989), 176.
46. Lopez, "Community Resistance," 467.
47. Ibid.
48. Becky Nicolaides, *My Blue Heaven: Life and Politics in the Working Class Suburbs of Los Angeles* (Chicago: University of Chicago Press, 2002), 27.
49. Ibid.
50. Lopez, "Battle for Chavez Ravine," 85.
51. Ibid., 85–86.
52. Ibid.
53. Lopez, "Community Resistance," 469.
54. Ibid.
55. Lopez, "Battle for Chavez Ravine," 89.
56. Negrete White, "Power vs. the People," 102.
57. Ibid.
58. Newmark, *Chavez Ravine*, 53.
59. "Testimonies," *Los Angeles Times*, September 4, 1981.
60. Newmark, *Chavez Ravine*, 133.
61. *Torch Reporter*, September 1957. Excerpt included in Edward Roybal Collection, 847 (Special Collections, Charles Young Research Library, UCLA), box 6, folder 6.
62. Ibid.
63. *Torch Reporter*, October 1957. Roybal Collection, box 6, folder 6.

64. Ibid.
65. Ibid.

Chapter 4

1. Don Parson, *Making a Better World: Public Housing, the Red Scare, and the Direction of Modern Los Angeles* (Minneapolis: University of Minnesota Press, 2005), 110–17.

2. Dorothy Healey and Maurice Isserman, *California Red: A Life in the American Communist Party* (Urbana: University of Illinois Press, 1993), 104–9.

3. For HUAC's hearings on the movie industry and the blacklisting of the Hollywood Ten, see Larry Ceplair and Steven Englund, *The Inquisition in Hollywood: Politics in the Film Industry, 1930–1960* (Garden City, NY: Doubleday, 1980).

4. Karl M. Schmidt, *Henry A. Wallace: Quixotic Crusader* (Syracuse, NY: Syracuse University Press, 1960); Alonzo L. Hamby, *Beyond the New Deal: Harry Truman and American Liberalism* (New York: Columbia University Press, 1973), chap. 17.

5. For a discussion of red-baiting in L.A. in the early twentieth century, see Robert Gottlieb and Irene Wolt, *Thinking Big: The Story of the Los Angeles Times, Its Publishers and Their Influence on Southern California* (New York: G. P. Putnam's Sons, 1977), chaps. 4–6.

6. Hamby, *Beyond the New Deal*, 415–33. For an analysis of the influence of the military-industrial complex in Orange County, see Lisa McGirr, *Suburban Warriors: The Origins of the New American Right* (Princeton, NJ: Princeton University Press, 2001).

7. James Thomas Keane, *Fritz Burns and the Development of Los Angeles* (Los Angeles: Historical Society of Southern California, 2001), 179.

8. Parson, *Making a Better World*, 107.

9. Don Parson, "The Decline of Public Housing and the Politics of the Red Scare: The Significance of the Los Angeles Public Housing War," *Journal of Urban History* 33, no. 3 (March 2007): 409.

10. Parson, *Making a Better World*, 104–6.

11. Don Parson, "'The Darling of the Neo-Fascists': The Bombastic Political Career of Councilman Edward Davenport," *Southern California Quarterly* 80, no. 4 (Winter 1999): 477–78.

12. *Los Angeles Times*, December 4, 1951.

13. Parson, *Making a Better World*, 106–7.

14. Ibid., 109.

15. Ibid., 114; Tom Sitton, *Los Angeles Transformed: Fletcher Bowron's Urban Reform Revival, 1938–1953* (Albuquerque: University of New Mexico Press, 2005), 171–72.

16. *Los Angeles Times*, January 7, 2001.

17. Thomas Hines, "Housing, Baseball, and Creeping Socialism: The Battle of Chavez Ravine, 1949–1959," *Journal of Urban History* 8, no. 2 (February 1982): 130–37.

18. Parson, *Making a Better World*, 118.

19. *Los Angeles Times*, August 30, 1952.

20. Edward Barrett, *The Tenney Committee: Legislative Investigation of Subversive Activities in California* (Ithaca, NY: Cornell University Press, 1951), 95.

21. Senate of California, *Seventh Report of the Senate Fact-Finding Committee on Un-American Activities* (Sacramento: California Senate Printing Office, 1953), 59–60.

22. Stanley Moffatt to Howard L. Holtzendorff, September 1, 1952, Frank Wilkinson Collection, Southern California Library for Social Studies and Research, series 3, box 1, folder 1.

23. Parson, *Making a Better World*, 121–22.

24. Elaine Woo, "Jean Wilkinson dies at 96; one of the first Los Angeles teachers to be fired during Red Scare," *Los Angeles Times*, January 6, 2011.

25. Ibid.

26. Eve Goldberg, "Frank Wilkinson and the Battle of Chavez Ravine," *Magazine Americana*, November 19, 2010, 1.

27. Ibid.; Robert Sherrill, *First Amendment Felon: The Story of Frank Wilkinson* (New York: Nation Books, 2005), 96–97.

28. Sitton, *Los Angeles Transformed*, 168.

29. Parson, *Making a Better World*, 121.

30. Ibid.

31. For the persecution of homosexuals in Los Angeles in the 1950s, see Daniel Hurewitz, *Bohemian Los Angeles and the Making of Modern Politics* (Berkeley: University of California Press, 2007), chaps. 3–5.

32. Parson, *Making a Better World*, 120.

33. Ibid.

34. Senate of California, *Seventh Report*, 61.

35. Parson, "The Darling of the Town's Neo-Fascists," 478.

36. Ronald Lopez, "The Battle for Chavez Ravine: Public Policy and Chicano Community Resistance in Post War Los Angeles, 1945–1962" (PhD thesis, University of California at Berkeley, 1999), 118.

37. Ibid., 119.

38. Ibid.

39. Sherrill, *First Amendment Felon*, chaps. 4–9.

40. Edward Ross Roybal Papers, Collection 847, Department of Special Collections, Charles Young Research Library, UCLA, box 32, folder 3.

41. Goldberg, "Frank Wilkinson," 1.

42. I searched through various collections of Wilkinson's papers for evidence of his opinions and did not find any evidence of personal conversations with individual homeowners in Chavez Ravine. His life and work are extensively documented in Sherrill, *First Amendment Felon*; Goldberg, "Frank Wilkinson"; Parson, *Making a Better World*; Lopez, "The Battle for Chavez Ravine"; Wilkinson's "Oral History" in Special Collections at the Charles H. Young Research Library at UCLA; and his personal collection of papers at the Southern California Library for Social Studies and Research.

43. Goldberg, "Frank Wilkinson," 1.

44. Sherrill, *First Amendment Felon*, chaps. 1–2.

45. Goldberg, "Frank Wilkinson," 2.

46. Norris Poulson, "Oral History," Special Collections, Charles Young Research Library, UCLA, 155.

47. Parson, *Making a Better World*, 127; Gottlieb and Wolt, *Thinking Big*, 263.
48. Gottlieb and Wolt, *Thinking Big*, 264.
49. Parson, *Making a Better World*, 127.
50. Sitton, *Los Angeles Transformed*, 185.
51. Don Parson, "Los Angeles' Headline-Happy Public Housing War," *Southern California Quarterly* 65, no. 3 (September 1983): 271.
52. Parson, *Making a Better World*, 128.
53. Ibid., 130.
54. Parson, "Los Angeles' Headline-Happy," 272.
55. William G. Bonelli, *Billion Dollar Blackjack* (Beverly Hills, CA: Civic Research Press, 1954), 213.
56. Parson, *Making a Better World*, 131.
57. Ibid.
58. Parson, *Making a Better World*, 132.
59. Keane, *Fritz B. Burns and the Development of Los Angeles*, 182–83.
60. Poulson, "Oral History," 218.
61. Lopez, "The Battle for Chavez Ravine," 132.
62. Don Normark, *Chavez Ravine, 1949: A Los Angeles Story* (San Francisco: Chronicle Books, 1999), 21.
63. Parson, *Making a Better World*, 132.
64. Ibid.; Lopez, "The Battle for Chavez Ravine," 132–33. For efforts by civil rights activists to desegregate the Los Angeles housing market, see Thomas J. Sugrue, *Sweet Land of Liberty: The Forgotten Struggle for Civil Rights in the North* (New York: Random House, 2008), 241–47.
65. Gary S. Henderson, "Los Angeles and the Dodger War, 1957–1962," *Southern California Quarterly* 62, no. 3 (Fall 1980): 262; Gottlieb and Wolt, *Thinking Big*, chap. 19.
66. Henderson, "Los Angeles and the Dodger War," 261. See also Eric Avila, *Popular Culture in the Age of White Flight: Fear and Fantasy in Suburban Los Angeles* (Berkeley: University of California Press, 2004), 156–61.
67. "Wyman's Historic Effort to Bring Dodgers to Los Angeles," http://www.walteromalley.com/feat_wyman_index.php.
68. Ibid.
69. Lopez, "The Battle for Chavez Ravine," 160 (italics added). Another supporter of the conspiracy theory is Rodolfo F. Acuna. See his *A Community Under Siege: A Chronicle of Chicanos East of the Los Angeles River, 1945–1975* (Los Angeles: UCLA Chicano Studies Research Center Publications, Monograph no. 11, 1984), 58–60.
70. Lopez, "The Battle for Chavez Ravine," 160–62.
71. Ibid., 161.
72. Poulson, "Oral History," 341–42.
73. The best accounts of the negotiations between L.A. and Walter O'Malley are contained in Henderson, "Los Angeles and the Dodger War," and in Neil J. Sullivan, *The Dodgers Move West* (New York: Oxford University Press, 1987), chaps. 5–7.
74. For an account of this event, see Manuel Garcia Griego, *The Importation of Contract Laborers to the United States, 1942–1964: Antecedents, Operation, and Legacy* (La Jolla: University of California Press, 1980), 43–52.
75. Lopez, "The Battle for Chavez Ravine," 340–43.

Chapter 5

1. Neil J. Sullivan, *The Dodgers Move West* (New York: Oxford University Press, 1987), 32–57. For more on O'Malley's career and business aims, see Michael D'Antonio, *Forever Blue: The True Story of Walter O'Malley, Baseball's Most Controversial Owner, and the Dodgers of Brooklyn and Los Angeles* (New York: Riverhead Books, 2009).
2. Sullivan, *The Dodgers*, 31–40.
3. For a study of Robert Moses's influence on the development of New York, see Hilary Balon and Kenneth T. Jackson, eds., *Robert Moses and the Modern City: The Transformation of New York* (New York: W. W. Norton, 2007).
4. Sullivan, *The Dodgers*, 48; Cary S. Henderson, "Los Angeles and the Dodger War," *Southern California Quarterly* 62, no. 3 (Fall 1980): 261–89.
5. Sullivan, *The Dodgers*, 48.
6. Ibid.
7. Ibid., 71–75.
8. Eric Avila, *Popular Culture in the Age of White Flight: Fear and Fantasy in Suburban Los Angeles* (Berkeley: University of California Press, 2004), 160.
9. Sullivan, *The Dodgers*, 77–78.
10. Henderson, "Los Angeles and the Dodger War," 264.
11. Sullivan, *The Dodgers*, 78–80.
12. Don Parson, *Making a Better World: Public Housing, the Red Scare, and the Direction of Modern Los Angeles* (Minneapolis: University of Minnesota Press, 2005), 172.
13. Ibid., 94–95.
14. D'Antonio, *Forever Blue*, 205.
15. Ibid., 206.
16. Ibid., 219–23.
17. Norris Poulson, "Oral History," 1969, Special Collections, Charles Young Research Library, UCLA, 343.
18. Henderson, "Los Angeles and the Dodger War," 273–74.
19. Ibid., 274.
20. Ibid.
21. Avila, *Popular Culture*, 164–65.
22. *New York Times*, October 18, 1958.
23. Avila, *Popular Culture*, 165–66.
24. Henderson, "Los Angeles and the Dodger War," 275–76.
25. Ibid.
26. Avila, *Popular Culture*, 166.
27. Parson, *Making a Better World*, 173–74.
28. Ibid.
29. Ronald Lopez, "The Battle for Chavez Ravine: Public Policy and Chicano Community Resistance in Post War Los Angeles, 1945–1962" (PhD thesis, University of California at Berkeley, 1999), 169.
30. Ibid.
31. Ibid.
32. Parson, *Making a Better World*, 174.
33. Ibid.

34. Ibid.
35. Ibid., 175.
36. Some of these Mexican baseball clubs were recruited from the players' places of work, like "Los Chorizeros," whose members worked in an East L.A. sausage factory. See Francisco E. Balderrama and Richard A. Santillan, "Los Chorizeros: The New York Yankees of East Los Angeles and the Reclaiming of Mexican American Baseball," *Baseball History* 1, no. 2 (Summer 1987): 47–49.
37. *Los Angeles Times*, April 6, 2006.
38. Balderrama and Santillan, "Los Chorizeros," 47–49.
39. *Los Angeles Times*, April 6, 2006.
40. Lopez, "The Battle for Chavez Ravine," 168–69.
41. Parson, *Making a Better World*, 175.
42. Lopez, "The Battle for Chavez Ravine," 170–71.
43. The best general accounts of the final evictions are given in Lopez, "The Battle for Chavez Ravine," 169–78, and Avila, *Popular Culture*, 166–70.
44. Lopez, "The Battle for Chavez Ravine," 172.
45. Ibid., 173.
46. Ibid., 173–74.
47. Ibid., 174.
48. Avila, *Popular Culture*, 167.
49. Lopez, "The Battle for Chavez Ravine," 176.
50. Avila, *Popular Culture*, 167.
51. Lopez, "The Battle for Chavez Ravine," 176.
52. Ibid., 177.
53. Avila, *Popular Culture*, 168.
54. Parson also notes that during the 1930s and 1940s organized labor united white, black, and Mexican workers in support of public housing and other reforms sanctioned by the New Deal. During the conservative 1950s, however, many white trade unionists, especially well-paid craftsmen in the building trades, abandoned the cause of public housing after they moved to the L.A. suburbs. This left poor, inner-city, minority workers as its main champions. Parson argues that this division within the labor movement was one of the main reasons why support for public housing collapsed during the fifties. See Don Parson, "Organized Labor and the Housing Question: Public Housing, Suburbanization, and Urban Renewal," *Environment and Planning* 1 (1984): 75–86.
55. Avila, *Popular Culture*, 169.
56. Lopez, "The Battle for Chavez Ravine," 179–91.
57. Ibid., 181.
58. Ibid., 182.
59. Ibid., 181.
60. Ibid., 182.
61. Ibid., 187–88.
62. *Los Angeles Times*, May 12, 1959.
63. Lopez, "The Battle for Chavez Ravine," 190.
64. *Torch Reporter*, June 1, 1959.
65. Ibid.

66. Parson, *Making a Better World*, 176.
67. Lopez, "The Battle for Chavez Ravine," 197.

Chapter 6

1. Walter O'Malley: The Official Website, "Opening Day: April 10, 1962," http://walteromalley.com/stad_open_index.php.
2. Eric Avila, *Popular Culture in the Age of White Flight: Fear and Fantasy in Suburban Los Angeles* (Berkeley: University of California Press, 2004), 171.
3. Michael D'Antonio, *Forever Blue: The True Story of Walter O'Malley, Baseball's Most Controversial Owner, and the Dodgers of Brooklyn and Los Angeles* (New York: Riverhead Books, 2009), 294.
4. See, e.g., *Torch Reporter*, November 8, 1959, Michelle Kholos Brooks Collection of Manazar Gamboa's Papers, Collection 88 (Chicano Studies Research Center, UCLA), box 1, folder 28.
5. Walter O'Malley, "Building O'Malley's Dream Stadium," http://walteromalley.com/stad_hist_page6.php.
6. Walter O'Malley, "Biography," http://walteromalley.com/biog_short_page14.php?lang=eng.
7. Walter O'Malley, "Biography," http://walteromalley.com/biog_short_page12.php?lang=eng.
8. Walter O'Malley, "Biography," http://walteromalley.com/biog_short_page13.php?leng-eng.
9. Samuel O. Regalado, *Viva Baseball! Latin Major Leaguers and Their Special Hunger* (Urbana: University of Illinois Press, 1998), 170.
10. Regalado, *Viva Baseball*, 172–82; Neil J. Sullivan, *The Dodgers Move West* (New York: Oxford University Press, 1987), 211–14.
11. Avila, *Popular Culture*, 176.
12. http://walteromalley.com.
13. *Si Vault*, August 29, 2001.
14. *Chavez Ravine*, PBS Talkback, January 4, 1979.
15. Ibid., August 5, 1984.
16. Ibid., June 9, 1986.
17. Ibid., July 8–9, 1986.
18. Ibid., July 17, 1986.
19. Ibid.
20. *Los Angeles Business Journal*, May 25, 1985.
21. Don Normark, *Chavez Ravine, 1949: A Los Angeles Story* (San Francisco: Chronicle Books, 1999), 127.
22. Interview by author with Alicia Brown, February 20, 2013.
23. *Los Angeles Times*, October 29, 2000.
24. Ibid.
25. *Los Angeles Times*, May 9, 2011.
26. For a general study of Latino deterritorialization, see Albert Camarillo, *Chicanos in a Changing Society: From Mexican Pueblos to American Barrios in Santa Barbara and Southern California, 1848–1930* (Cambridge, MA: Harvard University Press, 1979).

27. See, e.g., "Private Corporations Conspire to Destroy Barrio," *Eastside Sun*, May 2, 1968.

28. *Chavez Ravine Remembered*, PBS Talkback, June 19, 2008.

29. Rodolfo Acuna, *Occupied America: A History of Chicano Los Angeles* (New York: Harper and Row, 1988).

30. Ibid., chap. 4.

31. William David Estrada, *The Los Angeles Plaza: Sacred and Contested Space* (Austin: University of Texas Press, 2008), 219.

32. Scott Kurashige, *The Shifting Grounds of Race: Blacks and Japanese Americans in the Making of the Multicultural Los Angeles* (Princeton, NJ: Princeton University Press, 2008), chap. 7.

33. Raul Homero Villa, *Barrio-Logos, Space, and Place in Urban Chicano Literature and Culture* (Austin: University of Texas Press, 2000), 8.

34. For the development of Boyle Heights, see George A. Sanchez, "'What's Good for Boyle Heights Is Good for the Jews': Creating Multiracialism on the Eastside During the 1950s," *American Quarterly* 56, no. 3 (September 2004): 633–61.

35. Villa, *Barrio-Logos, Space, and Place*, 45–46.

36. Edward J. Escobar, *Race, Police, and the Making of a Political Identity: Mexican Americans and the Los Angeles Police Department, 1990–1945* (Berkeley: University of California Press, 1999), 42–49. For the Magonistas, see W. Dirk Raal, *Revoltosos: Mexico's Rebels in the United States, 1903–1923* (College Station: Texas A & M University Press, 1981).

37. Estrada, *The Los Angeles Plaza*, 8.

38. Ibid., chap. 6.

39. Rosalio Munoz, "Our Moving Barrio: Why?" *La Gente*, April 5, 1973, 5.

40. Mario Barrera and Geraldo Vialpando, eds., *Action Research: In Defense of the Barrio* (Los Angeles: Aztlan, 1974), 5.

41. Munoz, "Our Moving Barrio," 5.

42. Don Parson, *Making a Better World: Public Housing, the Red Scare, and the Direction of Modern Los Angeles* (Minneapolis: University of Minnesota Press, 2005), chap. 5.

43. Guillermo V. Flores, "Race and Culture in the Internal Colony: Keeping the Chicano in His Place," in *Structures of Dependency*, ed. Frank Bonillo and Robert Girling (Palo Alto, CA: Nairobi Bookstore, 1973), 198.

44. Parson, *Making a Better World*, 147.

45. Ibid., 151–52.

46. Ibid., 150.

47. Community Redevelopment Agency, *Bunker Hill Urban Renewal Project: A History and Plans for Completion* (Los Angeles: Community Redevelopment Agency, 2012).

48. Parson, *Making a Better World*, 152.

49. Mike Davis, *City of Quartz: Excavating the Future in Los Angeles* (New York: Verso, 1990), 230.

50. Ibid., 232–33.

51. Peter F. Eisinger, "Black Mayors and the Politics of Racial Economic Advancement" in *Culture, Ethnicity, and Identity: Current Issues in Research*, ed. William C. McReady (New York: Academic Press, 1983), 95–109; Mike Davis, "'Chinatown Part

Two'? The Internationalization of Downtown Los Angeles," *New Left Review*, no. 164 (July/August 1987): 1–24.

52. *Eastside Sun*, December 4, 1998.

53. Ibid.

54. David Geffner, "Inevitably, Renewal Leads to Gentrification (Who Owns Downtown?)," *Los Angeles Business Journal* 28 (March 2005): 81.

Chapter 7

1. Frank Wilkinson, "Oral History," Special Collections, Charles Young Research Library, UCLA, 341.

2. "There's Nothing Sentimental About Your Cash Register," Architecture and Urban Planning Collection, 1880 (Special Collections, Charles Young Research Library, UCLA), box 10, folder 14.

3. On the complacency of city planning officials, see Herbert J. Gans, "The Failure of Urban Renewal," in *Urban Renewal: The Record and the Controversy*, ed. James Q. Wilson (Cambridge: MIT Press, 1966), 537–57.

4. Don Parson, *Making a Better World: Public Housing, the Red Scare, and the Direction of Los Angeles* (Minneapolis: University of Minnesota Press, 2005), 165–72.

5. Dana Cuff, *The Provisional City: Los Angeles Stories of Architecture and Urbanism* (Cambridge: MIT Press, 2000), 47.

6. For an account of African Americans who migrated to Los Angeles in the 1940s in search of wartime jobs, see Josh Sides, *L.A. City Limits: African American Los Angeles from the Great Depression to the Present* (Berkeley: University of California Press, 2003).

7. Mindy Fullilove, *Root Shock: How Tearing Up City Neighborhoods Hurts America, and What We Can Do About It* (New York: Ballantine Books, 2004), 245, note 8.

8. Ibid., chaps. 3–8.

9. Katherine Underwood, "Process and Politics: Multiracial Electoral Coalition Building and Representation in Los Angeles' Ninth District, 1949–1962" (PhD thesis, University of California, San Diego, 1992), 226–27.

10. See, e.g., Martin Anderson, *The Federal Bulldozer: A Critical Analysis of Urban Renewal, 1949–1962* (Cambridge: MIT Press, 1964). The gist of his argument is reproduced in Wilson, *Urban Renewal*, 143–48.

11. Jane Jacobs, *The Death and Life of Great American Cities* (New York: Random House, 1961), 124.

12. Ibid.

13. Max Miller, ed., *Ideas That Matter: The Worlds of Jane Jacobs* (Washington, DC: Island Press, 1997), 23–24.

14. Quoted in Jacobs, *The Death and Life*, 14.

15. Miller, *Ideas That Matter*, 25.

16. For the inner-city riots of the 1960s and 1970s, see Teaford, *The Rough Road*, chap. 5.

17. Quoted in Jack Melzer, "A New Look at the Urban Revolt," *Journal of the American Institute of Planners* 34, no. 4 (1958): 255–59.

18. Quoted in John R. Chavez, *Eastside Landmark: A History of the East Los Angeles Community Union, 1968–1993* (Stanford, CA: Stanford University Press, 1998), 11.

19. Ibid., 114–17.

20. Robert Bauman, "The Black Power and Chicano Movements in the Poverty Wars in Los Angeles," *Journal of Urban History* 33, no. 2 (January 2007): 277–95.

21. Parson, "The Development of Redevelopment," 408.

22. Parson, *Making a Better World*, 188.

23. "Trouble Plaguing City Renewal Agency," *Los Angeles Times*, September 24, 1967 (Architecture and Urban Planning Collection), box 1, folder 5.

24. Ibid.

25. Quoted in "Speedup Ordered for Watts," *Los Angeles Times*, November 2, 1965, Architecture and Urban Planning Collection, Coll. 92, Special Collections, Charles H. Young Research Library, UCLA, box 1, folder 4.

26. Quoted in ibid.

27. "Delays in USC Project Worsen Blight Picture," *Los Angeles Times*, January 14, 1969 (Architecture and Urban Planning Collection), box 1, folder 5.

28. Quoted in ibid.

29. Quoted in ibid.

30. Teaford, *The Rough Road*, chap. 7.

31. *California Redevelopment Policy: A Summary of California Redevelopment Law, Its Application in Los Angeles County, and Policy Issues Developed During the California Redevelopment Workshop Series* (Los Angeles: Los Angeles Community Design Center, 1977), 6–13.

32. Quoted in ibid., 7.

33. Quoted in ibid., 8.

34. Quoted in ibid., 7.

35. Chavez, *Eastside Landmark*, 114–17.

36. Jennifer Woloch, "From Global to Local: The Rise of Homelessness in Los Angeles During the 1980s," in *The City: Los Angeles and Urban Theory at the End of the Twentieth Century*, ed. Allen J. Scott and Edward W. Soja (Berkeley: University of California Press, 1996), 404.

37. Edward Soja, "Los Angeles, 1965–1992: From Crisis-Generated Restructuring to Restructuring-Generated Crisis," in *The City: Los Angeles and Urban Theory at the End of the Twentieth Century*, ed. Allen J. Scott and Edward W. Soja (Berkeley: University of California Press, 1996), 445–46.

38. Quoted in Woloch, "From Global to Local," 401.

39. Ibid., 403–4.

40. Ibid., 401–2.

41. *Community Redevelopment Agency: Progress Report, 1983–1984* (Los Angeles: Community Redevelopment Agency, 1986), 9.

42. Ibid., 10.

43. Ibid.

44. Ibid., 53.

45. Quoted in Edmund M. Burke, "Citizen Participation Strategies," *Journal of the American Institue of Planners* 34, no. 6 (1958): 287–94.

46. Dan Soen, "Citizen and Community Participation in Urban Renewal and Rehabilitation—Comments on Theory and Practice," *Community Redevelopment Journal* 16, no. 2 (1987): 54.

47. Quoted in ibid., 55.

48. For a general discussion of the problems of gentrification of formerly degraded urban areas, see Loretta Lees, Tom Slater, and Elvin K. Wyly, *Gentrification* (New York: Routledge, 2007).

49. David Ley, *The New Middle Class and the Remaking of the Central City* (New York: Oxford University Press, 1996), 52–58.

50. *Los Angeles Times*, June 27, 2008.

51. "A Plan for the Gentrification of the Broadway Commercial Corridor in Downtown Los Angeles," http://www.downtownlagentrification.com.

52. Peter D. Salins, "Comment on Chester Hartman's 'The Case for a Right to Housing': Housing Is a Right? Wrong," *Housing Policy Debate* 9, no. 2 (1998): 226.

53. Quoted in CRA/LA2011-2012 *Annual Report*, http://www.crala.org.

54. Raphael Bostic and Tony Salazar, "LA's Real Housing Problem," *Los Angeles Times*, February 4, 2013.

55. Quoted in *Los Angeles Times*, February 14, 2013.

56. Quoted in ibid.

57. Some of the suggestions that follow are taken from Paul S. Grogan and Tony Proscio, *Comeback Cities: A Blueprint for Urban Neighborhood Revival* (Boulder, CO: Westview Press, 2000).

58. Ibid., 94–103.

Chapter 8

1. *El Clamor Publico*, June 4, 1850.

2. Leonard Pitt, *The Decline of the Californios: A Social History of the Spanish-Speaking Californians* (Berkeley: University of California Press, 1970), 280.

3. Valerie Sherer Mathes, *Helen Hunt Jackson and Her Indian Reform Legacy* (Austin: University of Texas Press, 1990), 81–84, 95–101.

4. Quoted in Douglas Monroy, *Thrown Among Strangers: The Making of Mexican Culture in Frontier California* (Berkeley: University of California Press, 1990), 269.

5. Raul Homero Villa, *Barrio-Logos: Space and Place in Urban Chicano Literature and Culture* (Austin: University of Texas Press, 2000), 98.

6. Ibid., 103.

7. Judy Baca, http://en.wikipedia.org/wiki/Judy_Baca.

8. Ron Arias, *The Road to Tamazunchale* (Reno, NV: West Coast Poetry Review, 1975).

9. See, e.g., *Los Angeles Times*, October 21, 2003.

10. Karl Germeck, "'Speaking with' the Ravine: Representation and Memory in Five Cultural Productions of Chavez Ravine" (PhD thesis, Utah State University, 2011), 35–36. See also Michelle Kholos Brooks Collection of Manazar Gamboa Papers, Collection 88 (Chicano Studies Research Center, UCLA), box 5, folder 5.

11. Shifra M. Goldman and Tomes Ybarra-Fausto, eds., *Arte Chicano: A Comprehensive Bibliography of Chicano Art, 1965–1981* (Berkeley: University of California Press, 1985), 42–43.

12. For these two leaders of the Mexican Revolution, see Robert L. Scheina, *Villa: Soldier of the Mexican Revolution* (Washington, DC: Brassey's, 2004) and Samuel

Brunk, *The Posthumous Career of Emiliano Zapata: Myth, Memory, and Mexico's Twentieth Century* (Austin: University of Texas Press, 2008).

13. Judy Baca, http://en.wikipedia.org/wiki/Judi_Baca.

14. Ibid.

15. Ibid.

16. Ibid.

17. Eric Avila, *Popular Culture in the Age of White Flight: Fear and Fantasy in Suburban Los Angeles* (Berkeley: University of California Press, 2000), 185.

18. Ry Cooder, *Chavez Ravine*, June 7, 2005, Nonesuch/Perro Verde Records 79887–2.

19. Ron Arias, http://en.wikipedia.org/wiki/RonArias.

20. Ry Cooder, "Poor Man's Shangri-La," *Chavez Ravine*.

21. Ry Cooder, "Don't Call Me Red," *Chavez Ravine*.

22. Ibid.

23. Tara J. Yosso and David N. Garcia, "'This Is No Slum!' A Critical Race Theory Analysis of Community Cultural Wealth in Culture Clash," *Aztlan: A Journal of Chicano Studies* 32, no. 1 (Spring 2007): 147.

24. Ry Cooder, "El U.F.O. Cayo," *Chavez Ravine*.

25. Germeck, "'Speaking with' the Ravine," 38.

26. Arias, *The Road to Tamazunchale*, 13–14.

27. Ibid., 14.

28. Ibid.

29. Ibid., 29–45.

30. Ibid., 46.

31. Ibid., 67–107.

32. David Gumaro Garcia, "The Evolution of Critical Race Theater: Culture Clash and Chicano/a Performance, 1965–2005" (PhD thesis, UCLA, 2006), 2–6.

33. Ibid., 174.

34. Ibid., 178.

35. Ibid., 179.

36. Ibid., 169.

37. Ibid., 181.

38. Ibid., 183.

39. Yosso and Garcia, "'This Is No Slum,'" 142–45.

40. Germeck, "'Speaking with' the Ravine," 53.

41. Ibid., 53–54.

42. Ibid., 55–56.

43. Elaine Woo, "Manazar Gamboa, Poet Who Wrote About Chicano Experience," *Los Angeles Times*, January 7, 2001.

44. Manazar Gamboa, "Cell E-304: Prison Manuscript, 1974," #2–18, Michelle Kholos Brooks Collection of Manazar Gamboa's Papers, Collection 88 (Chicano Studies Research Center, UCLA), box 4, folder 4.

45. Manazar Gamboa, "Cell E-304: Prison Manuscript, 1974," #2–16, Brooks Collection, box 4, folder 4.

46. Michelle Kholos Brooks Collection of Manazar Gamboa's Papers, Collection 88 (Chicano Studies Research Center, UCLA), box 4, folder 13.

47. This and the following excerpts from "Ponchi" are taken from "'Ponchi,' A Short Story by Manazar Gamboa," Brooks Collection, box 5, folder 5.

48. Ibid.

49. For a discussion of the use of "Chicano vernacular," which mentions the Culture Clash authors, see Lauren Nicole Mason, "Identity Formation in Chicano Comedy" (MA thesis, UCLA, 2004), 34–51. See also David G. Garcia, "Transformations through Teatro: Culture Clash in a Chicana/o Classroom," *Radical History Review* 102 (Fall 2008): 111–30.

Epilogue

1. Frank Wilkinson, "Oral History," Special Collections, Charles H. Young Research Library, UCLA, 723.

2. Don Parson, *Making a Better World: Public Housing, the Red Scare, and the Direction of Modern Los Angeles* (Minneapolis: University of Minnesota Press, 2005), 173.

3. Lee Jenkins, "The Day That Damned the Dodgers," *Si Veult*, March 31, 2001.

4. Ibid.

5. *Chavez Ravine Again*, PBS Talkback, April 4, 2008.

6. Interview with Alicia Brown, April 24, 2013.

7. Interview with Carol Jacques, May 2, 2013.

8. Parson, *Making a Better World*, 162.

9. *City of Los Angeles v. Howard Holtzendorff*, May 1, 1967, case no. 44–94236 (Los Angeles City Archives).

10. Robert Sherrill, *First Amendment Felon: The Story of Frank Wilkinson, His 132,000 Page FBI File, and His Epic Fight for Civil Rights and Liberties* (New York: Nation Books, 2005), chap. 16, 30–37.

11. Peter Dreier and Jan Breidenbach, "Frank Wilkinson's Legacy," *Shelterforce* 145 (Spring 2006): 2.

12. Tom Sitton, *Los Angeles Transformed: Fletcher Bowron's Urban Reform Revival, 1938–1953* (Albuquerque: University of New Mexico Press, 2005), 197.

13. Ibid., 199.

14. Norris Poulson, "The Untold Story of Chavez Ravine," *Los Angeles Magazine* 3, no. 4 (April 1962), 15.

15. *Los Angeles Times*, October 29, 1963.

16. *Biographical Dictionary of the U.S. Congress, 1774–Present* (Washington, DC: Government Printing Office, 1983), 224.

17. Quoted from http://www.lindadelmar.com.

18. Elaine Woo, "Manazar Gamboa; Poet Wrote About Chicano Experience," *Los Angeles Times*, January 7, 2001.

19. *Los Angeles Times*, December 18, 2000.

20. Interview with Dixie Swift, October 12, 2012.

Further Reading

Those who wish to study the history of Chavez Ravine further should consult the following works.

Eric Avila, *Popular Culture in the Age of White Flight: Fear and Fantasy in Suburban Los Angeles* (Berkeley: University of California Press, 2004).

Richard Griswold del Castillo, *The Los Angeles Barrio, 1850–1890: A Social History* (Berkeley: University of California Press, 1979).

William David Estrada, *The Los Angeles Plaza: Sacred and Contested Space* (Austin: University of Texas Press, 2008).

Ronald William Lopez, "The Battle for Chavez Ravine: Public Policy and Chicano Community Resistance in Post War Los Angeles, 1945–1962" (PhD thesis, University of California at Berkeley, 1999).

Don Normark, *Chavez Ravine, 1949: A Los Angeles Story* (San Francisco: Chronicle Books, 1999).

Don Parson, *Making a Better World: Public Housing, the Red Scare, and the Direction of Los Angeles* (Minneapolis: University of Minnesota Press, 2005).

———, "The Decline of Public Housing and the Role of the Red Scare: The Significance of the Los Angles Public Housing War," *Journal of Urban History* 33, no. 3 (March 2007): 407–29.

Raul Homero Villa, *Barrio-Logos: Space, Time, and Place in Urban Chicano Literature* (Austin: University of Texas Press, 2000).

Index

Note: Page numbers in *italics* represent photographs/illustrations; page numbers in **bold** represent maps.

About the Author

John H. M. Laslett is a research professor of history at the University of California, Los Angeles. He is the author of many books, including most recently, *Sunshine Was Never Enough: Los Angeles Workers, 1880–2010* (University of California Press, 2012), which won the Gold Shield prize for the best book on California history in 2012 from the Commonwealth Club of San Francisco. Laslett's research focuses on U.S. history, American labor and social movements, minority immigration, and Euro-American history.